THE STANDARD GUIDE TO THE LINCOLN CENT

Third Edition, 1992

SOL TAYLOR
13515 Magnolia Blvd.
Sherman Oaks, Ca. 91423

3rd Edition 1992

PURPOSE OF THIS BOOK

It was recognized in 1982 that no one book contained a well-rounded and comprehensive look at the Lincoln Cent. The first edition published in 1983 explored the potential for a comprehensive collector's guide to the Lincoln Cent. The 1988 edition expanded that arena considerably. And so much has been written and discovered since 1988 that this enlarged and edited third edition has come into being.

The purpose is to keep the collecting of this most common of United States coins alive and well into the next century. It is intended to be the handbook of the beginner, the advanced collector, and every dealer. It contains details as well as highlights of every date and mintmark and many of the recognized varieties.

The contributions of many members of The Society of Lincoln Cent Collectors, including: Steve Benson, Bill Fivaz, J.T. Stanton, Chuck Benko, Carole Kelsey, Lou Coles, Harry Ellis, and others cited in the text are invaluable in making this edition possible. The process does not end, as SLCC publishes six times a year and new material is always included in each issue.

This edition is dedicated to the hundreds of active members of SLCC and the thousands of collectors of Lincoln Cents who make this venture worthwhile.

Since 1988, much has happened in the field of collecting small cents. The grading and especially the encapsulation of coins has been highlighted in the numismatic press, in auctions, and in LINCOLN SENSE, The Journal of the Society of Lincoln Cent Collectors. Unlike other series of coins, the grading of copper coins requires the additional information of color which is a valuation factor. Thus when a copper (or bronze) coin is encapsulated (called "slabbed"), the imprinted grade will read, "1924D MS64RD".

That means the coin grades as uncirculated (60-70 scale of uncirculated) and the color is red. Since red is more valuable than reddish brown and reddish brown is more valuable than brown, the color assigned to a grade is almost as important as the grade numeral. Various examples are pointed out in the date section with recent selected coins sold or offered for sale.

SLCC member, Kenneth Cable published an article in the February, 1992 issue of THE NUMISMATIST and article suggesting a system of "spectral grading" to account for the variations in colors which determine copper (bronze) coinage values. The highest such color, commonly referred to as "blazing mint red" would be designated as Color Grading Index CGI-1. This is the highest quality for a particular date--whether it be cherry red, golden red, or pale yellow gold. The next color grade of CGI-2 would show some mellowing (chemical oxidation) but would be primarily red in color. Many dates in the 1920s started out with these colors. The next red grade of CGI-3 would apply to coins which are more red than other shades and a mixture of colors with red, or reddish hues, the primary. The grade of CGI-4 would show duller hues and shades of red and mixed with other colors. The next grade of CGI-5 would be what is now usually called "red-brown", but lustrous enough to indicate much red (1/3 or more). The next CGI-6 would be what is now "red-brown" but more brown and traces of red or other mint hues. The final grade of CGI-7 would be what is now called "brown" which usually means little or no red showing and little or no mint luster.

Since this proposal has not filtered down through the system, only time will tell whether such a color grading scale would eventually be applied to small cents.

Also, since 1988, two of the major grading services, Professional Coin Grading Services (PCGS) and Numismatic Guarantee Corporation (NGC) have published "Population Reports" of the coins they have encapsulated. These data are useful insofar as they reflect the numbers of coins encapsulated and thus their relative scarcity. Population data are shown in the chapter of dates (Ch. 5). Thus, coin values have changed dramatically since 1988 based partially on the dual impact of color requirements and population data.

For information on THE SOCIETY OF LINCOLN CENT COLLECTORS write to: SLCC, 13515 Magnolia Blvd., Sherman Oaks, CA 91423. Enclose a large-sized envelope with $0.52 postage to cover the return mailed information package and application form.

The author does not buy or sell coins. Please do not send coins for attribution or sale to the author or SLCC.

Published by KNI Publishers, Anaheim, CA, 1992.

About the author. . . .

Dr. Sol Taylor began his collecting career in 1937 with his first "penny board" purchased at a downtown New York City coin shop. In 1953 he began a mail order business in coins and stamps and in more recent years had been active as a bourse dealer in many local and regional coin shows. He is a former president of the Numismatic Association of Southern California (1975), life member of the American Numismatic Association (LM805), and life member of the Numismatic Literary Guild, Society for International Numismatics, Tokens and Medals Society, and the Whittier Coin Club. He also holds memberships in several other numismatic organizations.

Dr. Taylor was a contributing editor to the Private Coin Collector, a contributor to the ANA Grading Guide, and a frequent contributor to many numismatic publications. He had conducted the annual grading seminar for the ANA in 1975, 1976, and 1977 and has been a frequent speaker on the subject at seminars and numismatic meetings.

He is a former associate professor of education at Chapman College having retired in 1982 and holds a doctorate in education from the University of Southern California. He also holds a BA and MA degree from Brooklyn College, an administrative credential from Long Beach State College, and additional postgraduate work from the University of California, Berkeley. He is a former science teacher and school administrator having served a total of seventeen years in the New York City schools and in the Whittier Union High School District (California).

This handbook is a study of the development of the Lincoln cent from its origins to its status as a popular collector and investor item. The data include primary references and publications covering almost each year of issue. In addition, several thousand coins were examined and these findings are reflected in the year-by-year analyses shown in Chapter 5.

LINCOLN SENSE is the journal of the Society of Lincoln Cent Collectors. Each issue contains information related to the Lincoln Cent. In this edition a separate chapter "Current Status of the Lincoln Cent" has been added. It includes some excepts from CAB's corner, a review of major auctions by Charles A. Benko. It includes various finds and information furnished by other SLCC members.

Prices reflect sales and list prices from sources dating from 1991 and early 1992. Sellers are reminded that retail prices, auction prices, and mail bid results do not reflect what the dealers would pay collectors for very similar coins.

An additional phenomenon of the late 1980s and early 1990s has been "Teletrade". This completely automated selling system was initiated to sell collectors' and dealers' encapsulated coins by telemarketing. Bidding is done by telephone and so is the billing and accounting. A weekly sale is published in one or more of the numismatic publications. Bidders then enter bids via a touch-tone system. Final results are available via a published list. These sales data reflect the market value of slabbed coins and often set the tone for fixed price lists and auction sale results. Some of these recent sales figures are shown in Chapter 5. For a complete operation of Teletrade, write to Teletrade, 885 Third Ave., New York, NY 10022, or call 213-355-5040.

POPULATION REPORTS - A Phenomenon of the 1990s

Just as the phenomenon of the 1980s was encapsulation (slabbing), that has led to a newer phenomenon, The Population Reports. Started by the Professional Coin Grading Service in 1987 and the Numismatic Guarantee Corporation of America (NGC) both issue monthly reports of the coins they have encapsulated. These reports are being used more frequently as another valuation base for dealers and collectors alike. These reports do not reveal the actual or even the majority of pieces known date-by-date, but they do reflect the population of encapsulated coins. And for many coins, these studies add something to the valuation of certain coins. For some series where many thousands rank as MS65, the overall value has leveled off or even dropped -- as with many BU Morgan Dollars and hoarded coins such as the 1938D Buffalo nickel. With many Lincoln Cents, however, the population of certain dates in MS65 are small numbers often even single digits. For several dozen Lincoln Cents, the total population data reveal less that ten coins each in MS65 Red. These reports provide another device in the ongoing process of placing values on coins.

In each date section of Chapter 5, recent data from PCGS Population Reports are included to illustrate the survival of the uncirculated specimens for each date and mintmark.

As is disclosed in the PCGS Population Report the numbers reflect only the coins which PCGS has encapsulated. Some coins have been submitted more than once and that may cloud the data if the grading service was unaware of resubmissions. Some coins have been resubmitted between services until the highest possible grade was finally obtained. Here again, the data cannot precisely reflect the actual number of submissions--but most authorities feel the data provide collectors and dealers with a valuable tool.

Coins graded by ANACS and accompanied by a certificate are not included in Population Report data.

Hold On to Lincoln Pennies!
No More "V.D.B.'s" Coined

5,000,000 of the New Coins Ordered by Outside Banks—"'Run" Continues.

Lay away your Lincoln pennies.

They're going to be worth something—something more than a cent apiece—after all.

Word came from Washington yesterday that Secretary of the Treasury McVeagh had ordered the minting of the coins to be stopped for the present, while new dies are being made.

The initials, "V. D. B.," standing for Victor D. Brenner, the designer, have been deemed too prominent a feature of the cent pieces, and, on the new Lincoln coins—those to be issued a few days from now—Mr. Brenner will be represented by a microscopic "B." concealed in some inconspicuous place.

Soon Will Be "Freak" Issue.

Therefore the V. D. B. coins will soon be regarded as a "freak" issue, and will be in demand by coin-collectors all the world over. And with the lapse of time they will grow more and more valuable.

The rush of coin-brokers was renewed yesterday with redoubled interest, when it became known that the pennies with the three initials were to be no more. An army of men and boys besieged the Sub-Treasury when it opened, and soon the lines were so long that police reserves had to be called out to keep them in order. As soon as they obtained their dime's worth or dollar's worth of pennies, they rushed to street corners and placed them on sale, as they had done on the previous day.

Clamor at the Banks.

The ruling price was three pennies for a nickel, in the Wall Street district; but in less populous quarters prices ranged from two for a nickel to a nickel, and even a dime, apiece. Nearly every bank in town found its customers were demanding the new coins as souvenirs. The banks sent their messengers to the Sub-Treasury early in the day. Each messenger was allotted ten dollars' worth.

The Sub-Treasury was obliged to remain open until 5 o'clock to attend to the rush. Besides handing out the coins over the counters, it received more than $50,000 in drafts from out-of-town banks which wanted the new copper engraving of Lincoln. This was equivalent to an order for 5,000,000 coins.

According to figures received from Washington, $265,000 worth of the initialled pennies bearing the martyred President's head had been struck off up to yesterday. That means 26,500,000 of the copper coins. Of this amount, $76,000 worth went to Washington, where they were nearly all disposed of by the Treasury. The rest were distributed mainly throughout Philadelphia and this city.

This cartoon from the NEW YORK AMERICAN dated August 6, 1909 tells the story of the new Lincoln cent shortly after its issue. Courtesy of Steve Nelson of Buffalo, NY who located the original copy in the library.

TABLE OF CONTENTS

Chapter 1 — Collecting the Lincoln Cent
by Dr. Sol Taylor

I began my coin collecting career and avocation in 1937. I had received three brilliantly uncirculated 1937 cents in change at the corner candy store and put them away in my toy box along with the usual assortment of things. Shortly thereafter, I bought my first coin board at Hans Sergl's shop on Fulton Street in lower Manhattan. In just over two years, I had found each and every coin in change necessary to fill the holes in the board from 1909 to 1940, except for the 1931S. Living in New York City at the time meant that all "S" mint and most "D" mint coins were hard to find in circulation.

Thus to complete my first "penny" board, I went to Al Fastove's coin shop in the old Williamsburg Savings Bank building in downtown Brooklyn in the summer of 1940 and spent 45¢ on an uncirculated 1931S cent. My set was now complete. By that time, I had several other penny boards, all near completion—usually lacking two or three coins—and all found in change! But that was before World War II.

Today, in the 1990s, the Lincoln cent is still the most widely collected coin. However, unlike the 1940s, one cannot find too many dates in circulation. In fact, any Lincolns before 1959 are quite scarce, while any dates before 1940 are extremely unlikely—even though they are far from rare—over the years they have been 99.99% pulled out by collectors. Up until a few years ago, I used to assist young collectors in getting their hobby going by buying bags of cents from vending machine companies and going through them coin-by-coin. And for every 5,000 coins (in 1975), fewer than ten were pre-1950. There were often more dimes in the bag than early Lincoln cents. However, there were mint errors, mint mark varieties, and relatively scarce modern dates such as the 1969P, 1974S, and 1960D small date found in each bag. However, one cannot expect to complete even one-third of a Lincoln set by this method today. Thus,

1

the collector has to turn to the coin dealer for his Lincoln cents, who in turn is always buying them from other collectors who put them away years ago.

The Lincoln cent thus becomes a collector's challenge—to complete the set in the best possible condition. A choice BU set is entirely possible—but at a rapidly rising price. Complete circulated sets are readily available, and in the past few years at modestly rising prices per set.

The challenge for the young collector as well as the advanced investor is to assemble a choice uncirculated set (with proofs for those years where circulation coins were not released). Fortunately for both groups, many rolls of Lincoln cents were hoarded for many years of issue making a supply available to future generations of collectors and investors. Unfortunately, hoarders rarely paid attention to the quality of their "mint condition" rolls and for many years (listed in Chapter 5) these rolls contain only mediocre to poorly struck coins. Also, during the years from 1911-1924 very few uncirculated rolls were put away, and for some of the years in that period, no BU rolls are known. However, roll collecting or hoarding became more in vogue again in the late 1920s, and rolls of such dates as 1929S, 1929D, and every year thereafter are fairly easy to come by—however, often with some poor specimens of mint coinage. It was not until the late 1940s that more care was seen in the assembling of BU rolls of Lincoln cents. Thus, on price lists, the prices one will see for "original BU rolls" often seems quite reasonable as compared to prices of the single coins listed in "MS65". This is due to the fact that most of these "original rolls" were assembled from bags without close visual inspection and contain weakly struck coins, spotted coins, and often scratched coins—although they are all technically, "uncirculated".

With the advent of the bookshelf-styled coin albums in the 1960s, impetus was given to Lincoln cents after some years of quiet activity. The prices even for circulated coins began to rise sharply in 1964 when coin collecting hit a peak of activity.

Roll collecting became the rage and many pages of ads in the numismatic press featured rolls of every coin minted from 1934 to date in BU condition. Prices of many common coins rose dramatically. The scarce 1960P small date cent rose to $500 a roll. The scarce 1950D Jefferson nickel reached $1000 a roll. Both rolls are available now some twenty eight years later at less than half of those astronomical prices. Likewise, prices for proof Lincoln cents from 1955 to 1964 were also very strong. The commonest 1960-1964 proof Lincolns were selling for $2.50 to $3.00 per coin— today they are available at less than 50 cents each. And for most of the past decade, prices for Lincoln cents generally have languished—moving up and down but making slow gains over the long run after the big slump at the end of the 1960s. (See Chapter 4 for details).

The most popular of the Lincoln cents, the so-called "keys"—1909S VDB, 1909S, 1914D, 1922 "plain", 1924D, 1931S, 1955 double die, and 1972 doubled die—have had only minor ups and downs in their history with a generally strong upside trend over the years. They are the coins the collectors all need and want—in all grades. They are the coins the investors all want usually in the best grades, pref- erably in MS65 or better. Thus, with the constantly rising demand and the shrinking supply, the "keys" continue to do well over the long run. However, not far behind are coins known as "semi-keys" which in many cases are turning out to be quite valuable in mint state as recent auction records reveal. These coins include: 1910S, 1911D, 1911S, 1912D, 1912S, 1913D, 1913S, 1914S, 1915, 1921S, 1922D, 1923S, 1926S, 1931D, and 1933D. While these coins are all readily available in roll quantities, they are scarce to quite rare in MS65 condition (See Chapter 4).

When the new zinc alloy cent came into play in 1982, there was another spurt in Lincoln cent interest. As in the past, at each changeover, or design modification, the interest in the series moved forward. The Lincoln cent is now the longest running design of any United States coin passing the 69 years set by the Liberty Head $5 gold piece, 1839-1908. And in light of its inexpensive cost (per coin), it will probably continue to be the most popular collectible United States coin.

3

DOUBLED DIES

1963-D 1¢ MS63	1970-S 1¢ PF65
I-O-VII — Overdate 1963/3	3-O-VI

A Must For Every Collector	All Lettering, Extra Thickness
$7.50	$175.00

1970-S PF 1¢ PF65	1971-PF 1¢ PF63
Tripled Die Obverse	One of My Favorites

1-0-II

7-O-I — A Super Coin!	
$195.00	$475.00

1972 1¢ MS63	1982 L.D. 1¢ AU
I-O-I	A New Listing — 5-O-II

The Biggie	
$175.00	$35.00

Chapter 2 — The Origin of the Lincoln Cent

As early as 1907, plans were underway to honor the centenary of the birth of America's best known hero—Abraham Lincoln. In 1908 Congress had approved a bill to issue a special two cent commemorative stamp in his honor to be released on February 12, 1909. Although Lincoln had been honored on postage stamps as early as 1866 (Scott's No. 77 issued April 14, 1866), and again the regular issues of 1869, 1870, 1873, 1879, 1883, 1890, 1894, 1895, and 1902-03, the 1909 issue was the first to be specially designated as a commemorative.

In 1908, President Theodore Roosevelt was sitting for his likeness for the medal commemorating the building of the Panama Canal. The artist, a young Lithuanian immigrant named Victor D. Brenner, had impressed the president sufficiently to have him named as the artist who would design the new Lincoln cent for 1909. Born Viktoras Barnauskas in 1871, he emigrated to the United States in 1890 and shortly found work as a craftsman with the National Academy in New York designing medals, plaques, and awards. After he became a naturalized citizen, he legally changed his name to Victor David Brenner. In 1907 he designed a plaque honoring Abraham Lincoln—not knowing that it was the same bust that would be used on the new cent in 1909. President Roosevelt met with his Secretary of the Treasury, George B. Cortelyou, and directed that Brenner be commissioned by the Treasury to design the new cent for the Lincoln centennial.

The design as we know it was essentially completed in late 1908. The original galvanos contained the name "BRENNER" in small block letters at the lower rim on the reverse. The Treasury officials requested it be removed as it detracted from the design and in its place placed the initials, "V.D.B."

This minor design change placed the issuance date well past the hoped-for February 12, 1909 deadline. The Indian head cent continued to be minted into the spring of the year until the working dies for the new Lincoln cent were ready for production at the Philadelphia and San Francisco mints. Final approval for the design, the dies, and production was given by Treasury Secretary Franklin MacVeagh on July 14, 1909. The first coins to be issued through the bank came out on August 2, 1909. Stories in the newspapers indicated a strong demand with lines of people waiting to obtain the new coins; some banks limiting customers to 100 coins or less. A similar story was repeated the day the Kennedy halves were issued in 1964. The public widely accepted the new coin and words of praise came in to the Mint and the Treasury generally favorable to the new design.

One stream of criticism came in aimed at the initials, "V.D.B." In an August, 1909 news article Treasury Secretary MacVeagh reported that he believed that the initials, "V.D.B." were to be incused, not raised and thus were too conspicuous. He reported that they would be removed and replaced with an incused "B". However, the current dime, quarter, and half dollar all had an incused "B" representing Charles Barber, the chief U.S. Mint Engraver. The initials were removed in September of 1909, and the major balance of the coins issued in 1909 had no initials.

The following is in part a letter written by Victor D. Brenner to Farran Zerbe shortly after the new cent was issued:

My Dear Mr. Zerbe:

It is mighty hard for me to express my sentiments with reference to the initials on the cent. The name of the artist on a coin is essential for the student of history as it enables him to trace environments and conditions of the time said coin was produced. Much fume has been made about my initials as a means of advertisement; such is not the case. The very talk the initials has brought out has done more good for numismatics than it could do me personally.

The cent not alone represents in part my art, but it represents the type of art of our period.

The conventionalizing of the sheafs of wheat was done by me with much thought, and I feel that with the prescribed wording no better design could be obtained. The cent will wear out two of the last lines in time, due entirely to the hollow surface.

The original design had Brenner on it, and that was changed to the initials. Of course the issue rests with the numismatic bodies . . .

Very sincerely Yours,
(signed)
Victor D. Brenner

In 1918, the initials "V.D.B." were restored to the truncation of the bust of Lincoln, barely visible to the naked eye. It had already been established that coins bore the initials of the designer; the Mercury dime in 1916 had initials "AW", the Buffalo nickel had an "F", the Liberty Standing quarter had an "M", and the Liberty Walking half dollar had the monogram "AW". Even the predecessor Indian head cent had the initial "L" in the design honoring the designer Longacre. Thus, the Lincoln cent had every right to its designer's initials. After the return of initials in 1918 there was no negative response from the public and there they have remained to this date.

NEW "LINCOLN" PENNIES DELIGHT MANY CHILDREN

Crowd So Great at U. S. Subtreasury That Sale of Coins Is Stopped.

Did you get any of the new "Lincoln" pennies at the U. S. Subtreasury, little boy and little girl?

If you didn't dozens of little boys and girls did. They crowded into the Subtreasury offices in the Federal building by the dozens, all seeking the bright new pennies of which they had read. They wanted the pennies in all amounts.

"Dimme a penny's wurf," some small lad or lassie would ask, and then a newsboy, intending to sell the pennies along with papers at a greatly advanced price, would buy a quarter's worth, a half dollar's worth or perhaps a whole dollar's worth.

Harry R. Flory, coin teller at the Subtreasury, began to think that all the little boys and girls in St. Louis were there to get the pennies. So large did the crowds become, nobody but the children could get to the coin teller's window, . Subtreasurer Whitelaw finally ordered that the issuance of the pennies be stopped. There were many disappointed youngsters when that announcement was made, for the press of children was so great that scores had no opportunity to buy their pennies before the sale was stopped.

LINCOLN PENNY STAYS.

Treasury Department Will Not Recall Issue in Spite of Artist's Initials.

WASHINGTON, Aug. 4.—The new issue of Lincoln pennies will continue in circulation despite the criticism that the initials of the designer appear rather conspicuously on the coins. That was the statement made at the Treasury Department to-day.

The objection was presented to the Treasury officials, and it was considered carefully. They have decided, however, not to recall the issue—at least not for the present, and the likelihood is that it will not be recalled at all—because it has been customary for many years for the designers of Government coins to place their initials upon them.

The "Lincoln pennies" were arranged for during the Administration of President Roosevelt, and the design was passed upon by the Treasury officials of that Administration. Some delicacy is felt, therefore, by the officials of the present Administration in taking up the matter.

"LINCOLN" PENNIES TO-DAY.

The Head Designed by Artist Victor Brenner, Once a Poor Match Seller.

The Philadelphia Mint will issue to-day the new "Lincoln" pennies, which the Treasury Department has caused to be designed and struck off in honor of the 100th anniversary of the late President's birth. The head of Lincoln which appears on the coin has been designed from a photograph in the possession of Charles Eliot Norton. The face is relaxed and smiling, the young artist having sought to reproduce particularly Lincoln's expression when talking to children.

This artist is Victor D. Brenner, a 27-year-old Russian, who came to this country as a boy, sold matches in the street, and studied art at night at Cooper Union. He saved up enough money to continue his studies in Paris, and on his return opened a studio. He had always been an admirer of Lincoln's anti-slavery policy, and when he heard that the Government was finding that the Indian head on the cent was too easily counterfeited and that a Lincoln head was being talked of for some coin he began seeking a suitable photograph of Lincoln, and after obtaining Dr. Norton's sent a design to Washington, which was accepted.

The oldest officials of the Sub-Treasury cannot remember when there has been such a popular demand for any coin as the new Lincoln pennies have called out. Before the Sub-Treasury doors on Pine Street, near Nassau, opened yesterday, morning there was a line of men, women, and boys extending down Pine Street nearly to William. When Assistant Treasurer Terry arrived at his office he called on the police of the John Street Station to keep order in the line, and all day long the clerks in the old building at Wall and Nassau Streets were busy changing coin from pennies up to dollars for the new one cent pieces.

Although the financial district was glutted with the new design on Tuesday, and the banks were able to get $10,000 lots on Tuesday and all day yesterday the stories printed yesterday morning that the entire issue might be recalled because of the appearance of the initials of the designer, Victor D. Brenner, on the reverse side of the coins, there was an unusual demand for new pennies yesterday in the belief that they might eventually sell at a premium.

Assistant Treasurer Terry made a rule yesterday morning that no one applying at the coin windows in the Sub-Treasury should receive more than $1 in pennies. Most of the applicants were small boys whose demands were for a dime's worth or less. The first applicant at the window, in fact, had only two battered pennies, which he traded for the newer coins.

Assistant Treasurer Terry said yesterday that he had had no word from Washington that the new issue would be recalled, and the coins were doled out until 4 o'clock, which is an hour later than the regular closing time of the Sub-Treasury.

Copies of articles from various newspapers in August, 1909 describing the new Lincoln Cent.

Chapter 3 — Design Changes

In its long life, the Lincoln cent has undergone two major design changes, and some minor cosmetic changes.

Type I. 1909-designs with V.D.B. on reverse.

Type II. 1909-1917-designs without initials.

Type IIa. *1918-1958-initials restored to truncation of bust.*

Type IIaI. 1943-coins issued in zinc-coated steel.

Type IIa2. 1944-1946-coins issued from shellcase brass alloy.

Type III. 1959-date-reverse design changed to Lincoln Memorial.

Type IIIa. 1969-1972-Lincoln bust reduced slightly and sharpened.

Type IIIb. 1973-date-Reverse design sharpened, FG initials enlarged.

Type IIIbI. 1982-Alloy changed to 97.6% zinc: 2.4% copper.

These design changes and content changes all reflect the nature of the times. When the cent was first designated to be 3.11 grams of bronze alloy back in 1864, the value of such alloy was perhaps 1/20th of a cent. Today the value of the same alloy is ⅔-¾ of a cent and once in 1974 actually exceeded one cent. Thus the 1982 changeover to a zinc alloy was warranted, keeping the overall coin dimensions with only a loss of 19% in weight. It was recommended in 1974 at the Assay Commission that aluminum cents be used to replace the bronze cents. However, the aluminum cent was much lighter than the bronze cent and would not work in vending machines and would probably have low public acceptance. The copper-plated alloy looks much like the bronze cent and was readily absorbed into commercial channels.

In 1943, due to the wartime critical shortage of copper, the Mint switched to an emergency alloy of zinc-coated steel for the cent. It was an overall failure. The alloy was magnetic and did not work in many vending machines. The highly corrosive zinc coating rapidly deteriorated into a whitish powdery oxide of zinc and often the steel started to rust. Furthermore, newly minted coins often confused people who thought they were dimes. After less than a year, the Mint decided to resort to an alloy of copper for the balance of the war and chose the shell casing from ammunition which is a brass-bronze alloy primarily of copper, zinc, and tin. This alloy was used successfully from 1944-1945. The normal bronze alloy of 95% copper and 5% zinc and tin was restored in 1946. In 1962 the small percentage of tin used in cent blanks was dropped, and all cents minted since then have been 95% copper and 5% zinc until the 1982 changeover.

An astute student of the Lincoln cent could examine each year in turn from 1909 to date and notice the subtle, yet evident, changes in both sides of the coin from year to year. For example after 1918, each year tended to have a little less distinctiveness to Lincoln's hairstyle, less definition in his coat, and weakness in the letters "O" in ONE and "C" in CENT. The wheat stalks on the reverse shows annual progression toward mushiness from about 1920 through 1930, often the kernels becoming less distinct. Often a BU roll of 1930S or 1929S cents will fail to show one coin with clearly defined wheat lines or wheat kernels. In 1930, some die changes brought out some sharply defined coins until about 1934 when again, the fuzziness of detail became evident throughout the year. Through much of the 1930s, coins show weakness in both sides. In 1943, new dies with very sharp details come on line and well-struck 1943 coins are the rule, not the exception. However, average to below average coins are the rule in 1944-1947. Not until 1950 is more definition noted in the cent. By 1954 and 1955, the "O" on ONE is about half gone. In 1956, it reappears until the end of the "wheat back" type in 1958.

With the Memorial reverse cent appearing in 1959, it too began to decline each year thereafter until in 1968, Mint Director, Mary Brooks, ordered the working dies redone to give Lincoln a better appearance. In 1969 a smaller, but sharper image of Lincoln appeared and the reverse sharpened up on details of the Memorial. But, after a few years, it was evident in 1972 that more work was needed to keep the coin looking aesthetically sharp. So in 1973 the Memorial was reworked, the initials, FG (Frank Gasparro, the designer of the reverse) was enlarged, and Lincoln got a face lift again. The legends were sharpened and the lettering was squared off—many letters were getting a rounded corner appearance.

It appears that after two or three years of work, the master hubs which produce all the working dies lose a little of their sharpness and thus the coinage begins to lack detail. Thus, about every three years or so, the Mint will examine its master hubs and make what changes seem necessary to insure a quality product for the public. Each modification would not qualify as a design change, and thus most catalogues and albums only show three types of Lincoln cents—the VDB, the Wheat Back, and the Memorial type, and possibly the 1943 steel cent as a variety, not a design change. In actuality, each year and mint mark is distinctive and one could argue that each one is another type. But most collectors would stick with three types—if they just were intent on Type Coins.

"SLABBED COINS" A Phenomenon of the 1980s

The March, 1988 display ad below shows a high quality 1909 S VDB cent in a hard plastic case provided by PCGS (Professional Coin Grading Service of Newport Beach, California). These certified coins are known as "slabbed coin" because of the rigid case. PCGS coins are encased in a hard plastic case and also have the guarantee of PCGS member dealers to buy and sell such slabbed coins at the grade indicated.

Refer to Chapter 8 for additional comments on certification services.

Chapter 4 — The Numismatic Track Record

Prior to the issuance of the Red Book, A GUIDE TO UNITED STATES COINS, by Richard S. Yeoman, in 1947, the only regular publication with regularly issued prices for United States coins was the NUMISMATIC SCRAPBOOK. The first set of data reveals the track record of uncirculated Lincolns published in three different years. Bear in mind, "uncirculated" in those years simply meant "not circulated"—not MS60, MS63, MS65, or MS67.

One should examine the 1934 data since it reveals something very important about the availability of uncirculated Lincoln cents. Note that for 25¢ you could buy a 1909SVDB, but several other coins which are now considered fairly common cost considerably more nearly 50 years ago, including: almost all coins from 1910 through 1924—which illustrates the point about hoards—most early rolls of Lincolns were put away in 1909. Mint roll hoarding did not resume until the late 1920s. Thus, if in 1934 anyone wanted a BU 1909SVDB, they were readily available at 25¢ each—since dealers and collectors had rolls put away. Note the two most expensive BU coins in 1934 were the 1914S and 1914D. That should tell us something about those two dates in BU.

Also note, some dates dropped in price between 1934 and 1941, again showing that quantities were put away and when they surfaced, the prices dropped. The 1947 figures show that a larger population of collectors entered the field and prices moved up sharply for most issues. This was the first post-war boom in coin collecting and collectors were no longer able to find the early key coins in change and the rolls put away in 1909 and 1910 were being parceled out so that more and more collectors could have their own BU 1909SVDB. It was then in 1947 that the 1909SVDB established itself as the key coin in the series and its popularity, not its rarity, has kept its price high ever since.

Year and Mint	Catalogue prices Uncirculated			Year and Mint	Catalogue prices Uncirculated		
	1934	1941	1947		1934	1941	1947
1909P	.15	.20	.35	1921S	.75	2.50	12.50
1909VDB	.15	.10	.20	1922D	.50	1.25	2.50
1909S	.25	2.50	4.00	1923P	.35	.25	.50
1909SVDB	.25	3.00	15.00	1923S	1.50	5.00	10.00
1910P	.25	.25	.75	1924P	.25	.50	1.75
1910S	.50	.35	1.50	1924S	1.00	4.00	7.50
1911P	.25	.25	.50	1924D	1.00	5.00	7.50
1911S	.35	2.50	3.50	1925P	.20	.25	.50
1911D	.35	1.25	2.50	1925S	.40	4.00	6.00
1912P	.25	.35	.50	1925D	.40	1.50	2.00
1912S	.60	2.00	4.00	1926P	.30	.50	.85
1912D	.65	3.00	5.00	1926S	1.50	5.00	7.50
1913P	.35	.50	.50	1926D	.35	1.25	2.00
1913S	1.00	4.00	5.00	1927P	.20	.25	.50
1913D	1.00	4.00	6.50	1927S	.40	2.50	5.00
1914P	1.25	2.00	2.50	1927D	.40	2.00	2.50
1914S	2.00	4.00	5.50	1928P	.20	.25	.50
1914D	2.00	6.00	12.50	1928S	.40	2.00	3.50
1915P	1.00	3.00	3.50	1928D	.40	1.50	3.00
1915S	.60	2.50	3.50	1929P	.10	.10	.40
1915D	.60	1.25	2.50	1929S	.25	.25	.40
1916P	.45	.25	.50	1930P	.10	.10	.25
1916S	.65	1.50	3.00	1930S	.25	.15	.50
1916D	.65	1.25	2.00	1930D	.25	.50	.60
1917P	.25	.35	.50	1931P	.10	.50	1.25
1917S	.65	1.50	2.50	1931S	.25	.40	1.50
1917D	.50	1.00	2.00	1931D	.25	1.50	3.00
1918P	.25	.45	.50	1932P	.10	.35	.85
1918S	.65	2.00	4.50	1932D	.10	.50	1.50
1918D	.60	2.00	3.50	1933P	.10	.50	.75
1919P	.25	.35	.50	1933D	.25	.10	.60
1919S	1.00	1.25	2.00	1934P	—	.10	.20
1919D	.60	1.25	1.50	1934D	—	.15	.30
1920P	.25	.25	.35	1935P	—	.05	.10
1920S	.60	1.50	4.00	1935S	—	.10	.25
1920D	.60	1.25	2.50	1935D	—	.10	.20
1921P	.25	.35	1.75				

The next set of data reflects catalogue valuations from the Red Book (dates shown) and the COIN DEALER NEWS-LETTER (dates shown). These figures reflect the faster paced marketplace of recent years as compared with those of the first set of figures in this chapter. They also reflect the demand for higher quality coins - thus the column for MS65 reflects the "choice uncirculated" coins versus the "average uncirculated" coin.

The grading numbers used conform to the current American Numismatic Association grading guide and the Sheldon numerical scale: Good-4, Very Good-8, Fine-12, Very fine-20, Extra fine-40, About uncirculated-50, Uncirculated MS-60, and choice uncirculated, MS-65. There are intermediate grades such as AU-55 and MS-63 which are also recognized legitimate grades under the ANA system, however, few catalogues list coins using the intermediate grades. The CDN lists MS-63 for most type coins, silver dollars, and commemorative coins and in its Monthly Summary also lists most issues in MS-60 as well as MS-65.

This portion of the chapter is subdivided into three sections:
Section 1: Tracking the key and semi-key coins,
Section 2: Tracking the BU rolls,
Section 3: Tracking the circulated roll market.

Refer to Chapter 5 for information regarding mintage figures, date specifics, and projections for each Lincoln issue.

Refer to Chapter 7 for detailed grading and storage information.

The major grading services use incremental grades for uncirculated coins including MS60, MS61, MS62, MS63, MS64, MS65, MS66, and for Proof coins, up to Pf69.

Prior to 1988, uncirculated grades were limited to MS60, MS63, and MS65 with rare higher exceptions. Proof grades included Pf66-69 specimens. Some grading services also have grades of AU50, AU53, AU55, and AU58. (AU is sometimes referred to as "MS".)

Section I: Tracking the Key and Semi-Key Coins

Red Book prices quoted: a - 1978 edition, b - 1980 edition, c -1986 edition n/l - grade not listed

		G-4	VG-8	Fine-12	VF-20	EF-40	MS-60	MS-63
1909VDB	a.	1.75	2.00	2.50	2.85	3.50	12.50	n/l
	b.	1.75	2.00	2.50	2.85	3.50	12.50	n/l
	c.	2.25	2.65	3.00	3.25	4.00	13.00	25.00
1909SVDB	a.	135.00	145.00	155.00	170.00	195.00	325.00	n/l
	b.	140.00	150.00	165.00	185.00	200.00	340.00	n/l
	c.	250.00	285.00	315.00	375.00	410.00	550.00	750.00
1909S	a.	25.00	27.50	32.50	38.00	48.00	85.00	n/l
	b.	26.00	29.00	33.00	40.00	50.00	90.00	n/l
	c.	45.00	50.00	60.00	70.00	110.00	225.00	300.00
1910S	a.	5.75	6.75	7.75	9.00	12.00	52.50	n/l
	b.	5.75	6.75	7.75	9.00	12.00	53.00	n/l
	c.	8.00	9.00	10.00	11.00	18.00	95.00	150.00
1911S	a.	9.00	10.00	11.50	14.50	20.00	75.00	n/l
	b.	9.00	10.00	11.50	14.50	20.00	75.00	n/l
	c.	11.00	13.00	15.00	18.00	30.00	115.00	240.00
1911D	a.	2.50	3.50	5.00	8.50	16.00	60.00	n/l
	b.	3.50	3.80	4.90	8.40	17.50	60.00	n/l
	c.	3.50	4.25	6.00	10.00	25.00	100.00	170.00
1912S	a.	8.00	9.00	11.00	14.75	23.00	75.00	n/l
	b.	8.00	9.00	11.00	14.75	23.00	75.00	n/l
	c.	10.00	11.00	13.00	17.00	35.00	110.00	175.00
1912D	a.	2.50	3.50	5.25	11.00	20.00	70.00	n/l
	b.	2.50	3.50	5.25	11.00	20.00	70.00	n/l
	c.	4.00	5.00	6.00	12.00	31.00	110.00	175.00
1913S	a.	5.00	6.00	7.25	8.50	16.00	67.50	n/l
	b.	5.00	6.00	7.25	8.50	16.00	67.50	n/l
	c.	8.00	9.00	10.00	13.00	23.00	100.00	225.00
1913D	a.	1.35	1.90	3.00	7.00	17.50	67.50	n/l
	b.	1.35	1.90	3.00	7.00	16.50	67.50	n/l
	c.	2.00	2.50	4.50	7.00	17.50	70.00	145.00
1914S	a.	6.50	7.50	8.50	11.00	20.00	92.50	n/l
	b.	6.50	7.50	8.50	11.00	20.00	92.50	n/l
	c.	9.00	10.00	12.00	18.00	31.00	165.00	425.00
1914D	a.	47.50	55.00	65.00	100.00	200.00	750.00	n/l
	b.	55.00	60.00	70.00	105.00	210.00	750.00	n/l
	c.	80.00	90.00	110.00	150.00	350.00	1,000.00	1,650.00
1915S	a.	5.00	5.75	7.00	8.50	17.00	65.00	n/l
	b.	5.00	5.75	7.00	8.50	17.00	65.00	n/l
	c.	7.75	8.50	9.00	12.00	22.00	100.00	200.00
1915D	a.	.60	1.00	1.50	5.00	11.00	37.50	n/l
	b.	.60	1.00	1.50	5.00	11.00	37.50	n/l
	c.	.60	1.00	1.50	3.00	10.00	45.00	110.00

1921S	a.	.60	.85	1.25	3.00	11.00	195.00	n/l
	b.	.60	.85	1.25	3.00	11.00	195.00	n/l
	c.	.60	.85	1.50	3.00	10.00	125.00	300.00
1922"P"	a.	50.00	60.00	100.00	150.00	275.00	1,850.00	n/l
	b.	90.00	110.00	140.00	190.00	325.00	2,250.00	n/l
	c.	200.00	250.00	325.00	425.00	750.00	3,100.00	7,500.00
1922D	a.	4.75	5.75	6.75	9.00	16.00	65.00	n/l
	b.	4.75	5.75	6.75	9.00	16.00	65.00	n/l
	c.	4.75	6.00	7.00	9.50	19.00	80.00	150.00
1923S	a.	1.40	1.75	2.50	4.75	14.00	260.00	n/l
	b.	1.40	1.75	2.50	4.75	12.00	260.00	n/l
	c.	1.40	1.60	2.10	3.25	10.35	142.00	975.00
1924D	a.	8.00	9.00	11.00	16.00	28.50	300.00	n/l
	b.	8.00	9.00	11.00	16.00	28.50	300.00	n/l
	c.	9.50	11.00	12.50	16.35	32.50	205.00	1,050.00
1926S	a.	3.00	3.60	5.00	6.00	12.50	185.00	n/l
	b.	3.00	3.75	5.50	6.50	12.50	195.00	n/l
	c.	3.00	3.60	5.00	6.00	12.00	100.00	170.00
1931S	a.	25.00	27.00	30.00	32.50	35.00	52.50	n/l
	c.	31.00	35.00	40.00	45.00	50.00	90.00	135.00
1955/55	a.	n/l	n/l	n/l	215.00	250.00	550.00	n/l
	b.	n/l	n/l	n/l	215.00	250.00	550.00	n/l
	c.	n/l	n/l	n/l	375.00	475.00	MS65=3,500	
1972/72	a.						115.00	
	b.						225.00	
	c.						MS65=350.00	

One can readily see that in the past few years, the semi-keys tended to remain fairly steady until 1981 when the interest in Lincolns picked up and they advanced in prices only in the higher grades. Many lower grades slipped in book value since so many circulated specimens were hoarded over the years. The MS65 grade which has been listed for the past few years by CDN and not the Red Book shows anywhere from a 4x to 6x premium over MS60. In Chapter 5 note carefully the characteristics for each date which make the difference in the mint state coins. The key coins generally have been moving right along in recent years especially in MS65, while lesser grades have not done as well.

Section 2: Tracking the BU Rolls—

The listing of rolls is taken from three issues of the COIN DEALER NEWSLETTER—April 1980, March 1983 and February 1988. The figures reflect the progress or regression of each issue.

(Only the bid prices are listed)

	April 1980	March 1983	February 1988	May 1992
1934P	240.00	260.00	160.00	200.00
1934D	1,300.00	1,800.00	1,275.00	900.00
1935	90.00	100.00	90.00	110.00
1935D	125.00	295.00	188.00	190.00
1935S	410.00	1,000.00	400.00	450.00
1936	54.00	65.00	57.50	75.00
1936D	100.00	165.00	135.00	165.00
1936S	115.00	175.00	135.00	140.00
1937	68.00	110.00	35.00	42.00
1937D	105.00	130.00	110.00	72.50
1937S	85.00	130.00	100.00	75.00
1938	53.00	75.00	67.00	70.00
1938D	86.00	125.00	77.00	87.50
1938S	110.00	150.00	85.00	70.00
1939	35.00	45.00	26.00	35.00
1939D	235.00	210.00	128.00	120.00
1939S	125.00	115.00	95.00	55.00
1940	29.00	27.50	26.00	41.00
1940D	50.00	75.00	41.00	50.00
1940S	50.00	125.00	36.00	42.50
1941	45.00	44.00	46.00	52.00
1941D	86.00	152.50	94.00	105.00
1941S	210.00	160.00	87.00	90.00
1942	17.00	26.00	20.00	28.50

-continued-

	April 1980	March 1983	February 19888	May 1992
1942D	16.00	30.00	23.00	22.00
1942S	235.00	220.00	180.00	190.00
1943	40.00	45.00	24.00	35.00
1943D	51.00	90.00	70.00	49.00
1943S	65.00	120.00	85.00	85.00
1944	6.00	9.75	16.00	27.00
1944D	15.00	30.00	11.00	11.50
1944S	15.00	17.00	10.50	10.50
1945	5.25	7.75	9.00	19.50
1945D	21.00	26.00	32.00	13.00
1946	6.35	9.25	9.00	15.00
1946D	8.00	8.75	8.50	6.50
1946S	18.00	17.00	13.00	13.50
1947	27.00	30.00	16.00	52.50
1947D	14.00	16.00	7.00	7.00
1947S	16.50	27.50	12.00	14.00
1948	12.00	18.50	15.00	20.00
1948D	6.00	30.00	14.00	14.50
1948S	23.00	38.00	21.00	23.50
1949	26.50	47.50	21.00	20.00
1949D	13.25	34.00	21.00	22.50
1949S	57.00	76.00	60.00	52.50
1950	17.50	47.50	19.00	22.00
1950D	11.00	9.50	9.00	9.50
1950S	18.00	30.00	18.00	20.00
1951	37.00	35.00	20.00	24.00
1951D	5.00	13.00	10.50	10.00
1951S	62.00	50.00	23.00	27.00
1952	19.00	18.00	17.00	19.00
1952D	6.00	23.00	5.75	7.50
1952S	32.00	29.00	19.50	22.00
1953	6.00	9.00	4.75	6.00
1953D	2.20	18.00	5.25	5.50
1953S	10.00	17.00	10.00	12.00

-continued-

	April 1980	March 1983	February 1988	May 1992
1954	17.00	18.00	13.00	15.00
1954D	3.60	8.00	3.25	6.00
1954S	8.00	7.25	3.50	6.00
1955	4.75	5.25	3.00	5.00
1955D	4.00	5.25	2.00	2.50
1955S	18.00	15.00	11.00	12.00
1956	2.15	7.00	2.25	4.35
1956D	1.55	3.65	1.75	2.85
1957	1.75	4.00	1.75	2.95
1957D	1.40	2.25	1.50	2.35
1958	1.85	2.35	1.50	3.00
1958D	1.35	2.05	1.15	2.50
1959	0.65	1.00	0.80	1.00
1959D	0.65	1.00	0.80	1.10
1960	0.65	0.90	0.70	1.00
1960 Sm	130.00	105.00	72.00	80.00
1960D	0.70	1.10	0.70	1.00
1960D Sm	3.25	2.20	1.10	1.00
1961	0.85	1.15	0.85	1.00
1961D	0.65	1.50	0.75	1.00
1962	0.75	1.70	0.85	1.00
1962D	0.75	1.20	0.85	1.00
1963	0.70	0.90	0.80	1.00
1963D	0.70	0.95	0.80	1.00
1964	0.65	0.80	0.70	1.00
1964D	0.85	1.00	0.85	1.10
1965	1.15	1.50	1.90	2.25
1966	1.25	7.00	3.20	3.00
1967	1.40	6.25	3.35	2.50
1968	2.00	5.25	3.10	2.70
1968D	0.85	1.60	1.00	2.70
1968S	0.65	1.30	0.80	1.00
1969	7.00	17.00	6.00	9.75
1969D	0.70	0.80	1.50	1.10

-continued-

	April 1980	March 1983	February 1988	May 1992
1969S	0.90	2.05	0.95	1.25
1969S Pf	8.00	37.50	25.00	45.00
1970	1.30	11.50	2.80	4.00
1970D	0.80	3.20	1.20	1.25
1970S	1.80	2.05	1.05	1.30
1970 Sm	215.00	380.00	530.00	700.00
1970S Pf	10.00	39.00	22.00	45.00
1971	1.55	7.00	8.50	6.50
1971D	0.95	5.00	7.25	8.00
1971S	2.35	7.50	3.40	5.50
1971S Pf	9.00	39.00	23.00	25.00
1972	0.80	1.60	0.80	1.75
1972D	1.00	3.40	2.25	2.95
1972S	0.95	1.10	0.95	2.65
1972S Pf	9.00	37.50	23.00	29.00
1973	0.70	0.80	0.70	1.45
1973D	0.60	0.90	0.85	1.20
1973S	0.70	1.35	0.90	1.35
1973S Pf	12.50	37.50	22.00	
1974	0.75	0.75	0.75	1.00
1974D	0.65	0.70	0.70	1.00
1974S	1.20	3.85	2.00	2.85
1974S Pf	12.50	37.50	23.00	
1975	0.75	1.15	0.85	1.25
1975D	0.90	1.75	1.15	2.75
1975S Pf	360.00	330.00	185.00	150.00
1976	0.60	0.90	0.95	1.60
1976D	0.60	2.50	1.05	4.50
1976S Pf	95.00	115.00	75.00	95.00
1977	0.65	1.25	0.80	1.35
1977D	1.10	1.00	0.90	1.25
1977S Pf	97.50	105.00	76.00	95.00
1978	0.65	3.00	1.10	1.80
1978D	0.65	2.20	1.20	1.50

-continued-

	April 1980	March 1983	February 1988	May 1992
1978S Pf	130.00	145.00	80.00	100.00
1979	0.65	0.85	0.70	1.50
1979D	0.65	0.95	0.90	1.15
1979S Pf (I)	140.00	150.00	70.00	90.00
1980	--	0.75	0.65	1.60
1980D	--	0.75	0.70	1.60
1980S Pf	--	80.00	40.00	75.00
1981	--	0.75	0.70	1.50
1981D	--	0.65	0.60	1.50
1981S Pf (I)	--	120.00	40.00	60.00
1982 Zinc Lg	--	1.25	0.70	1.65
1982 Zinc Sm	--	1.25	0.70	1.10
1982 Br Lg	--	1.00	0.65	1.00
1982 Br Sm	--	4.75	2.50	1.65
1982D Zinc Sm	--	1.10	0.75	1.00
1982D Zinc Lg	--	7.95	4.50	5.25
1982D Br Lg	--	0.75	0.65	0.80
1982S Pf	--	185.00	100.00	75.00

The track record in recent years for the BU rolls has been very erratic to say the least. In the peak of the market of 1979-1981, many records were set only to fall back as profit taking and the effects of the recession were felt across the board. Prices however, for the majority of issues from 1970 to date have shown steady growth since they were not caught up in the buying frenzy. See chapter 5 for specific suggestions regarding some of these roll issues.

Section 3: Tracking the Circulated Roll Market

Most Lincoln cents are commonly traded by the circulated roll—except for the most expensive coins. A look at some of the prices ("Bid" prices mostly taken from the Coin Dealer Newsletter for selected issues). The figures represent the bid prices shown in January, 1980, March, 1983 and March, 1988.

	January 1980	March 1983	March 1988	May 1992
1909VDB	56.00	100.00	90.00	120.00
1909	10.00	22.50	24.00	20.00
1909S	1,100.00	2,100.00	1,750.00	1,850.00
1910	3.00	6.00	5.00	3.50
1910S	192.50	300.00	250.00	200.00
1911	3.75	6.50	5.00	3.00
1911D	97.50	162.50	145.00	180.00
1911S	330.00	507.50	440.00	375.00
1912	9.00	13.50	10.50	8.00
1912D	105.00	172.50	160.00	150.00
1912S	280.00	437.50	425.00	350.00
1913	5.00	11.00	11.50	7.50
1913D	55.00	87.50	75.00	50.00
1913S	185.00	297.50	195.00	150.00
1914	5.00	12.50	13.50	8.50
1914S	245.00	395.00	325.00	400.00
1915	21.00	35.00	18.00	24.00
1915D	15.00	27.50	24.50	27.50
1916-20 ea.	1.60	3.50	3.00	3.50
1916D	6.00	8.50	6.00	7.00
1916S	22.50	35.00	24.50	18.00
1917D	5.25	7.50	6.00	7.00

-continued-

	January 1980	March 1983	March 1988	May 1992
1917S	8.75	12.00	7.50	10.00
1918D	4.75	7.00	10.50	10.00
1918S	6.65	9.00	11.50	12.50
1919D	3.35	5.75	5.00	5.00
1919S	2.75	3.20	2.80	2.50
1920D	4.65	6.00	10.00	8.00
1920S	3.15	6.25	9.00	10.00
1921	4.25	4.75	6.25	7.50
1921S	15.00	30.00	37.50	40.00
1922D	120.00	192.00	140.00	150.00
1923-30 ea.	1.60	2.85	4.00	4.00
1923S	50.00	70.00	50.00	55.00
1924D	300.00	520.00	475.00	450.00
1924S	17.50	27.50	30.00	25.00
1925D	6.25	7.50	6.50	6.00
1925S	3.00	4.00	5.00	4.50
1926D	5.25	5.75	4.50	4.50
1926S	87.50	125.00	145.00	135.00
1927D	3.50	4.50	5.00	5.00
1927S	14.00	19.50	24.50	21.00
1928S	2.70	4.00	4.00	4.50
1928S	8.00	10.00	8.00	9.00
1929D	2.25	3.85	4.50	4.00
1929S	2.00	3.20	3.00	3.00
1930D	2.75	3.65	3.60	3.25
1930S	5.50	6.00	5.00	4.00
1931	11.00	20.00	14.00	12.50
1931D	70.00	92.50	88.00	100.00
1931S	1,000.00	1,500.00	1,340.00	1,400.00
1932	50.00	60.00	46.00	40.00
1932D	18.00	32.00	27.50	30.00
1933	11.00	35.00	27.50	30.00
1933D	60.00	70.00	65.00	60.00
1934-39 ea.	1.10	3.50	2.85	2.50
1934D	4.25	5.00	3.35	3.00

-continued-

	January 1980	March 1983	March 1988	May 1992
1935D	2.15	3.00	3.50	3.50
1935S	2.65	4.10	4.00	4.50
1936D	1.85	2.95	3.00	3.00
1936S	3.20	4.00	4.00	4.00
1937D	1.85	2.80	3.50	3.50
1937S	2.10	2.85	3.50	3.50
1938D	4.25	6.50	6.00	5.00
1938S	6.50	7.50	6.50	5.50
1939D	11.00	15.00	14.00	15.00
1939S	1.80	2.75	2.50	2.50
1940D	1.50	2.25	2.00	2.25
1940S	1.65	2.25	2.00	2.25
1940-58, except as listed "P" mint				
	1.00	1.75	1.85	1.50
1941D	1.95	2.10	2.00	2.00
1941S	1.75	2.25	2.00	2.00
1942S	2.25	2.50	2.25	2.50
1943	2.50	2.50	2.75	3.50
1943D	10.00	5.50	7.00	8.00
1943S	10.00	5.50	7.75	10.00
1949S	2.20	2.50	2.75	3.00
1954	1.50	1.60	2.15	3.00
1955S	6.25	11.50	6.50	6.50
All other Wheat dates not listed				
	1.00	1.50	1.50	1.60

Conclusions from Chapter 4:

a. Key coins move up regularly, sometimes slowly, sometimes rapidly.

b. Semi-key coins and common coins move slowly and often regress.

c. Uncirculated rolls are subject to speculation and rapid changes in prices both up and down.

d. Circulated rolls (as listed) tend to show a cyclical movement and a shrinking supply to replace those that have been broken down. The assembling of circulated rolls apparently was in vogue in the past, but not to any extent in the past 10-15 years resulting in smaller supplies each year. Those left in circulation are too few to count and those hoards that have come onto the market have been readily absorbed by dealers and collectors alike. Prices do not reflect supply as much as demand.

The market in both uncirculated as well as circulated Lincoln Cents is changing and in future years may not be an issue as more collectors break down these rolls for the best coins for their collections and dealers do likewise for their stock books. At one time in the early 1970s rolls were readily available for almost all coins form 1934 to date and for Morgan and Peace dollars almost the entire series (save a few rare dates), prices were quoted for rolls. Since the late 1980s rolls have been shrinking in numbers and those remaining are lower end circulated rolls and the uncirculated rolls often tend to be "rejects" from culled over rolls.

Chapter 5 - Vital Statistics

The data in this chapter come from many sources. The mintage figures are from the annual U.S. Mint reports, and for many issues are rounded off to the nearest thousand. In cases where the actual mintage is not reported, it is shown as an estimated number, such as the mintage of the 1960P small date cents.

The prices shown for 1992 are based upon varied reliable sources - including our own mail bid sale results, advertised price lists, auction results, private transactions, and various newsletter data. For the very inexpensive coins, the prices are shown in the nearest whole cent - and for later years, prices are shown by the roll rather than decimal values per coin.

These prices are not an offer to buy nor sell. They are prices that one can expect to pay for the specific coins listed in the specific grade at the time of publication - prices do tend to fluctuate and the actual numbers then become relative rather than absolute. Any projections made by the author about future trends are projections, not predictions and are not designed to guide specific collectors or investors toward certain coins. The author does not stock coins and is not promoting any coins on behalf of anyone.

In some cases of very rare of choice coins, the prices may vary widely on specific transactions. A case in point relates to the 1922 plain cent which was sold for $16,000 at an auction in Texas in 1981 and a matching piece brought $7,500 at a later auction. We tend to report the lower price. Similarly, MS65 1909SVDB cents have been sold at recent auctions at prices ranging from $750-1450. See the final chapter on Grading to clarify these variances in prices.

Many roll prices of issued after 1935 are lower in 1992 as compared to 1983. The basic reason is that 1992 rolls, by and large, are the lower quality rolls. The vast majority of rolls in the past five years have been broken down to singles.

GENUINE MATTE PROOF 1909 CENT
Obverse and Reverse views

This chapter is devoted to the data of each year of the Lincoln Cent. Where some special feature of the date is indicated, it will be expanded for collector interest. Special thanks go to Carole Kelsey, Chuck Benko, Steve Benson, and Bill Fivaz for their input on this chapter.

The mintage data come from U.S. Mint sources and are believed reliable. The Population Data come from 1991 PCGS data reports. Population Data reflect a slice of the pie, and are statistically valid inasmuch as they reflect the whole. Thus, when there is a coin such as the 1926S which shows none in MS65Red, it can be assumed that there are indeed few or none of such coins known. As the population data continue to grow--slowly for most dates, the relative position of the very scarce and rare pieces remains unchanged. It is also known that in a few cases, coins which were once included in a Population Report were subsequently removed form the plastic and resubmitted in the hopes of obtaining a better grade. The actual number of such resubmissions is unknown and may affect the total number of slabbed pieces, but by some small increment. Again, these data are used by collectors to qualify their top pieces as compared to others known to be certified by a given grading service. SLCC member Stewart Blay exhibited "The World's Finest Certified Lincoln Cents Collection" at the American Numismatic Association Centennial Convention in Chicago in 1991. This set (in 1991) represented the best known coin of each date and mint and thus the best total set ever assembled. Only one coin was less than MS65Red and that was a 1926S MS65RB. That list is reprinted in Chapter 8.

The actual number of coins available for each date cannot be determined. This is especially true for circulated coins, since most circulated Lincoln Cents are not certified and are not included in any population data studies. Even the uncirculated and proof coins are not totally represented. Among the later dated coins, only a minuscule fraction are ever submitted for certification since their value is often less than one dollar and the cost of the service is at least $20 per coin.

—1909—

MINTAGES:
1909VDB — 27,995,000
1909VDB — Matte Proof — 420 Pieces
1909 — 72,702,618
1909SVDB — 484,000
1909 — Matte Proof — 2,198 Pieces
1909S — 1,825,000

AVAILABILITY:

As seen in the clippings in the introduction, the 1909 Lincoln Cent generated a considerable stir. Collectors and Lincoln fans scooped up large numbers of the new coins and stored them away. Some have only recently appeared on the market after 75 or more years in storage. Though the 1909 VDB was minted for a scant few days, the total mintage of 27 million makes it fairly common. Many tens of thousands remain in mint condition. Nearly 2,000 were slabbed by PCGS and graded as mint state as of late 1991. More are submitted regularly.

Since the working dies saw so little use, most specimens are early die state coins, full of mint red and golden hues and show considerable detail in the hair, beard, coat, and wheat stalks.

The 1909 SVDB also saw very little production time-- perhaps as few as five days or less and a total mint output of 484,000. Since San Francisco was far from most channels of commerce, these pieces saw very little service outside the West Coast. Again, hoards were know well into the 1960s. San Francisco dealer Robert Johnson had two BU rolls in his shop from a purchase back in 1964. Several other dealers have handled full uncirculated rolls well into the 1970s. Since then, only small groupings and single coins have shown up in old estates. They usually show bright mint luster, full mint red and golden hues, strong die details, and even wire rims. Prices however, have remained strong since there is a steady demand for a choice to gem uncirculated 1909 SVDB.

Prices for such pieces have ranged form just under $1,000 in the mid-1980s to over $2500 in 1991. Auction sales typically run in the $1250 to $1450 range in the 1990s.

The two matte proof issues of 1909 are both quite scarce and the 1909 VDB matte proof is the lowest mintage Lincoln Cent recorded in the U.S. Mint records. In recent sales specimens have gone for $1500 up to $7500. As of 1991, PCGS had certified only 45 pieces.

The 1909 matte proof is also quite scarce with only 2,198 pieces minted. The distinctive satin finish of the matte proof with the squared rim, separated letters and granular field makes the matte fairly easy to identify. However, some early struck BU coins can be mistaken for matte proofs. A diagnostic study by Leonard Albrecht is essential to help identify each dated matte proof by specific die features. And as most authors write, attribution or certification is recommended for all matte proof cents.

The 1909 cent is readily available in mint state and circulated grades, including roll quantities. For many years, specimens could be found in change well into the 1960s. The high mintage of the 1909 (72 million) keeps it out of the scarce category even after these many years.

The 1909S cent is a semi-key coin and always in demand in all grades. Though hoarded in small numbers, many apparently did circulate. Only 1.8 million were minted and few managed to migrate across the nation to eastern cities. BU hoards showed up at major coin shows for many years until the supply trickled out by the early 1980s. Most are well struck and full reds are not hard to locate. PCGS reported (Nov. 1991) nearly 400 in MS red with 35 as MS66--a very high number if one goes right down that column in the population data and the HIGHEST number of MS66 Reds for any San Francisco minted coin until well into the 1930s.

One very interesting mint variety of the 1909S shows up in sales. It is the 1909S/S with the under S in the horizontal position. This is known as RPM#1, "S over horizontal S".

Breen lists it as "scarce" and prices tend to run about 10-20% over usual price for this variety.

Two obverse doubled dies are found in this date. First discovered in 1978 (published by Wexler), it is clearest in doubling the RTY and 190 of the date. BU specimens have sold in SLCC mail bid sales from $125 to $450. In searching through more than 1,250 pieces (circulated rolls) this author found two circulated specimens. In very fine, sales have been made at $40 and in extra fine, sales have been made at up to $65. The coin is featured in the Cherrypicker's Guide. The other doubled die is less obvious with the main features small die breaks in B and R and thicker numerals in 190 of the date. This variety brings about $10 in circulated grades and up to $75 in choice uncirculated.

Breen lists a 1909 obverse doubled die not included in Wexler and listed as "very rare". (Breen #2056).

Wexler lists a minor reverse doubled die which shows thickened end stalks of wheat.

Breen reports a major hoard of 1909S VDB cents bough by John Zug at the San Francisco Mint in 1909 and resold in 1918 at $1.75 cents each. The hoard reportedly contained 25,000 coins. Also reported by George Fuld in the Van Cleave Sale of Kagins on 2/1/86.

Because of the popularity of the 1909S VDB and the 1909S, both coins have been extensively faked--both with added mint marks as well as cast counterfeits, and other forgeries. Thus, certification is highly recommended for uncirculated specimens. Even circulated 1909S VDB coins have been faked.

V.D.B. and DOTS

The various dies used for the V.D.B. reverse show the periods in eight configurations ranging from none, Var. #8 to all three Var. #1. A few collectors have assembled BU sets including one of each of the eight variants. Varieties 5, 6, and 7 appear to be scarce while the others appear more commonly.

No. 1 — V.D.B.

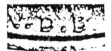
No. 2 — V.D.B

No. 3 — V.D B.

No. 4 — V D.B.

No. 5 — V.D B

No. 6 — V D.B

No. 7 — V D B.

No. 8 — V D B

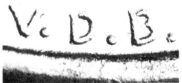

1909-S VDB Cent—Mintmark: Serifs are vertical and parallel to each other. There is an lump in the lower left part of the upper curve. On high-grade coins a groove can be seen in the upper serif.

1909-S VDB Cent—Designer's Initials: The center and bottom bars slope downward diagonally to the left. The tops of the initials are sometimes weakly struck, almost nonexistent, and one or more of the periods may be missing.

34

COLLECTORS TIPS:

There are eight variations of the **VDB** on the **VDB** cents. Each one varies according to the location and number of periods in the initials—ranging from three to none. See p. 32.

There were three working dies used for the 1909S **VDB** obverse. These are: 1 high left, 2 high right, and 3 low right. Type I tilts a bit to the right. Type 2 also tilts a bit to the right pointing toward the 0 in the date. Type 3 lies almost directly beneath the 0 in the date as is vertical. In each case, the S itself is somewhat thick and lacks clear loops. It has a stubby serif at each end of the S.

There are six variations of the S on the 1909S cents. Three are the same as the 1909SVDB, and the other three are: medium high tilted right, low tilted far right, and far low far right.

1909-VDB 1¢ 1-O-III

DOUBLING: The second hubbing is spread West-Northwest and shows on the 190 of the date, Lincoln's lips and on LIBERTY.

MARKERS: The obverse has a die crack (spiked head) running from the ear North to the rim at approximately K-12. The reverse die has a small die break from the base of the D in V.D.B. It is possible that further study will prove this variety to be a Class IV doubled die rather than a Class III variety.

—1910—

MINTAGES:
1910-P — 146,801,218
1910 Matte Proof — 2,405 Pieces
1910S — 6,045,000

Since the reverse dies of many 1910 cents show workover at the lower rim, it is assumed that dies from 1909 with the V.D.B. were carried over for 1910 strikings. One 1910S specimen was sold to a Brooklyn coin dealer who had it examined by Walter Breen in 1985 and Breen indicated there are traces of the "V.D.B." on the reverse. Another specimen sold through SLCC in 1991 now is in a New Jersey collection. Bill Fivaz discovered a slabbed 1910 matte proof which shows a trace of the "B". It was sold via SLCC in 1991 to a Nevada collector. This coin was featured in an article in COIN WORLD in 1991.

The 1910 cent was apparently hoarded since full mint red specimens still appear on the market in the 1990s. Over 200 have been certified by PCGS by late 1991 and more than 50 were graded as MS66 with 3 as MS67. They come in varying shades of mint red, lustrous golden red, golden orange, and pale red. Most strikings appear to be early die states.

The 1910S cent with a mintage of over 6 million made its way into commercial channels as most specimens available in the 1990s are lower grade circulated coins. The combined PCGS population of mint state 1910S coins late in 1991 was over 500 pieces with only 8 MS66 Red. Another 162 rated MS65 Red. Small hoards were known well into the 1970s.

The 1910 matte proof cent had a total mintage of 2,405 pieces. The original surface color was described by contemporary collectors as "golden tan", "satiny red", and "brassy red".

Since most were stored in paper, the present surfaces tend to appear woody toned--mixtures of reddish and brown hues. The full mint red seen in business strikes is not the color one expects on matte proof cents. Over 130 pieces have been certified by PCGS as of late 1991. Only 46 rated a "red" designation.

The 1910S is characterized by two repunched mintmark variants. They are both fairly clear under low magnification--RPM#1 shows the under mintmark to the south and RPM#2 shows the under mintmark to the north. Both add some 20% additional value to the 1910S cent.

—1911—

MINTAGES:
1911P — 101,177,787
1911 - Matte Proof — 1,733 pieces
1911-D — 12,672,000
1911-S — 4,026,000

AVAILABILITY:

The 1911D cent was the first U.S. copper (bronze coin) minted at the Denver Mint. The dies were prepared at the Philadelphia Mint and shipped to Denver for the mintmark and general production. The mintage of 12 million made for a wide variation in quality of mint coins. Though early die state coins are known in mint state, the more common uncirculated coins tend to be average or even late die state quality. As a result the MS65 Red population reported by PCGS late in 1991 is only 31 coins. The MS64 Red is 57 coins. In circulated grades, the extra fine coins tend to be average to late die state, indicating a combination of factors leading to less than pristine die states.

The 1911 cent was reduced from the 1910 production in Philadelphia from 145 million to 101 million--perhaps allowing the Denver production to meet the midwest demand. Though not seen in large numbers, choice BU early die state 1911s are available. PCGS showed 88 MS65 Red, 18 MS66 Red, 75 MS64 Red, and some 50 other MS graded pieces as of late 1991. Though most certified specimens are early die state, there are numerous average and even late die state coins around. Numerous "raw" (uncertified) 1911 coins are known in MS63 and other MS grades less than MS65 Red. The later die state coins perhaps do not warrant the expense of certification.

The 1911S cent was the largest mintage of any San Francisco cent to date--with over 12 million minted. However, for many, the quality was well below the 1909S level and today the majority of mint state specimens are average to late die state coins and far more red-brown than red. The PCGS population of MS66 Red - 5, MS65 Red - 24, MS64 - 32, and MS63 Red - 2. The total of MS coins in red-brown certified for the same report was 90. Many of the "raw" 1911S cents appear to be MS64 quality or less and most seem to be red-brown versus full mint red. The number of newly certified pieces as of early 1992 appears to be single digit increments per month. In circulated grades, the 1911S is even available in roll quantities from grades of about good on up to extra fine, indicating this dated coin saw wide use over the years. It is a popular early date mintmarked coin and had always commanded a premium.

The 1911 matte proof is very similar to the 1910 matte proof. Many existing specimens were stored in paper wrappers or envelopes and some have a distinctive purple hue--perhaps a sulphur reaction to the copper surface. Mishandled specimens still bring over $150 at auction and gem specimens (spotless and lustrous surfaces) bring well into the $500 range. Only 1,733 pieces were minted and no doubt some were lost, spent, or mishandled to lower grades than mint state. This author has found a few matte proof coins in coin folders in slots reserved for the "P" mint coin of that date.

PCGS had certified by late 1991 Pf64 Red - 8, Pf65 Red - 12, and Pf66 Red - 3 and Pf67 Red - 1. The total number of red-brown and brown 1911 matte proofs was 119.

A 1911S RPM#1 is listed in Wexler. It brings about a 50% premium in all grades.

—1912—

MINTAGES:
1912P — 68,153,000
1912 Matte Proof — 2,145 pieces
1912D — 10,411,000
1912S — 4,431,000

AVAILABILITY:

The 1912 cent is available in all grades and commands a premium only in the highest MS grades in mint red. A total of 13 were certified as MS66 Red in the November 1991 PCGS Population Report. Another 88 listed in MS65 Red and 61 in MS64 Red. A fair number still in "raw" state are available on various dealer price lists and in various sales catalogues.

The 1912D, similar to the 1911D shows some late die state effect and choice early die state coins are the exception, not the rule. Only 19 were graded MS65 Red by PCGS late in 1991 and none higher. Another 38 were graded MS64 Red. Both are small numbers. Late die state BU coins probably make up the bulk of known BU 1912D.

From the circulated collections and circulated rolls examined, the weakness in the features typify the quality of this issue.

The 1912S shows similar weaknesses in die features, though well-struck specimens do exist. PCGS data show: MS65 Red - 12, MS64 Red - 25 and MS63 Red - 6. A total of 66 listed in MS63-65 BN certified pieces. Chances are such brown pieces are not prime candidates for encapsulation and can be readily found in many dealers' files.

The 1912 matte proof is similar to the 1911 with some more granulation (orange peel effect) in the field. In Albrecht's study (THE NUMISMATIST, October, 1983), two die states are described. Both show diagonal die polish lines in the field. The usual colors found range from deep tan to purplish brown. Red is not at all common. Only 4 were graded by PCGS as Pf65 Red. Another 4 as Pf64 Red. In red-brown and brown, the total rises to 101 including Pf63-66. The "red" seen in the matte proofs typically are russet brown or brownish rust or wood-toned red. They do not match mint state business strikes.

Some early die state 1912 cents can be mistaken for matte proofs. The key is the squared rim on matte proofs and the separation between the rim and the letters. Raw coins should be checked against Albrecht's listings or purchased subject to certification.

A 1912S RPM#1 is listed in Wexler. It brings a 33-35% premium in all grades.

—1913—

MINTAGES:
1913P — 76,532,000
1913 - Matte Proof — 2,848 pieces
1913D — 15,804,000
1913S — 6,101,000

AVAILABILITY:

The 1913 Philadelphia mint coin is still found in choice and gem mint state and often in early die state. The choicest pieces tend to be pale golden yellow versus mint red and often have a gold-like quality. In the PCGS Population Report of October, 1991, there were 2 MS67 Red, 12 MS66 Red, 61 MS65 Red, 34 MS64 Red and 4 MS63 Red. SLCC has handled several gem red 1913 cents which were not slabbed which surely fall into these categories. In fact, the encapsulated red coins outnumber the combined red-brown and brown MS coins. Though late die state 1913 cents are known, they are less common than the early and average die state coins.

The 1913D cent is a case where the early die state coin is the exception. The majority of certified pieces are average to late die state. PCGS has certified 4 in MS66 Red, 28 in MS65 Red, 29 in MS64 Red and 4 in MS63 Red. The total of the other MS pieces is 50.

"A Guide to Die States" by Della K. Romines in the January, 1991 issue of THE NUMISMATIST exemplifies the die states of the Lincoln Cent. He uses the terms as herein except for "MDS" - Mid Die State for ADS - Average Die State.

The 1913S cent is a low mintage branch mint coin and because it was well-circulated, being found in all grades, it is one of the "semi-key" dates. Collectors in the early 1950s were able to locate well worn (AG-G) specimens in change.

This author even found several in New York City in the period from 1937-1960. None was much better than a grade of good. However in mint state, this date is quite scarce--regardless of die states. In PCGS, 1991 data only 14 were MS65 Red, 25 MS64 Red, and 4 MS63 Red. In red-brown there were 13 MS65, 35 MS64, and 17 MS63. From those examined most were MDS to LDS. None is graded MS66 or higher.

The S punches used for the 1913S cent apparently were the same (if not the same style) as used from 1909 through 1915. This diagnostic helps one identify altered S mint cents of this era where the mintmark was lifted from a later dated coin or created from the field.

Discussions with the late Abe Kosoff, Lou Friedman, and Maurice Gould all indicated that the 1913S was not a coin ever seen in BU hoards or rolls.

The 1913 matte proof as its predecessors was a low mintage collector piece with only 2,848 pieces struck. The surviving population is probably one-fourth that number with only 175 encapsulated by PCGS and a lesser number by the other services. Perhaps the total is higher, but as with other matte proofs, some have been misidentified and reside in collections as BU coins, not matte proofs. It is typified by fine mint polish, well struck, and several distinctive die striae seen in Albrecht's photographs. Colors typically range from light reddish tan to deep brownish purple. Though PCGS had graded several as "red" including 7 Pf66 Red and 1 Pf67 Red, the actual surface colors are more russet-tan.

—1914—

MINTAGES:
1914 — 75,238,000
1914 - Matte Proof — 1,365 pieces
1914S — 4,137,000
1914D — 1,193,000

The 1914 cent is available, at a price, in high states of preservation and early die states as well. Small hoards and BU rolls were seen at major shows up through the 1960s. In the late PCGS 1991 Population Report, there were: 1 MS67 Red, 13 MS66 Red, 58 MS65 Red, 76 MS64 Red and 9 MS63 Red. Several raw BU red 1914 cents were handled by SLCC in mail bid sales. Others have been seen at recent coins shows. The 1914 red-brown unc show: 1 MS66, 19 MS65, 56 MS64 and 21 MS63. Most are seen as early die state. Circulated rolls from AG to XF are known and available from various dealers.

The 1914D cent is considered by many as the "Number 2" coin in the series behind the 1909S VDB. This is more due to the low mintage of 1.193 million and not as much as die state, color, or other value factors. In fact, Breen reports a BU hoard of 700 pieces in the stock of a dealer in the early 1950s. Thus BU coins are available as raw or certified. The popularity of the date was recognized early on and most price lists show a premium in all grades. The PCGS data show: 1 MS66 Red, 14 MS65 Red, 22 MS64 REd, 8 MS63 Red, 9 MS65 RB, 53 MS64 RB, 40 MS63 RB and 29 other MS coins.

Because the coin is valuable in less than mint grades, a sizeable number is also known encapsulated. Further, because the coin has been extensively forged with false mintmarks, altered dates, and even die struck counterfeits, many circulated specimens are slabbed. This is not typical for other dates except for the 1922 "plain".

Early price lists reflected the scarcity of mint state 1914S cents. In fact, in 1934 price lists, the highest priced Lincoln Cent was the 1914S. Today, there is one known PCGS MS66 Red, and only 7 MS65 Red. The total number of mint state 1914S coins listed with PCGS in late 1991 was 97 coins. A 1992 price list published a price of $12,500 for a MS65 Red 1914S. This indicates the value rarity of such a coin.

The 1914 matte proof had a total mintage of 1,365 pieces. One diagnostic is a small die chip atop the 1 in the date and a myriad of raised die striae below the beard and above the date. The surface is a fine granular field similar to the 1912 and 1913. Again, colors tend to have a woody tan color often with iridescent hues. A total of 28 1914 matte proofs are certified by PCGS as "red" from Pf63-Pf66.

Since the 1914D has been extensively altered, counterfeited, and otherwise faked, certification is highly recommended, even for specimens grading very fine to extra fine. If 1944D cents were altered, there is a wide gap in the date and the VDB on the truncation of the shoulder is visible or scraped off. The D on the 1944D is larger and has longer serifs than the genuine D. Die struck counterfeits are known.

—1915—

MINTAGES:
1915P — 29,092,100
1915 - Matte Proof — 1,150 pieces
1915S — 4,833,000
1915D — 22,050,000

AVAILABILITY:

The 1915 Philadelphia mint cent was reduced in mintage by more than 60 percent from the prior two years. If this knowledge precipitated hoarding or not is not known from contemporary accounts, but hoards did exist and the Population Report data seems to support this. Most uncirculated pieces examined tend to be early die state coins with sharp details and some even proof like. Dave Bowers writes that through an auction bidding error some 50 years ago, the 1915 cent took off as being more valuable than its availability would indicate and somehow that image has persisted. In late 1991 population data there are 12 MS66 Red, 75 MS65 Red, 60 MS64 Red, and 3 MS63 Red. These are very similar to 1914 data--a date considered to be quite a bit less valuable in fixed price lists and auction results. The total mintage of 29 million is far from a "low" mintage. The fact that many circulated specimens exist in all grades indicates the coin circulated widely.

The 1915D cent with a mintage of 22 million was the highest Denver mintage of any cent to that date. However, from specimens currently encapsulated and from many coins examined over the years, late die state mintage was far more the rule than not. A few early die state coins have been certified and high grade circulated coins also show early die state features. The population data in late 1991 show: 8 MS66 Red, 69 MS65 REd, 59 MS64 REd, and 11 MS63 REd. Another 98 pieces are listed in mint state red-brown and brown.

The 1915S cent is another semi-key coin which was always difficult to locate in circulation and especially so in mint red state. The earliest price lists (see Chapter 8) often did not have more than the lower grade pieces for sale. The number of encapsulated red specimens is rather low a s compared to other early date Lincolns. There were: 1 MS66 Red, 13 MS65 Red, 8 MS64 Red, and 1 MS63 Red. The other mint state pieces totaled only 43 as of late 1991. Few "raw" pieces have been seen in the past few years--chances are most have already been slabbed. No hoards have been described in the literature.

The 1915 matte proof was reduced from the previous years to 1,150 pieces. The surface was less granular and more satiny than the 1914. Some early business strikes look remarkably like matte proofs, thus attribution is essential. Also, many specimens show a purple toning probably from sulphur infused paper used to ship the coins. The population numbers for Pf Red show: Pf67 - 2, Pf66 - 1, Pf65 - 6, and Pf64 - 5. The scarcity of this coin is clear. Most of the remaining encapsulated pieces in red brown and brown total 90 coins. Auction results do not seem to differentiate this piece as scarcer than the other more available matte proofs.

—1916—

MINTAGES:
1916P — 131,833,677
1916 - Matte Proof — 1,050 pieces
1916D — 35,956,000
1916S — 22,510,000

AVAILABILITY:

The 1916 cent is one of the early dates which seemed to always be available in quality as well as quantity. Gem bright golden yellow early die state specimens are still available from fixed price lists, encapsulated and raw, and in private collections. Other than 1909, the 1916 Philadelphia mint cent shows higher numbers in population data than any until 1920. In ultra-high grades of MS66 Red there were 39 and MS67 Red there were 7 graded by PCGS late in 1991. In MS65 Red there were 185, MS64 Red 115, and MS63 Red 15. Compared to other dates, these higher numbers reflect the availability of high quality coins. The dies show as much detail as the early 1909 coins and in some cases, early strikes can be confused with the much scarcer matte proofs of the same date. Since the market value drops off strongly below mint state 63 levels, chances are many lesser grade 1916 cents are never submitted for certification. The Population Report data support this. Circulated rolls ranging form lowest grades up through extra fine are available from various recently-published dealer price lists. Since 131 million were minted, supplies are readily available.

The 1916D cent has never been considered a semi-key date since rolls of circulated specimens are readily available form several dealers at any given time. However, for mint state specimens, that is another story. The majority of mint red coins examined are medium to late die state and the colors less than bright mint red--more often dull red, reddish brown, and streaky as well. This may well account for the low population data of MS Red coins: 0 in MS66 or higher, 12 in MS65, 42 in MS64 and 4 in MS63.

Coins of lesser grades are prices less than what it would cost to encapsulate. In MS RB grades, the late 1991 data show: MS65 - 17, MS64 - 28, and MS63 - 19. Uncertified uncirculated specimens seen in recent years tend to fall into the MS63 RB category--barely higher, but often lower. Again, if the cost of submission exceeds the fair market value of the coin, the owner would be reluctant to have the coin encapsulated. This factor can be repeated for almost any low dollar value coin which also shows a very small number of certified pieces in a Population Report.

The 1916S has been a borderline semi-key since early collecting days. Few were found in circulation and usually just the lowest grades. It was rare to find a circulated roll of very fine to extra fine 1916S for sale, In mint state, they have always been scarce, perhaps as scarce as most the "semi-keys". The majority of mint state coins appear to be less than full red, most are reddish brown. Streakiness is common. In the PCGS Population Report of October, 1991, the numbers were: 0 above MS65, 5 MS65 Red, 25 MS64 Red, and 4 MS63 Red. In red-brown the figures were approximately doubled for each grade.

The 1916 matte proof was the last officially made matte proof. The demand had declined and only 1,050 pieces were made. As with earlier proof issues, these were made on order and as orders declined, production declined. The Mint did not sell these over the counter, except as a few surplus pieces remained. Except for the 1909 VDB matte proof, this date is the most difficult to locate in red grades--only 9 were so listed in the 1991 PCGS data.

—1917—

MINTAGES:

1917P — 196,429,000
1917 - Matte Proof — One confirmed by ANACS. Perhaps
  two exist.
1917D — 55,120,000
1917S — 32,620,000

AVAILABILITY:

The 1917 Lincoln Cent is a high mintage (196 million) widely circulated issue. Early die state uncirculated pieces are found regularly along with medium to late die state coins. The PCGS data in late 1991 showed for MS REd coins: MS67 - 2, MS66 - 30, MS65 - 113, MS64 - 49, and MS63 - 2. Coins grading less than MS64 have too little premium to warrant the cost of encapsulation. Thus the number of red-brown and brown uncs combined is only 40 pieces.

The 1917D is more often than not found in late die stages in mint coins. The details in the obverse tend to be soft with considerable metal flow evident. Even early die state pieces lack the sharpness seen in the 1917 Philadelphia pieces. Though never considered a "semi-key", the 1917D in nice mint red is always hard to located. In low grades, this date can be found on several dealers price lists in singles as well as roll quantities. Fewer than 100 have received PCGS rating of MS Red with 3 rating MS66 Red.

The 1917S also has not been rated as a "semi-key" due to its high mintage of over 32 million and its relative availability in roll quantities in circulated grades. However, for select and choice uncirculated grades, it has always been rated highly. Most of the uncirculated pieces seen tend to be red-brown, average to later die states and thus the population data show very few in MS Red - 0 MS65, none higher, 12 MS64, and 3 MS63. Another 80 pieces rated MS63-65 Red-Brown.

The 1917 matte proof is not listed in Mint records, but in 1977 ANACS certified one specimen. Albrecht spoke of the piece at the Mid-Winter ANA show in Tucson in 1983. It was believed to have been produced by or for a Mint official along with a Buffalo nickel and Standing Liberty quarter. A fixed price list from dealer Joel Rettew advertised the 1917 matte proof nickel for $7500 around 1984. Dealer "Doc" Cline featured the quarter in one of his 1991 ads with the price on request. Breen refers to the piece as "clandestine" and believe there are two such pieces in existence. When ANACS was resubmitted the piece a few years ago to put into a Cache (ANACS version of the slab), it was returned.

In a 1991 sale by Superior Coin Company, the 1917 matte proof was offered for sale. The high bidder (plus 10% bidders fee) was $3,960. Apparently the consignor placed a minimum bid of $12,500 on the coin. SLCC member, Dennis Blackall furnished the information as he bid on the coin and after the sale was offered the coin by Superior for $12,500. He returned the coin. The catalogue description included a memo from Walter Breen indicating the coin may have been dipped once. A letter from Breen dated July 24, 1988 confirms the coin as matte proof. This was the same coin described by Albrecht earlier.

A very clear doubled die obverse is known of the 1917. First discovered by Andrew Frandson in 1977, it is listed by Breen as #2081 and "very rare". Three uncirculated pieces have been traced by SLCC with one MS63RB specimen sold in 1988 for $526. A less obvious doubled die is also known, but of much lesser value. The clearly doubled date variety (as in Breen) is the desirable variety. This variety rarely shows up in price lists or auctions. As with other doubled dies, the estimated mintage varies from the low thousands to tens of thousands. No estimate has been offered on the 1917/17.

—1918—

MINTAGES:
1918P — 288,104,000
1918D — 47,830,000
1918S — 34,680,000

AVAILABILITY:

The 1918 year marks the return of the V.D.B. to the Lincoln Cent. Located at the truncation of the bust, it is barely visible without a magnifier--and in many dates, not even visible under magnification. Once Charles Barber had left the service of the Mint, the issue of the initials was moot and they were restored. Barber's initials "B" appeared on the 1892-1916 series of dimes, quarters and half dollars. His nickel (1883-1913) did not bear any initial. He objected to the use of another artist's initial "B" on a current U.S. coin. Refer to Brenner's letter on the subject in Chapter 2.

The 1918 Lincoln Cent was a very high mintage coin for the time--288 million. It was the highest total of any coin from any U.S. Mint to that time, and considerably higher than the previous year's mintage. This fact alone accounts for the relatively large number of mint specimens still available. The quality of most mint specimens examined tend to be early to average die state with some very nice flashy mint red coins available. The PCGS population data for the end of 1991 showed: MS67 Red - 3, MS66 Red - 18, MS65 Red - 102, MS64 Red - 60 and MS63 Red - 6. In red-brown only 41 specimens had been certified--a fact related more to the low market value of less-than-red-red-brown "raw" coins. SLCC handles several a year at its six mail bid sales.

The 1918D cent is a relatively scarce coin in mint state despite its mintage of 47 million. Most specimens examined tend to be not only late die state, but very late die state. SLCC had offered several such MS64 Red VLDS coins in recent sales. There apparently were no hoards reported of this date and most specimens are dull golden and russet mint red. The advanced die wear takes these coins far out of the prices one would have to pay for an early die state MS64 Red or MS65 Red. In circulated grades, it is a common coin and available on various dealers' price lists. In early die state grades, PCGS listed: MS66 - 4, MS65 - 15, MS64 - 29, and MS63 - 4. In red-brown and brown the total certified comes to only 50 coins--again, the VLDS makes the value of such a coin far less than the plastic holder. Thus most of these coins are available "raw". A 1990 dealer price list offered at PCGS MS65 Red for $748 and a MS64 Red for $165. Another 1918D PCGS 64 Red PQ (premium quality) was listed in the same list at $192. (LS 1/91 p. 4).

The 1918S is not on the "semi-key" list of Lincolns, but in mint state, it is an elusive coin. Many are in late to very late die state, but there are a very few early to average die state coins known, usually in reddish brown, The low population numbers (1991) show: MS65 Red - 2, MS64 Red - 9, and MS63 Red - 3. The total for red-brown mint state grades is only 46 pieces. This coin represents a case where scarcity alone does not command superior prices because of popularity (or lack thereof). It is considerably scarcer than higher priced coins such as 1909S and 1911S for example.

—1919—

MINTAGES:
1919P — 392,021,000
1919D — 57,154,000
1919S — 139,760,000

AVAILABILITY:

The year 1919 set all sorts of records for coin production. The largest number of cents minted at the three mints was recorded. The 1919 cent topped 392 million. Thus it is not unusual for mint specimens to exist today in quantities--though choice uncirculateds are quite scarce.

The PCGS population data show far more choice MS66 Red and MS67 Red than any year since 1909 and more than any year until 1926. Early struck and early die state coins are not difficult to locate--at a price. Original mint coins tend to be golden red versus coppery red. PCGS showed 185 MS65 Red and 74 MS64 Red in their October, 1991 Population Report. Mint rolls were seen at conventions throughout the 1960s and in the early 1970s. However, since then, existing rolls most likely have been scoured over for the choice coins cited in the population data and a good number still available uncertified. In the March, 1991 issue of LINCOLN SENSE, Dr. Fred Tweet reported prices on slabbed Lincolns and there was a 1919 PCGS MS66 listed at $390. The Teletrade data for the same piece showed a rather large number of fourteen such pieces sold by Teletrade at prices ranging from a low of $160 to a high of $340. (Refer to Ch. 8 for more information on Teletrade.) the number 14 represents the only figure in double digits for a MS66 Red Lincoln sold via Teletrade.

This would support the concept that of all the uncirculated 1919 cents, the choicest ones have been submitted for encapsulation in the hopes of obtaining a grade of MS66 or higher.

Since the 1919D circulated so widely and was readily available in all grades up to mint state (though mediocre quality), it never got the status of a semi-key date or a scarcity in choice BU. In a 1991 dealer fixed price list a 1919D PCGS 65 Red was listed for $890, (LS 11/91 p. 10). The MS Red data show MS65 - 24 with 0 higher, MS64 - 45, and MS64 - 11. In red-brown 48 pieces are listed in the recent data. In brown, only 7 again, not due to scarcity but to value--1919D pieces in brown are valued at less that $20 thus precluding most collectors from having these coins encapsulated.

The typical mint state 1919D is a late die state strike with mushy letters, weak date, and very soft wheat ears. The rims tend to be rounded and most show darker colors. Thus a truly scarce piece would be a high grade early die state MS Red 1919D.

The 1919S cent is very common in circulated grades and despite its record mintage of 139 million (a record for a branch mint at the time), choice BU coins are very elusive. Late die state coins are the rule. The PCGS population date show: MS65 Red - 6, and none higher, MS64 Red - 11, and MS63 Red - 1. These are very small numbers and reflect the scarcity of high quality mint state 1919S coins. In red-brown, the total is 46, also a very small number. However, in about uncirculated or extra fine, the 1919S is readily available in quantity. As a note, over the years this author has found in circulated rolls (pre-1970) in every other roll, at least one low grade 1909S would be found and in one case after searching through over 200 rolls, a 1909S VDB was found.

—1920—

MINTAGES:
1920P — 310,165,000
1920D — 49,280,000
1920S — 46,220,000

AVAILABILITY:

Mintages for 1920 dropped from 1919 at all three mints. The Philadelphia production of 310 million was still large enough to permit hoards and rolls of BU coins to be put away for decades. the number of uncirculated 1920 cents still available in 1992 is quite large compared to earlier and even later dates up to 1930. Thus choice and gem 1920 cents do not command a large premium even for early strike (EDS) and full mint colors. The majority of BU 1920 cents seen over the years tend to be golden hues rather than mint red. And most 1920 cents are early to average die state. The PCGS numbers reflect the submissions which have been given high ratings: MS66 Red - 17 none higher, MS65 Red - 141, MS64 Red - 135, MS63 Red - 20. Late die state BU specimens have been seen but priced low. Likewise, PCGS has not certified any MS BN specimens--the market value being less than the encapsulation costs.

The 1920D cent is difficult to locate in early die state. The specimens certified by PCGS in 1991 show: MS66 Red - 1, MS65 Red - 35, MS64 Red - 73, and MS63 Red - 8. Due to the late die state and off-colors most seem to exhibit, many of the MS64 Red submissions were probably once considered "MS65" before they were slabbed. Some 70 others have been graded in MS RB. True early die state MS65 coins are unknown.

This is due to both color and die state. SLCC sold a choice BU 1920D as "MS65 Red" (due to bright multicolored hues), but it went to a grading service and came back MS64 RB. Still it was among the nicest seen of the date. The ones seen in slabs tend to be off-color (mixed reds, iridescent colors, and streaky), and average to late die state. None has compared to a 1920P MS65 Red or even a 1920P MS64 Red.

The 1920S is an exceptionally scarce coin in mint state red and rarely found in early die state. Thus it is entirely expected that the PCGS population data show small numbers: MS65 Red - 5 with none higher, MS64 Red - 4, no other MS Red. This places the 1920S as one of the most difficult to locate MS65 Red Lincolns. Mint red coins are available, but the late die state usually downgrades most such coins to MS60 status. SLCC had two such for sale in the past two years.

Circulated rolls of the 1920D and 1920S were commonplace in many dealers' stock up through the 1980s. Though still available today, most contain few coins above fine in grade and rarely very fine. A premium is charged for extra fine coins and nicely struck AU coins sell for more than MS60 coins.

—1921—

MINTAGES:
1921P — 39,157,000
1921S — 15,274,000

AVAILABILITY:

The year 1921 was an off year for Mint production due largely to the efforts and time needed for the huge silver dollar production. The cent production dropped radically from the previously busy three years. The relatively low mintages for both mints resulted in fewer choice coins available for collectors. The 1921 cent however, does come in early die state and full blazing mint golden color and full mint golden red. The majority of uncirculated specimens seen however indicate that medium to late die state is more common than the early die state. The PCGS population data indicate a fair number (related to mintage) of coins rated high red mint state grades: MS66 - 3, MS65 - 43, MS64 - 66, and MS63 - 8. In red-brown (due to lower market value) only 54 coins were certified by PCGS as of late 1991. For the same reason a singular piece was graded MS65 BN, most likely a lustrous early die state coin. SLCC has handled at least three choice golden mint blazers which rated MS65 - Red in the past three years.

Since the 1921 did circulate widely, rolls are available from several dealers in grades ranging up to fine. Considerably scarcer are the rolls with only very fine or extra fine coins. Choice AU 1921 cents can bring as much or more per coin than the mint state red-brown coins under MS64.

The 1921S represents one of the "semi-key" dates in the series. The mintage of 15 million was low enough to mean few would be hoarded. In the earliest retail price lists the BU 1921S always rated a premium. In 1934 for example, a BU 1921S was listed at $0.75 and a BU 1909S VDB listed for $0.25 and the BU 1909S also was listed for $0.25. (See Ch. 4 for more details.) In 1947, the apparently scarcer 1921S moved up in rankings to where it was matched by the BU 1914D and topped only by the 1909S VDB. In an April, 1992 COIN WORLD ad a PCGS64 Red was listed for $795. The majority of 1921S cents examined have usually come with a faintly impressed mintmark. The overall die states tend to be below average often into late die states. The PCGS population data for late 1991 showed in mint stated red: none above MS65, MS65 - 9, MS64 - 14, and MS63 - 4. In red-brown mint state the total rises to 114 with 61 MS64 RB. In brown only 15 had been submitted in mint state. The coin is fairly common in circulated condition and rolls still can be found on a number of dealers' price lists. One interesting factor, related to the weak mintmark, is that in searching through rolls of 1921P cents, at least one 1921S was found per roll. In lower grades, the S is much weaker than one expects and easily missed. High grade circulated 1921S cents are hard to find and do command a premium.

This phenomenon was first reported by this author in 1975 and chances are unsearched rolls today still have hidden 1921S cents in rolls marked "1921". However, it is quite possible that most rolls have been carefully culled over just for that reason.

SLCC member Monty Millard reported a PCGS 1921S 65 Red sold at the Heritage Dallas Sale February 26, 1992 for $1900 + 10% buyer's fee. He commented that it was a "nice coin".

—1922—

MINTAGES:

1922D — 7,160,000

1922 — No mint mark (Plain), actually minted in Denver, but the mint mark was misapplied. Estimated mintages range from a low of 20,000 to a high of 60,000.

AVAILABILITY:

As for annual output, the year 1922 stands out as the lowest output of cents in the series. The total of just over 7 million includes the few thousand estimated "no D" cents. The 1922D comes in a variety of mint state conditions but mostly medium to late die state, average to dull luster and reddish brown to mixed colors. The number of encapsulated mint state red coins is on par with other years, but most are not the high quality of 1920 or 1919 Philadelphia issues and similar in quality to those minted in Denver in 1920 and later years through the end of the 1920s.

The PCGS population data showed at the end of 1991 in mint state red - 3 - MS66, 39 - MS65, 72 - MS64, and 19 - MS63. In mint state red-brown and brown combined some 150 coins have been certified. The larger number is due more to market values of mint state 1922D coins, than supply. Quite a few mediocre 1922D mint state coins exist "raw". If they are late die state, the market value is nominal.

The 1922 "P" has been the subject of considerable research and up until recent years, three distinct varieties were considered in the 1922 P category. However, in 1984 the American Numismatic Association decreed that only Variety 2--the strong reverse--is the official 1922"P" and the other two varieties (see photos) are die states of the 1922D in which the D has been excessively polished.

60

According to research done by A.D. Craig in 1967, the "true" 1922P die was actually made in Philadelphia and when shipped to Denver, no D was applied to the working die.

The diagnostics of the 1922 "P" include:
   a. the R in LIBERTY is fuzzy as compared to the other letters.
   b. the final 2 in the date has a flattened base.
   c. the first T in TRUST is the strongest letter motto.
   d. the L in LIBERTY is merged with the rim and only the base is clearly visible.

The other two "no D" varieties both show a diagonal die break through 0 in ONE and the wheat stalks are very indistinct--a very late die state condition.

Prices of choice uncirculated 1922 "plain" has always made news. In 1981 at a Steve Ivy sale, one went for $16,000 in MS65. Several other sales have been recorded in recent years close to $20,000. The finest known specimen graded PCGS MS65 RB was sold for $20,900 on November 4, 1988 at Vantage Auction Sale in Nevada.

PCGS had certified a total of 19 1922 "P" coins in all mint states from MS60 BN to 3 in MS64 RD. None received a higher grade. One was graded MS65 RB. It was the same coin previously certified as MS64 RD. The streakiness of the color made a color call very subjective. Based on die state, many feel there is no MS65.

There is a popular "weak D" or "broken D" variety which is a die state before the "no D" Variety 1 or Variety 3. It is worth a small premium over a comparable 1922D cent.

MORE ON 1922 No D

Two key references have studied and analyzed the 1922 "plain" cent as thoroughly as one would want - the July, 1982 issue of **THE NUMISMATIST**, pages 1763-64 and the study by Allen D. Craig in COIN WORLD August 30, 1967 and September 6, 1967. The "bottom line" seems to be that there were three die pairs used in the production of the "no D" varieties.

Die Pair 1: Second 2 in date is weaker than first 2. First T in TRUST is smaller and more distinct than the other letters. WE is very mushy. Reverse is very weak, usually with no lines in the wheat ears.

Die Pair 2: Second 2 in date is sharper than first 2. All letters in TRUST are sharp. WE is only slightly mushy. Reverse is sharp.

This is the "officially recognized 1922P."

"Jogging" Die Crack: Appears on die pair 1. Crack runs fron left half of L to upper edge of O, then "jogs" downward and continues on through the inside of the O. Appears on both "No D" and "Weak D" cents.

With the article on the 1922 plain in Vol. I No 1 of LINCOLN SENSE, and these items, the collector can feel confident about owning this coin.

Die Pair 3: Second 2 in date is weaker than first 2. TRUST is weak but sharper than IN GOD WE. Lower left part of O in ONE begins to spread into the field as the die deteriorates.

—1923—

MINTAGES:
1923P — 74,723,000
1923S — 8,700,700

AVAILABILITY:

The 1923 cent is available in various mint grades and even a few rolls traded hands in the 1970s and 1980s. Of the encapsulated pieces examined and other BU coins handled by SLCC and this author, choice early die state coins are available. PCGS had certified in mint state red: 4 - MS66, 60 - MS65 - 53 - MS64, and 8 - MS63. Lesser grades and RB graded coins have nominal value and thus very few are submitted for encapsulation.

The 1923S cent is on most lists as a "semi-key" date and is a premium value coin in all grades from good on up. The choicest mint state coins seen tend to be reddish versus bright mint red, late to medium die state, rarely better, and thus add up to a very scarce quality coin. Early price lists (see Chapter 4) point to prices comparable to the key dates in the series. The PCGS population data confirm this scarcity: MS65 Red - 12 and none higher, MS64 Red - 11, and MS63 Red - 7. In red brown and brown combined MS60-65 a total of 70 coins were encapsulated. This is another date where it is possible for a coin graded AU55 Red to be valued (i.e. priced and sold) higher than a MS63 RB or even MS64 RB coin of the same date and mintmark.

SLCC reported in 1991 a 1923S PCGS 65 Red for sale at $2,760. Since so few are known, fixed price lists rarely have an offering. An April, 1992 ad in COIN WORLD featured a PCGS65 Red for $2100. It indicated a PCGS population of 11 and NGC population of only 1.

—1924—

MINTAGES:
1924P — 75,178,000
1924D — 2,520,000
1924S — 11,696,000

AVAILABILITY:

Lincoln Cent mintages picked up from 1923 at the Philadelphia and San Francisco Mints. The Denver production dropped off to a small 2.5 million.

The 1924 cent was hoarded and even in the 1960s several BU rolls were offered by dealers. As the prices for choice mint singles climbed in the 1980s the rolls essentially vanished. Many early die state bright mint red coins were put away for collectors and when slabs became the rage in the late 1980s a goodly number were encapsulated. The 1991 data show for mint state red coins: 18 - MS66, 91 - MS65, 51 - MS64 and 7 MS63. This represents a small percentage of the pieces known in "raw" state still available from various fixed price lists. SLCC reported in January 1991, a NGC66 Red offered for $790. MS65 Red coins have been sold recently for considerably less--usually under $200.

The 1924S is not usually considered a "semi-key" and in circulated grades, rolls are available in 1992 from various dealers. This author bought five rolls in 1991 and selected out the few very fine pieces; no extra fine coins were found. In mint state, however, the coins seen tend to be late die state, dull red, and less than quality mint products. The PCGS data show a very small number of mint state red coins: 3 MS65, 7 MS64, and 1 MS63.

In red-brown, the numbers increase somewhat to: MS65 - 7, MS64 - 27, and MS63 18. In lesser mint grades there were 15 pieces encapsulated. The choicest MS65 Red pieces would command four figure prices when and if available.

The 1924D has always been recognized as a low mintage "key" date in the series. The mintage of 2.5 million ranks it fifth lowest in the series. In mint state it always was high on the price list. (Refer to Chapter 4 for early price data.)

In a 1991 fixed price list a PCGS MS65 Red was listed for $5,500. The PCGS data for late 1991 showed: MS65 - 5, MS64 - 14, and MS63 - 8. In red-brown, some 85 pieces have been encapsulated by PCGS. In the same price list above, a 1924D PCGS MS65 RB was listed for $850. Chances are it was a typical late die state coin as well. In fact, most 1924D cents seen are medium to late die state. Some softness is typical at the rims, mottoes, and wheat ears.

Since it is a key coin, a number of 1924 cents have been altered to look like 1924D by adding a mintmark. Such fakes usually are early die state which is one tip off. Close examination of a key date mintmark often will reveal fakery. Attribution and sales guarantees are strongly recommended in buying non-certified scarce dated coins.

As with earlier scarce late die state scarcities, a choice extra fine or AU coin with strong details would sell for a price compatible with a lower end mint state RB coin.

A DIE VARIETY OF 1924D

A number of collectors and dealers alike have noted a long die mark (believed to be a die scratch rather than a die break) on the reverse of some 1924D cents. Since this date is considered a key or semi-key coin by many, it warranted additional study. In COIN WORLD CLEARINGHOUSE dated April 27, 1983, six specimens were shown (including the one below) to illustrate the nature of the mark. At first, it was thought to be rather scarce, but samples are appearing all over the country as collectors and dealers check their stock and collections.

A close-up of the 1924D cent. The prominent line is a ridge and the area extending to the right of that ridge is raised.

—1925—

MINTAGES:
1925P - 139,949,000
1925D — 22,580,000
1925S — 26,380,000

AVAILABILITY:

Starting with 1925, rolls of most Philadelphia Mint coins were put away for either resale or long-term investment potential. Most of these rolls actively traded though the 1960s up to the mid-1980s when single coins were certified, graded, and often sold for large premiums over the roll pro-rata prices. As recently as 1990, more than one roll was still offered for sale in a fixed price list. These more than likely were low-end (though mint red) coins.

The 1925 often can be found in bright mint red and early die state as well. Some also exist in medium and also late die state. And some of these rate MS64 grades. In a 1991 fixed price list a PCGS65 Red was listed for $65, and a PCGS64 Red for $40. Another "high end" PCGS64 Red was listed at $50. Many singles can be found at a major convention at somewhat lesser prices than these.

The 1925D however, ranks among the "ugliest" of U.S. Mint issues. Most mint specimens are soft in details, rounded rims, and lackluster red. Thus it is no shock when prices quoted for gem 65 Red coins are in the four figures. From the same price list as before a PCGS64 Red was listed for $259. A PCGS63 Red was listed for $89. Having culled over many circulated rolls, no early die state coins have been located over the 50 years this author has spent on the series.

The PCGS data for 1991 show: MS65 Red - 10 and none higher, MS64 Red - 37, MS63 Red - 21. Fewer than 100 others are listed in mint state red-brown and brown. In an April, 1992 COIN WORLD ad a PCGS65 Red was listed for $1500 (p. 32 4-13-92).

The 1925S issue is another scarce date in upper grades. Circulated rolls are still available at many dealers. The mint state population data from PCGS show: 1 MS65 Red, 7 MS64 Red, and 1 MS63 Red. These are very small numbers for collectors to meet their needs. Gem raw 1925S cents are not known or reported as of this printing. Heritage Dallas Sale of February, 1992 had a 1925S NGC65 RB sell for $1400+10% buyer's fee. According to Monty Millard at the sale, it was a typical weak strike (late die state). A search of several 1992 price lists failed to uncover a single MS64 Red or MS65 Red 1925S for sale. It is actually of a high rarity when compared to coins which do show up in major sales or price lists.

There are three described repunched mintmarks of the 1925S. These are listed in Wexler as RPM1-3.

—1926—

MINTAGES:
1926P — 157,088,000
1926D — 28,020,000
1926S — 4,550,000

AVAILABILITY:

The 1926 cent can still be found in small hoards in choice and gem mint state grades. One recent fixed price list had a PCGS65 Red for $58 and another for only $42. A PCGS on the same list in MS64 Red was listed for $40. SLCC has handled a number of MS65 Red (or better) 1926 cents over the years. Due to the large number of gem coins, submissions to PCGS were very high and a whopping 106 rated MS66 Red, the highest number of MS66 Reds since the 1909VDB. One rated MS67 Red. and 465 rated MS65 (with several new ones being added each month). Red-brown pieces rate too little promise to warrant encapsulation. Thus the red-brown figures are relatively small--only 13 total and none in brown. With discounts offered on large submissions, the total of 1926 MS65 Red may rise into the thousands--since they are available.

The 1926D cent was widely circulated as seen in the number of rolls of circulated coins available. However, the original mintage consisted of late die state coins and so-so colors, thus in 1992 the population of choice uncirculated coins was: 9 MS65 Red, 122 MS64 Red, and 6 MS63 Red. A total of 55 others rated lower mint state ratings. As with the 1926D Buffalo nickel, the 1926D cent is generally found in late die state. The mint state red coins seen both raw and slabbed tend to be dark or dull red. True gem or choice 1926D cents are very scarce to rare.

The 1926S cent is listed by most authors as either a "key" date or "semi-key" date. The relatively low mintage of 4.5 million was low enough to make it sought after. The quality of the new cents was described as "weak" or "dull". Of the uncirculated specimens examined by this author and SLCC contributors, the rule is late die state to very late die state and so-so colors. Full red is very unusual. The PCGS population data show: 0 - MS65 Red, 7 - MS64 Red, and 7 MS64 Red making this the lowest PCGS mint state red Lincoln Cent. Prices tend to reflect that fact.

In Stewart Blay's Best Lincoln Cent Set (Ch. 8), the 1926S is the only coin rated less than MS65 Red; it is MS65 RB. In early price lists, the BU 1926S always carried a premium high among the series.

This author has identified six mintmark positions of the 1926S. Two of them are as low and right of the date as seen in any cent. With only 14 mint state red PCGS coins (as of late 1991), it is not unusual that none can be located in a current price list or auction sale. Chances are all have been put away by collectors or investors. Dealers have this coin high on their clients' lists of "wanted". In red-brown, the 1926S is quite scarce with only 46 pieces certified. SLCC offered a raw specimen in its March, 1992 sale and it brought $561.00. The coin was previously graded by ANACS with a certificate grade of MS65/65. However, the 1992 standards would probably have called the coin a MS64 RB.

—1927—

MINTAGES:
1927-P — 144,440,000
1927D — 27,170,000
1927S — 14,276,000

AVAILABILITY:

As with the 1926, the 1927 Philadelphia mint coins were hoarded away in roll quantities and seen for sale well into the 1980s. Many are golden mint hues and early die states as well. Though there are many uncertified pieces available, quite a few have been encapsulated. PCGS data show: 31 - MS66 Red, 124 MS65 Red, 51 MS64 Red, and 4 MS63 Red. Only a few mint state red-brown coins have been submitted due to the low market value of such coins. In a 1991 price list, a 1927 PCGS64 Red was listed at $50 and a PCGS66 Red listed at $290. MS65 Red coins have been seen at dealer's tables in recent shows for $50 to $75.

Della Romines reported a 1927 doubled die obverse which is illustrated in Wexler's book. The doubling is seen in LIB and 27 of the date. Breen lists it as "very scarce". Two sales noted in SLCC in 1989 and 1990 at $125 in MS63 RB and $145 in MS64 RB. No data on any pieces certified.

The 1927D cent is fairly common in circulated grades up to extra fine. However in higher grades it is scarce to very scarce. The mint specimens seen raw and encapsulated tend to be late die states and even very late die states and mushy off-colored. The PCGS mint state date show: MS66 Red - 1, MS65 Red 22, MS64 Red - 34, and MS63 Red - 8.

In red brown a total of 102 pieces have been certified. Due to the lack of sharpness, mint state pieces in red-brown or brown command little premium value over early die state extra fine coins.

The 1927S cent is somewhat scarcer than the 1927D and in most cases also medium to late die state. The PCGS population data show: 9 - MS65 Red, 26 - MS64 Red, 54 MS63 Red, and 6 - MS62 Red. Far fewer red-brown and brown coins were submitted. The nicest mint state coins seen compare poorly to the 1927 Philadelphia mint coins, thus one cannot compare 1927S to same year coins. They do compare to 1926S coins. Circulated rolls are available. This author bought four rolls in 1991 in search for extra fine specimens or early die state specimens and found none.

—1928—

MINTAGES:
1928P — 131,116,000
1928D — 31,170,000
1928S — 17,266,000

AVAILABILITY:

The 1928 cent was available in mint rolls at major coin shows well into the 1970s then disappeared. Many are seen in full mint red, golden red, and early die state. Thus choice BU coins are easy enough to come by. SLCC has handled several gems over the years. Due to modest market values, only the choicest have been submitted for encapsulation. PCGS data show: MS66 Red - 28, MS65 Red - 140, MS64 Red - 37, and MS63 Red - 1. In a 1992 price list two PCGS65 Red coins were listed, one for $92, the other for $75. In uncertified 2x2s, similar coins have been seen for $35-$45.

The 1928D cent can be found in mint state red and early to average die state, unlike the previous three years of Denver Mint productions. The PCGS population date reveal: MS66 Red - 2, MS65 Red - 28, MS64 Red - 43, MS63 Red - 3. In red-brown a total of 51 pieces have been encapsulated. SLCC reported in 1991 a 1928D PCGS65 RB for sale at $184, and PCGS MS65 Red for $990. An ANACS MS66 Red was listed for sale at $975 in 1991.

In circulated rolls, the 1928D is still available from various dealers' price lists. Most rolls however fail to yield any coins much better than fine.

The 1928S cent is a very scarce coin in mint state. The choicest specimens seen are mint red, average die state, and modest luster. True gems are unknown. In mint state red, PCGS data include: MS65 - 26, MS64 - 43, and MS63 - 8. The total for lesser mint state grades is 38.

A novel triple mintmark is known. It is a large S variety with two under mintmarks to the north. It is scarce and no recent price records available. Two other RPMs reported in Wexler. Two distinctive sized mintmarks used for the 1928S. See the article by John Merz (next page). Breen lists the large S variety as scarce.

1928 Large S and Small S Varieties

Have you ever noticed that the 1928S Cent entry in the Redbook is marked by a dagger? This refers to a footnote at the bottom of the page which says that large and small mint mark varieties exist, and directs the reader to page 59.

Page 59 of the Redbook gives more information on mintmarks, recounting how a hand punch is used to impress the mintmark in the die, resulting in occasional double punched mintmarks, over-mintmarks, lack of mintmark when it should be there, and lots of variety in size and location. The Redbook goes on to say that "a more or less standard size small mintmark was used on all minor coins starting after 1909, and on all dimes, quarters and halves after the Barber series was replaced in 1916. Slight variations in mintmark size occur through 1940 with notable differences in 1928, when small and large S mint marks were used."

I have a 50 power hand held microscope that I use to look at mintmarks. The reticle is calibrated in thousandths of an inch. I have measured the 1928 "normal S" at 25 milli-inches. I call this a "normal S" because it's about the same size as S mintmarks of other dates. I have measured a 1928 "large S" at 30 milli-inches, not a tremendous difference, but noticeable to the naked eye when the two coins are side-by-side.

Does anyone have any similar (or different) data? I have no idea which mintmark is the scarcer of the two. I, presently, own three 1928S cents, and two are the normal S and one is the large S. The Redbook also indicates that there are large and small mintmark varieties of 1941S, but I haven't had time to do any research on them yet.

> — John Merz, UNITY COINS,
> Clifton, VA, Jan. 1983

—1929—

MINTAGES:

1929P — 185,262,000
1929D — 41,730,000
1929S — 50,148,000

As with earlier Philadelphia Mint coins, the 1929 was available in mint rolls for many years well into the 1970s. Most of the rolls examined by this author were average die state tomato red coins. Many would grade MS64 Red by 1992 standards. But in the 1970s and even 1980s there was not much premium for single coins. They seemed so plentiful. With a mintage of 185 million they did circulate widely and many were also hoarded. From the choicest pieces sent for encapsulation, PCGS graded: 36 MS66 Red, 109 MS65 Red, and 46 MS64 Red. Lesser graded mint state coins total 15 indicating a lack of incentive to certify lesser graded 1929 cents. Several more high end pieces are submitted regularly as more dealers' stocks and rolls are scanned for possible submissions. Most MS65 Red coins seen are nice but not on par with the same graded 1926 and 1927 coins.

The 1929D was also apparently hoarded since as late as 1984 this author was offered ten BU rolls by a La Mirada coin dealer who bought them from a hoard presented by a customer. The Charles Ruby hoard of rolls included several hundred rolls dating from 1929 well up to 1939. Superior Coin Company bought his holdings about 1980 for well over one millions dollars. Other BU rolls have been offered by various dealers at major shows up to very recently.

The quality was well below Philadelphia Mint standards and the colors often were dull, dark, streaky, and reddish brown. Thus gem 1929D cents are truly unusual and very scarce. A few average die state pieces have been seen in choice grades. PCGS graded: 4 MS66 Red, 54 MS65 Red, 55 MS64 Red, and 11 MS63 Red. Lesser graded mint state coins certified by PCGS total only 20 pieces. Late die state pieces have little market or collector value.

The 1929S was apparently also hoarded as many rolls were offered well into the 1980s. As with the 1929D, only a very few were well struck and mint red. The majority were later die states, off-colored, and lackluster. From these hoards, several high quality pieces have been found and encapsulated. PCGS shows: 2 MS66 Red, 71 MS65 Red, 104 MS64 Red, and 7 MS63 Red. Lesser mint grades total only 16. These coins drop off rapidly in value below the grade of MS64 Red. A recent price list offers a PCGS 64 Red for $108. Similar raw coins sell for $20-$30. Gem 1929S coins have sold for up to $250. They are hard to find.

—1930—

MINTAGES:
1930P — 157,415,000
1930D — 40,100,000
1930S — 24,286,000

AVAILABILITY:

The 1930 cent is still available in mint rolls after over 60 years. Bags and rolls were actively traded in the 1960s and at major shows up to this year one or more rolls can still be found. In the Ruby hoard perhaps as many as 500 rolls were stored. Other hoards were also known. The start of the Great Depression after the Wall Street market crash of October, 1929 perhaps kept more coins (especially small denominations) in hoards in private hands as banks were closing and money became scarce.

So far over 200 (a record for the period) have been graded MS66 Red by PCGS. Other services have also encapsulated large numbers of gem red coins--including several MS67. PCGS has also graded nearly 600 MS65 Red and over 100 MS64 Red. More are being submitted regularly as rolls are scanned for the choicest coins.

Most BU coins are well struck early to average die state and flashy mint golden color. Some are bright red. Slabbed MS65 Red have been seen recently for as little as $30. PCGS has also graded a record of 8 MS67 Red. No Lincoln since 1909 has had that many graded 67 Red.

The 1930D cent closely parallels the 1929D cent in terms of quality of the mint product. The rolls examined in the past few years contained late die state, off-color, lackluster coins--often with spots as well. Fortunately for collectors, a quantity of early die state red coins were also hoarded and these make up much of the encapsulated population data. The lesser quality pieces can not only be found in singles but still in rolls. The PCGS data show: 25 MS66 Red, 164 MS65 Red, 84 MS64 Red, and 10 MS63 Red. Only 15 were encapsulated in red-brown and none in brown as their value is nominal.

The 1930S cent follow the pattern of the 1929S cent. Most rolls examined were reddish brown, glossy luster, and late die states. Again, some small hoards of early die state red coins have come to light and these make up most of the encapsulated PCGS pieces. The red-brown and average coins can still be bought by the roll. The PCGS data show: 12 MS66 Red, 242 MS65 Red, 99 MS64 Red, and only 17 in less mint states.

Wexler lists a minor doubled die obverse. Breen lists a die chip variety of the 1930D where the zero in the date is filled. It is listed as Breen #2121.

—1931—

MINTAGES:
1931P — 19,396,000
1931D — 4,480,000
1931S — 866,000

AVAILABILITY:

The 1931 cent was reduced in mintage as were most coinage issues following the Crash of 1929. However, over the next three decades, rolls were showing up on dealers' price lists and on exhibit floor tables at coin shows. Though not as numerous nor quality of the 1930 Philadelphia issue, still a fair number of BU red coins exist. Since the mid-1970s most singles seen were average die state, lustrous though not fiery red, and available with some looking. On a 1991 price list (LS Jan. 1991), a PCGS66 Red was listed for $334. The PCGS population data show: MS66 Red - 36, MS65 Red - 124, MS64 Red - 48, and MS63 Red - 3. Lesser graded mint state coins totaled 12, inasmuch as lesser uncirculated coins do not warrant encapsulation. MS64 Red coins can be found for under $25.

Rolls of 1931 cents were once plentiful, but are hard to locate on lists from dealers who specialize in circulated rolls. Prices have been steady over the past five years with minor increases so far in the 1990s. As a relatively low mintage Philadelphia coin (19.3 million) it was not commonly found in change.

The 1931D cent with a low mintage of 4.48 million was only hoarded by a few and by the 1970s it was apparent that in true mint red it was considerably scarcer than the more popular 1931S.

In fact, the Population Reports verified what dealers have known for many years--for every BU 1931D you would be able to locate four or five BU 1931S cents. The data show: MS66 Red - 1, MS65 Red - 29, MS64 Red - 32. MS63 Red - 3. Roughly equal numbers are found for coins graded as red-brown. The value drops off radically below mint state grades. Circulated specimens can often be found for under one dollar. On early price lists, the 1931D was priced higher than the 1931S in uncirculated grades.

The 1931S cent has an interesting track record and history. Because the production figures were known to be quite low (the lowest since 1909), many speculators and coin dealers stocked up large quantities in anticipation of a windfall. Very few even escaped into circulation. The price spread between circulated and uncirculated specimens has always been narrow reflecting the fact that BU coins are more common than extra fine copies.

Abe Kosoff bought ten rolls of BU 1931S cents at the ANA convention in 1937 for $10 a roll. The dealer who sold them had "many hundreds" of rolls for sale according to Kosoff. In 1940 Kosoff sold two of those rolls to Brooklyn coin dealer Al Fastove for $15 a roll. This author bought one of those brilliant uncirculated coins from Fastove in 1940 for $0.45. At the NASC convention banquet in January, 1980, this author told the audience of his purchase back forty years earlier. Kosoff was at the head table and told this author how Fastove came by those coins. Other uncirculated rolls were seen at coin conventions well into the 1970s when it became more practical to sell the coins singly and have the nicest ones certified. There more than likely are some more rolls stored away some 60 years which have yet to come on the market.

The 1931S cent has been widely altered from other dated S mint coins. However, since the 3 in 1931 was quite different (see photos) from later dates, such alterations can be easily detected.

Breen reports the Scharlack hoard of 200,000 uncirculated pieces perhaps many included in the ANA conventions of the late 1930s cited by Kosoff and others. Uncirculated rolls noted in dealer price lists well into the 1960s.

Genuine   *Altered*

—1932—

MINTAGES:
1932P — 9,062,000
1932D — 10,500,000

AVAILABILITY:

The 1932 cent also mired in the Great Depression was a low mintage. In fact it is the lowest mintage of any Philadelphia issue. It was not commonly found in change and circulated rolls have always commanded a good premium. They still do. As for uncirculated coins, small hoards apparently were put aside by collectors and dealers alike including the Ruby hoard which came to light in the 1970s and 1980s. Singles still can be easily found. They tend to be average die state, full mint red, and usually nice eye appeal. Lesser BU coins are also known but bring minimal prices. The PCGS data show: MS66 Red - 41, MS65 Red - 150, MS64 Red - 46. The total of lesser mint state coins is 10 as values drop off quickly in lesser grades. Most MS65 coins seen were early to average die state. Some MS64 Red coins seen were late die state.

Due to a lack of demand, the San Francisco Mint made no one cent coins until 1935.

The 1932D cent is the first case where a branch mint outproduced the Philadelphia Mint in one cent pieces--by almost one million. These coins closely parallel the numbers and quality of the 1932P issue--similar color, strike, and planchets. The PCGS data also closely follow: MS66 Red - 17, MS65 Red - 143, MS64 Red - 40, MS63 Red - 3.

—1933—

MINTAGES:
1933P — 14,360,000
1933D — 6,200,000

AVAILABILITY:

The 1933 issues are the last low mintage issue for Lincoln Cents. The Great Depression era and the bank closures left the need for new small coinage minimal from 1930-1933. Production rose sharply starting in 1934 and has never dipped to the Great Depression levels since.

Lincolns dated 1933 and 1933D have always been popular both in circulated and uncirculated grades. Some of the early "Penny Boards" had asterisks next to those holes which represented a challenge to locate in circulation. The 1933 and 1933D usually were both so marked.

Despite the low mintage, many 1933 cents were hoarded away in uncirculated rolls. The Chicago World's Fair saw many thousands of these BU cents used for souvenirs, the most popular being the encased cent--an aluminum framed 1933 cent with a surrounding inscription of "Century of Progress".

Because many rolls were only recently culled over since the mid 1980s, many early die state golden red gems have come to light. The PCGS data show: MS67 - 5, MS66 - 44, MS65 - 140, MS64 - 71, these are for MS Red coins. The lesser graded mint state coins totalled 14. None were certified as "brown". The value declines rapidly from MS64 Red downward.

Circulated rolls have always been available and always been a premium roll. Extra fine specimens typically bring about a dollar. Well used specimens in good bring about fifty cents. MS65 Red pieces typically fetch $50 and more.

The 1933D is a relatively low mintage coin and has always held a rating of "semi-key". It was not found in change in any numbers and rolls were never readily available. In circulated grades it ranges from about $1.50 in good to $3.00 in extra fine. However, for choice mint red coins, prices are quite a bit higher. Hoards apparently did exist until well into the 1970s and as the brighter, sharper pieces were submitted for certification, the rolls disappeared. Chances are some rolls still reside in bank vaults and other hiding places to hit the market as estates are liquidated. The PCGS data suggest many BU red coins are available: MS66 Red - 46, MS65 Red - 227, MS64 Red - 101, and MS63 Red - 6. Lesser mint state certified coins total 12. Values below MS64 drop sharply. Prices for MS65 Red seem to be in the $30-$35 range. Higher prices are known, but on fixed price lists--not actual sales.

1933 marks the end of the period in which Lincolns were not actively traded by the roll. In the hectic days of the early 1960s all Lincoln Cent issues were traded by the roll from 1934 to date. Prices for choice singles did not become popular until almost 1980--and then only for a very few dates between 1934 and 1939.

—1934—

MINTAGES:
1934 — 219,080,000
1934D — 28,446,000

AVAILABILITY:

The year 1934 marks the start of the modern roll collecting phenomenon which started in the early 1960s (or late 1950s) and has carried through with the advent of the COIN DEALER NEWSLETTER right up to the present. The relatively high mintages (as compared with earlier years) and the many hoards put away by investors, collectors, dealers, and plain folks who shunned banks all seemed to emerge after World War II and the start of the collecting frenzy shortly after the first edition of the RED BOOK (1947) came out and later reinforced with the issuance of a weekly coin newspaper in 1960, COIN WORLD. It seemed the ONLY way to collect U.S. coins was by the uncirculated roll.

The majority of BU 1934 cents seen raw and encapsulated are early to average die state (with some late die state as well) full mint red and generally nice eye appeal. These rolls have been trading in the $200 range but prices vary widely depending on the quality of the roll. Only a relatively few 1934 cents have been certified due to the relatively low market value even for choice BU coins. PCGS data show: MS67 Red - 3, MS66 Red - 47, MS65 Red - 59, and only 8 lesser graded pieces.

From a copy of an April 6, 1992 display ad in COIN WORLD, a dealer recently acquired choice BU rolls of 1934D cents. As many of the 1934D cents were early die state coins, these coins look like a good value. However, many certified 1934D cents are medium to late die state and command lower values in the marketplace. As time passes, probably more rolls now in hiding will emerge as estates come on the market. PCGS data show: MS66 Red - 46, MS65 Red - 509, MS64 Red - 301, and 128 of lesser mint state grades. The value drops rapidly below MS64 Red. Assuming the coins in this ad rate MS65 Red, the advertised slabbed coins at $75 and $85 seem a bit high. If these coins are MS64 Red, then the value of $17 is comparable to slabbed MS64 Red coins selling at $25 or so.

—1935—

MINTAGES:
1935 — 245,388,000
1935D — 47,000,000
1935S — 38,702,000

AVAILABILITY:

The 1935 cent may be the most readily available choice to gem BU cent of the 1930-1939 decade. Even recently, gem BU rolls were seen. The term "golden gem blazer" was most often applied to 1935P cents. Because of its relatively low market value only a few have been encapsulated and only those in mint red: PCGS shows: 3 - MS67, 58 - MS66, 68 - MS65, and 3 in lesser grades. Many come well struck (early die state), sharp details, golden copper color (not red), and often flawless surfaces. Of course rolls of lesser quality exist and these are the rolls (often called "original rolls") that are still seen for sale. Recent prices from 1991 and 1992 lists show asking prices from $90 to $125.

However, the 1935S cent suffers from average to late die state conditions, glossy surfaces, soft details, and brownish hues. Most rolls examined over the decades show this is the rule. A very few average die state pieces have been slabbed in the high end. PCGS data show: 3 - MS66 Red, 69 - MS65 Red, 61 - MS64 Red, and only 5 of lesser grades. The choicest red still pale by contrast to the nicer 1935P coins. Sales records of $75-$85 are known. Uncertified BUs often run at less than half those prices. The price is more akin to the coin's surface, details, and colors. True gems (MS65 Red) have not been examined but probably also pale in comparison to MS65 Red 1935P. BU rolls have been advertised recently at the $400+ level.

A 1935S/S exists and in choice mint red commands about a 25% premium. Few prices have been found except for some SLCC mail bid sale records for RB coins at $15-$20.

The 1935D lies somewhere between the 1935P and the 1935S in terms of mint state quality. Mint red coins exist, but average to late die state. A few gems have been certified by the grading service. PCGS data show: 2 - MS67, 58 - MS66, 60 - MS65. None in RB or BN has been reported as the value is too low to warrant certification. This date is also available by the roll and from the most recent price lists run from $150 to $200.

One minor 1935 obverse doubled die is reported in Wexler. It lists at $50 in BU and is listed as 1-0-V. A reverse doubled die listed as 1-R-VI is listed at $5 in BU. A 1935D is listed as 1-R-VI and catalogues at $10 in BU.

—1936—

MINTAGES:
1936 — 309,637,000
1936D — 40,620,000
1936S — 29,130,000
1936 — Brilliant proof 5,569

AVAILABILITY:

1936 marked the return of proof mintage coins after a hiatus of twenty years. The first run of 1936 proof cents (a small portion of the total of 5,569 pieces for the year) were satin finished, double struck, square rimmed coins. Apparently not well received, the mint finished the year's production of proof coins with only high polished mirror-like proofs. Though the satin-type (also known as Type I) proof is the scarcer of the two, it does not bring comparable prices to quality mirror-like proofs of the same year. In the January, 1991 issue of LINCOLN SENSE, two such examples were quoted from a recent ad: a 1936 Satin finish Pf65 PCGS was listed at $1250 and a Pf65 Type II was listed at $2450. Many of the 1936 proofs (both types) were mishandled, some were spent, and undoubtedly some were lost. Since the Mint wrapped these pieces in tissue paper which was not acid-free, many pieces over the years acquired a grainy darkened surface. Some turned black. Others spotted. Some have been seen with fingerprints (*chances are they were U.S. Mint employees). Thus the surviving gems total a very small number and the prices rise regularly as new gems hit the market. The total of Type I proofs certified by PCGS is: 94 and Type II is 275. Of that total only one rated a Pf66 Red and 29 Pf65 Red. For Type I 2 rated Pf66 Red and 18 received a Pf65 grade.

The 1936P cent like the 1935P cent is also readily available in "golden gem blazer" grades of MS65 and MS66. SLCC has handled many from the hoards of two late Los Angeles coin dealers who had put the rolls away in the 1950s. Most have been broken down to singles and up to 1991, they were still being sold by several Southern California dealers. Undoubtedly, some other roll hoards may still come to light as old timers pass away and their holdings come to light. Mostly well-struck, and flashy golden surfaces, they make close rivals to the gems of 1935. Average die state coins are also seen. Some of the average to late die state coins include the "broken "R" variety. In this case, the R in LIBERTY has a thin vertical stem. SLCC sold one in 1991. It is not shown in most guidebooks, but is a consistent die variety. It also is a die feature of one of the several doubled dies known for 1936. Three strong doubled dies are shown in Wexler and The Cherrypicker's Guide. BU specimens have sold from $100 for 3-0-V to over $500 for the strong 1-0-IV.

The 1936D is available in BU rolls and in early die state mint red. Recent roll prices quoted at $185-$225. Medium and late die state coins exists, but in rolls at a lower premium. Many surviving rolls show spots. Though a few have been encapsulated, there is too little premium to warrant many submissions.

The 1936S is available in BU rolls and recent Trends prices show bid of $140. The choicer rolls have long ago been broken down to gem singles. They come in all die states and run form gem red blazers to dull red brown late die state. At this time, very few (less than 1/4th compared with the 1936D) have been slabbed.

1936 DOUBLED DIE OBVERSE 3-0-V
Showing the doubling in the motto.

Photos by Bill Fivaz

1936 DOUBLED DIE OBVERSE 3-0-V
Showing the "broken" R in LIBERTY.

93

The 1936 2-0-V 1936 doubled die.
Listed at $300 in THE CHERRYPICKERS GUIDE.

Note the broken left leg on the "R" of the first hubbing.

—1937—

MINTAGES:
1937 — 309,179,320
1937D — 50,430,000
1937S — 34,500,000
1937 — Brilliant proof — 9,320

AVAILABILITY:

This author began coin collecting in 1937. The three new shiny 1937 cents received one day were the inspiration to become a life-long collector. Today, there are still rolls of these shiny golden bright 1937 cents for sale. Many more are hidden away to come to light one day. The 1992 Trends show 1937 BU rolls at $42.00. This price range has remained steady for the past four to five years since the quality rolls and gem singles have been steadily culled over for singles, sets, and hand-picked choice BU rolls which bring a huge premium over the Trends values. Many are early die state, though reddish, medium die state rolls have been seen at present price levels. Late die states are not common.

The 1937D cent with a mintage of 50 million is still available in BU red rolls. Though as with most rolls of the 1930-1939 era, they have been extensively culled over, new hoards pop up as old timers pass away and as estates are brought out of hiding. Most are early to medium die state and mostly fiery mint red. Late die state coins are also seen in some rolls--those usually the ones that Trend for $75. In 1988 the 1937D rolls were trading in the $110-$125 range. Thus, the BU choice coins have been mostly culled over.

The 1937S fits closely with the 1937D. More medium to late die state coins are known in BU but many choice singles have been culled out of the many rolls sold in the past 20-30 years. They come in fiery mint red, dull red, and streaky red-brown. BU rolls were quoted in April, 1992 Trends at $75. These most likely are culled over rolls. In 1988, Trends showed $100 minimum for 1937S rolls. Since gem singles have sold for $5 to $8 each, it pays to cull over BU rolls for the best looking coins and leave the rest. Original rolls are not common, but new hoards come to light almost every year. The Ruby hoard had several hundred rolls of each date form about 1934 through the 1940s. Many dealers in the 1960s had hundreds of BU rolls in stock. Manchester Coins in Los Angeles often advertised in the numismatic press full page ads in the early 1960s for BU roll and bag (100 roll) quantities of these rolls.

The 1937 proof cent is full mint brilliant mirror-like. Many were sold singly over the counter at the Philadelphia Mint for $0.16. Some of the 9,320 pieces were sold in sets through the mail. Over the years, many of these cents turned colors from mishandling, from Mint wrapping paper, and from the mailers used for sets. Most 1937 proof cents have been impaired and as such, the survivors rating Pf65 Red and better command strong prices. PCGS rated 20 - Pf66 Red, 127 - Pf65 Red, 260 - Pf64 Red, 60 - Pf63 Red, 10 - Pf62 Red. Sixty-one others rated less grades in red-brown and brown. Often the lesser grade includes hairlines, spots, irregular toning, and fingerprints.

A novel 1937 cent exists with full reeding closely matching that of a half dollar. About 100 such cents along with a reeded Buffalo nickel were made for the ANA convention in 1941. According to Breen they were not Mint made.

A matched pair was offered for sale at the 1990 Long Beach Convention for $2,500. Abe Kosoff claimed to have bought and sold several of the pairs ($0.01 and $0.05) for $5 in the 1950s.

No current sales data available on this item. The originals seem to trace back to Philadelphia coin dealer Ira S. Reed.

—1938—

MINTAGES:
1938 — 156,696,000
1938D — 20,010,000
1938S — 15,180,000
1938 — Brilliant proof — 14,734

AVAILABILITY:

The 1938 cent is still available in BU rolls, but as with earlier dates of 1934-1937, most seen recently have been culled over. Thus the 1992 Trends prices of $75 reflect the drop from recent highs of $100 in 1988 and peak prices in the mid-1970s. The gem BUs available to collectors are golden mint luster (rather than red), usually early to average die state and flashy eye appeal. Medium and late die state coins are also known and can be found in current re-packaged rolls. As with other rolls of the 1930s, undoubtedly hoards still await discovery.

The 1938D cent is readily available from various dealers in high mint state, usually golden mint hues, sometimes red. They run from sharp early die states to medium and even late die states. Rolls exist and BU prices in Trends show $85, about the same as in 1988 and down from mid-1970s highs of over $100. New supplies show up as estates are discovered.

There is an exciting variety of the 1938D. It is a repunched mintmark with two clearly visible Ds. One variant also is a reverse doubled die noted by a thickened motto. Recent BU sales have been in the $20-30 range.

The 1938S cent is also still found in BU rolls. However, they are culled over, usually late die state, and contain spotty coins. The Trends value of $70 is well below the highs of the mid-1970s and lower than the 1988 prices of $85-90.

Two popular RPMs are found n the 1938S. One is the S/S where both mintmarks are quite clear. The second is a triple S, apparently large S over S over a small S. Though scarce, they are still being found by scanning existing rolls. Prices recently for gem BU triple S have been in the $75 range for ANACS Cache slabbed pieces. Raw specimens sold by SLCC have run from as low as $10 to a high of $55. They are medium die state and show some minor die breaks, stress lines, and nice mint gold color. Even in circulated grades they bring a few dollars each for extra fine coins and about $1 for fine to very fine coins.

The 1938 proof cent is very similar to the 1937--high mirror finish, deep mint red, wire rim, early die state, and for many collector specimens, surfaces free of specks, spots, and fingermarks. However, most apparently have one or more such defects. This author bought one at the Mint in 1940 and unwrapped it in 1964 and it was glossy black, like obsidian. A dip in Nik-A-Lene ruined the coin for good leaving it brassy with a faded luster. No doubt many others in long storage suffered similar reactions and are now valueless. PCGS proof reds population data show: Pf67 - 1, Pf66 - 26, Pf65 - 206, Pf64 - 46, and 82 others in lesser grades. None has been certified as "brown". Lesser pieces command little or no premium as collectors prefer Pf64 Red or better. The high surviving population increases by a few pieces each year indicating more select to gem pieces are being submitted for certification.

Note: the major certification service that certifies RPMs and minor double dies is ANACS. Population data is not available on ANACS certified (certificate or Cache) coins. Thus any prices of slabbed RPMs or lesser doubled dies refer to ANACS Cache coins.

RPMs of 1938D, 1938S. Courtesy of Harry Ellis.

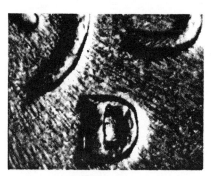

1938D 1¢ RPM #2
D/D West
Kramer 38W2, CONE E-01

1938S 1¢ RPM #2
S/S/S West and Northwest
Harnack III, CONE E-02

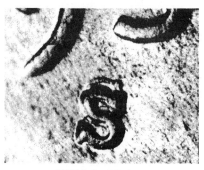

1938S 1¢ RPM #1
S/S North
RPM #1a
Harnack I, CONE E-01

RPM #1b
Harnack II, CONE E-01

—1939—

MINTAGES:
1939 — 316,479,520
1939D — 15,160,000
1939S — 52,070,000
1939 Brilliant proof — 13,520

AVAILABILITY:

The 1939 cent is also available in BU rolls from recent sales, they are still nice quality of MS64 Red overall. Lesser quality rolls are still making the rounds on dealer's tables at shows and price lists. Unlike the 1935-1938P issues, the 1939P is bright red, early to medium die state, and medium luster. The fiery luster seen on some issues of the 1940s is not typical. A few 1939Ps are known with polished fields (die polish) and even have a proof-like appearance, but not mistaken for proofs. BU rolls currently Trend for $35, about half their peak of 1979 and about the same for 1988. Nice single gem MS65 Reds go for about $5 each.

The 1939D represents the lowest branch mintage since 1934D. It was heavily hoarded, making circulated rolls hard to come by and thus raising the value of such rolls. BU rolls have always been available and were actively traded from 1964 to date. Having peaked at over $300 a roll, current Trends show a value of $120. There are gem singles going for $25, MS64 Reds for $10 and lesser quality coins for $5 and less. A retail ad shows a MS66 Red PCGS for $45.

A scarce 1939D/D RPM#1 (Wexler) is available at some 20% premium. They tend to be average die state, full red, and medium luster. Seems one or two can be found by searching red-paper "original" rolls. Rolls in square tubes probably have been culled over and "cherry-picked".

101

The 1939S does not compare to the other mints. Most are lackluster, medium to late die state, and reddish hues. True MS65 Red coins do not hold up to the 1939P or even the 1939D MS65 Reds. Rolls prices are down from 1988 to 1992 Trends of $55.

The 1939 proof comes in mirror surfaces, full light red, wire rims, and early die state. Many have toned a variety of hues. The premium coins are flawless surfaces. Almost matching PCGS numbers for 1938 show: Pf67 - 1, Pf66 - 29, Pf65 - 215, Pf64 - 310, Pf63 - 37, and a total of 37 others. Prices are strong for the MS65 Red and higher. Lesser grades bring less than half the Pf65 values. (Ref. to Ch. 8 for recent sales data.)

A doubled die obverse is described in Wexler as 1-0-I. It is most noted at the 19 in the date and the TY in LIBERTY. Fivaz quotes a private sale in MS63 in 1988 of $525.00. Apparently quite scarce, few sales can be traced. SLCC has not handled one.

—1940—

MINTAGES:
1940 — 586,825,000
1940D — 81,390,000
1940S — 112,940,000
1940 — Brilliant proof — 15,872

AVAILABILITY:

The 1940 cent is available in BU rolls, including many "shotgun" rolls (those wrapped by machine in red paper tubes). Prices have remained steady for the past five years in the $25 range. Most specimens tend to be golden red or reddish. Early die states are common and so are medium die states. Spotting is common in many of the red rolls. Culled over rolls tend to be sold in square plastic tubes. Gem singles have been sold via SLCC mail bid sales for up to $5. High quality pieces are available raw probably including MS66 grades.

1940D cents also are available by the roll. Prices of $80 in 1988 have slipped to $50 in 1992. However, gem singles have moved from $4 in 1988 to $8 in 1992. Hoards are known and both shotgun rolls and even bags are still awaiting closer examination. They do come in early as well as average die state. Late die state coins have little value even in mint red.

The 1940S comes both in Large S and small S varieties. According to Breen there is also a S/s, large over small S, also known as RPM#4 (Wexler). In BU rolls, most do not carry any mintmark size distinction. Prices have slid steadily for several years as rolls have been culled over. The 1988 Trends was $130 and in 1992 Trends is $42. Most are average to late die state.

The 1940 proof is readily available in all grades and more are submitted monthly so the totals increase steadily. Prices have held steady only for Pf65 and higher pieces. SLCC member Monty Millard reports a Pf67 Red sold at the Heritage Dallas sale of February, 1992 for $1,250+10% buyer's fee. Apparently only the very smallest Population Report numbers still bring record prices. As of November, 1991, PCGS has only certified one Pf67. Thus, the buyer (at this time) probably bought the highest graded 1940 proof cent. These single pieces suffer the same indignities of the 1936-1942 issues and still a fair number have survived to be certified at Pf64 levels and above. To date over 500 pieces have been so graded by the three major services combined.

NOTE: In grading proof cents, color and toning seem to have a stronger component in assigning a grade by the grading services. For example, an otherwise gem mint red coin with a small stain on the reverse, and no other defects might be assigned a Pf64 rating. For BU coins, many with a similar stain would still be called "MS65".

—1941—

MINTAGES:
1941 — 887,039,000
1941D — 128,700,000
1941S — 92,360,000
1941 — Brilliant proof — 21,100

AVAILABILITY:

The year 1941 saw the first year in which over one billion cents were minted. The majority of 887 million were minted at the Philadelphia Mint. As with other coins of this era, many rolls were hoarded away. Even in 1992 some original rolls in red wrappers are available for sale. However, examination of such rolls has shown they are darkened on the rims, top and bottom coins are very dark, and often the coins have small black spots (some ads refer to these as "leopard spots"). These rolls are the rolls often quoted in Trends. Choice BU coins fortunately exist in large enough numbers to meet collector demands. Choice culled over rolls in MS65 Red also are available, but at prices pro-rata for such nice singles. The 1941 cent tends to come in early die state, flashy mint red, and nice eye appeal. Many also come dull red, and medium to late die state. Choice pieces have sold recently for $5-8.

The 1941D also is available by the roll and recent Trends prices are quoted in the $105-115 level. These are less than full blazer red, average die state overall, and have the same problems as other red wrapped rolls of this era. Gem golden blazers have been sold by SLCC in recent mail bid sales for up to $10. PCGS has certified 10 in MS66 Red. Very few others have been submitted.

The 1941S is a moderately scarce coin by the BU roll. Often found in red-brown or dull red, medium die state, this coin brings a good premium for original BU MS65 Red or better coins. Breen points out the large and small S in the date with the large S the scarcer of the two. No comparable prices recently published to indicate the value difference between the two.

There are three prominent doubled die 1941 cents described in Wexler and Cherrypickers Guide. All three have sales records for BU in the $125 to $450 range. The 5-0-IV, which shows clear doubling in the TY of LIBERTY and 19 of the date apparently is the scarcest type. SLCC sold one which the consignor had in a 2x2 marked "1941 doubled date $5". It sold for $450.

As with most minor doubled dies ("minor" refers to those not listed in the Red Book and thus are not as well-known), sales figures are sparse and auction data are lacking most of these coins. There is further discussion of the lesser-known doubled dies in Chapter 8.

The 1941 proof cent is available to collectors in Pf65 and higher. Though many were mishandled, improperly stored, and even spent, enough survived without surface damage, spotting, hairlines, or discoloration. Many others however, have been treated to look nicer. The effect of treating a proof coin is tantamount to ruining it. See discussion in the preservation chapter. Nice mint red, mellowed red, fine lettering details, early die state, and squared rims are the feature of a quality 1941 proof cent. PCGS has encapsulated: 7 Pf66, 161 Pf65, 380 Pf64, 73 Pf63, and 81 others in lesser grades. Prices seen in sales, fixed price lists and auction results vary widely even for Pf65 Red. The actual color and eye appeal are major factors in pricing this and other 1936-1942 era proof cents.

—1942—

MINTAGES:
1942 — 657,828,000
1942D — 206,698,000
1942S — 85,590,000
1942 — Brilliant proof — 32,600

AVAILABILITY:

The 1942 Mint production of cents tapered off a bit dropping to under a billion coins. However, again the extensive hoarding of bags and BU rolls has enabled collectors to have choice and gem coins today of this date. The nicer BU rolls have yielded striking mint red well struck (early die state) coins. Some rolls examined in the past year have been of lesser quality with medium die state coins, reddish hues, darker luster, and often minor spotting. This is especially true of red wrapper rolls. For most early dates (pre-1960) the red wrapped rolls tend to become spotty in time. The edges of such coins also tend to become very dark even black. And the end coins which are exposed also become very dark in time.

The nicest BU red singles have been sold for up to $5 a coin in recent SLCC mail bid sales. The current Trends value of $30 does not assure that there will be a majority of choice mint state red coins.

The 1942D cent is also still available by the roll. The current Trends of $22 indicates that the majority of such rolls are lesser mint state coins. There are many choice singles in MS65 Red available, however, the remaining BU rolls have most likely been culled over to remove the better coins. SLCC has sold choice BU singles for up to $5.

They tend to be average die state, soft red, rarely bright mint golden red, and lacking some details especially in the hair, coat, and wheat ears. Minor die breaks are common.

For some years, the 1942S was highly touted as an investment coin especially in BU rolls. Prices peaked in the mid-1970s and at current Trends levels of $190 are less than half their highest value. Choice mint state singles are readily available and SLCC has sold many over the past five years at prices up to $10 a single coin. The existing rolls tend to be average die state and soft mellow red, versus the bright mint red found in the 1942P.

Breen and Wexler describe a 1942S doubled die obverse. It is considered rare and no prices have been found in recent price lists or auction results.

The 1942 proof was the last of the pre-war era proofs. As with earlier issues, many were sold singly over the counter and not in sets. The majority apparently have not fared well over the past 50 years and most offered for sale today (especially raw) have hairlines, spots, and often show evidence of cleaning. Many of the nicer pieces have been encapsulated both for protection against mishandling and for grading. PCGS had certified as of the end of 1991: Pf66 - 9, Pf65 - 161, Pf64 - 380, Pf63 - 179, Pf62 - 52 and 102 of lesser grades in mint state.

—1943—

Due to the unusual nature of the coinage of 1943, a little explanation is necessary. The shortage of copper for the war effort caused the U.S. Mint to switch to a zinc-coated steel planchet for the 1943 cents. This alloy was not adequately field tested and as a result proved to be unsuitable for long-term use. Zinc is highly reactive to the elements and readily reacts to moisture, oxygen, and most other gases to form whitish oxides. The steel was not a stainless variety and being iron, it too is reactive to moisture and oxygen and readily forms red and/or black oxides of iron. Thus, many of the coins produced in 1943 had already developed corrosive products seen as spots, pock marks, rust, granulation, and peeling. This process goes on and special care is required for the long-term safe storage of these coins. Also, due to the hardness of the planchet as compared with the bronze planchets, new dies had to be prepared with more detail in order to strike proper looking coins.

MINTAGES:

1943 — 684,628,000
1943D — 217,660,000
1943S — 191,550,000
No proofs were struck this year.

AVAILABILITY:

Because of the high interest in the off-metal cents struck in 1943, collectors probably know more about this mint-made error than perhaps any other U.S. coin, including the 1913 Liberty Head nickel.

The 1943 steel cent itself is also a novelty to collectors as it is the only coin made for circulation of this metal. Most have aged badly over the past half century and though a few choice pieces remain, the long range outlook is not optimistic. Because they were generally well struck and sharply defined, those pieces that have survived in pristine shape have been eagerly sought by collectors. PCGS has encapsulated a fair number considering their relatively low market value. The data show: 10 - MS67, 62 - MS66, 84 - MS65, and 18 - MS63.

Uncirculated rolls (almost always in square plastic tubes) are currently quoted in Trends for $35. Generally these are coins with some of the usual problems found in this year--spotting, pitting, and rust. At $0.70 each, one cannot expect quality or choice BU coins. SLCC has sold choice BU singles for up to $5 in recent mail bid sales. Many of the 1943 cents have also been replated and sold as "processed". These tend to look whiter than the normal BU 1943 steel cents and show less detail. Chrome-plated steel cents are also common, and worth a fraction of the usual BU coins. In time, the true BU 1943 cent should become very scarce indeed as the chemical processes which affect the zinc and steel components continue to act inexorably toward the coin's demise. Thus the few pieces which have been encapsulated may be insured of a much longer quality life.

The 1943D cent has the same history as the 1943P. Some are less than early die state with more evidence of die stress and planchet problems than the 1943P. However, choice BU coins do exist and the most recent Trends shows a quote of $49 a roll--about the same price level as four to five years ago. Again, these rolls typically contain coins rating MS64 and less.

Having examined many such rolls over the years, one thing is clear, the coins in the roll tend to age over the years by spotting, pitting, and rusting. In some cases, rolls first seen in the 1960s and reexamined in the late 1980s showed a whitish oxide of zinc on most of the coins--and these were stored in a bank vault some 30 years in a dry climate (Los Angeles). The various storage tips published about cents do not typically address the unique foibles of the steel cent. Also, as with the 1943P, a fair number of choice BU coins have been encapsulated and the PCGS data show: MS67 - 13, MS66 - 64, MS65 - 64, MS64 - 9. Lesser coins have nominal value. As before, a gem MS67 should be a true premium coin in the future as the number of BU coins shrinks. An April, 1992 COIN WORLD ad featured a 1943D NGC67 for $90 and a 1943S PCGS67 for $90. The 1943S is scarcest of the trio of steel cents and recent Trends quote a price of $85 per roll. However, rolls examined in recent years tend to be the culled over remnants form earlier years. One cannot expect to find MS65 coins in such rolls and often barely MS64 coins in a roll. The true BU coins have a bluish haze over a steel silvery surface. These are the gems which have been submitted for encapsulation. The record number of MS67 coins (by PCGS) illustrates the point that these were very sharp coins in 1943 and those that have made it to this point deserve some protection. The PCGS data show: 23 - MS67, 99 - MS66, 109 - MS65, and 23 - MS64. Lesser grades have nominal value. SLCC has sold such gem sets (raw) for up to $25 for the trio. Price for the 1943S in a recent ad was $120 in PCGS MS67 (LS 11/91 p. 10). The same ad featured a NGC MS67 1943D also for $120.

For those with rolls of steel cents, follow the suggestions in the chapter on preservation with special attention to anti-desiccants. Moisture is the ultimate enemy of coins, but especially so to 1943 steel cents.

1943 Bronze Lincoln Cent

1076 1943 Lincoln cent struck in bronze. EF, with some traces of mint lustre, closely approaching Mint State. 47.25 grains. Some areas of light oxidation are seen.

This example has an illustrious pedigree and is believed to have been the property of Chief Engraver John R. Sinnock of the Philadelphia Mint.

While occasionally 1943 "copper" cents have surfaced, nearly always they have proven to be copper-plated zinc issues or fabrications. The example offered here is an authentic specimen and is the finest we have ever seen or handled.

A 1943 copper cent is a coin of which legends and dreams are made, and 20 to 40 years ago tremendous amounts of ink were used to describe one or another find. Years ago, the 1943 bronze cent was featured on a matchbook cover—the nature of which we do not recall, but it was something of the exact context of which we do not recall, but it was something of the nature that the finder of such a piece in circulation could receive a large amount of money equivalent to a fortune!

Some interesting information concerning the 1943 bronze (and also 1944 steel) issue can be found on pages 226 and 227 of Walter Breen's *Encyclopedia*. Toward the end of 1942, some bronze blanks were left over in a hopper attached to one of the cent presses, and early in 1943 at least 40 bronze 1943-dated cents were struck, such being mixed in with the normal production run of zinc-coated steel cents (zinc-coated steel being used for normal cents of 1943, an expedient used in this year only).

One of the earliest specimens to come to light was the bronze 1943 cent found in change by Don Leuts, Jr., in 1947. Another was reported in *The Numismatist*, June 1947, page 434 by Dr. Conrad Ottelin.

A big flap occurred in 1958 when a coin discovered by the young Marvin

Beyer was consigned to Abe Kosoff for sale at the American Numismatic Association convention, held that year in Los Angeles at the Statler-Hilton Hotel. Beyer's father insisted at the last moment that the coin be withdrawn, which Abe Kosoff vehemently protested, as apparently mail bids well into five figures were already on the books.

Since then, over a dozen others have been authenticated, making a total population today of perhaps 15 pieces. The coin here offered, we offered this in our 1981 ANA sale as have been owned by Chief Engraver John R. Sinnock is specifically mentioned by Breen on page 226.

Further on the pedigree, as noted, we offered this in our 1981 ANA sale as Lot 414. The consignor obtained it from Harry J. Forman, the noted Philadelphia dealer on March 1961. Earlier it was the property of Philadelphia dealer William Grichin, [Grichin or Grinchin?] who obtained this piece and a companion 1944 steel cent from a lady friend of John R. Sinnock. She stated that the 1943 bronze cent was a Christmas present from him to her in 1943. Obviously, John R. Sinnock knew that he had a rarity on his hands!

Sinnock was well tuned to such subtleties as, for example, in 1936 he created a special Matte Proof 1936 Elgin Centennial half dollar for sculptor Trygve Rovelstad, and from time to time made other "special" pieces. It is not known whether Sinnock retrieved this 1943 bronze cent from a production run, or whether he simply furnished a bronze blank and had it struck specially. The point, we suppose, is moot.

From John R. Sinnock, chief engraver of the Mint, to a lady friend, to William Grinchin, to Harry Forman, to a private collector in 1961, to the Bowers and Merena Galleries ANA auction sale of 1981, through intermediaries, to the present consignor.

From the catalogue of Mid-America Auctions F.U.N. Sale January, 1986.

INCREDIBLY RARE AND POPULAR 1943 COPPER CENT, THE FIRST VERIFIED EXAMPLE, AND POSSIBLY "FINEST KNOWN"

475. 1943 About Uncirculated (55/55). The 1943 Copper Cent is one of the most dreamt-about, sought-after items in all of numismatics. Ads in major publications have prompted millions of people to examine their spare change in search of this elusive rarity, with little promise of ever finding one. It is estimated that only ten or so examples are known, in all grades. This piece is finer than the specimen which appeared in McIntire's 1985 Central States sale, which was touted as being "Finest Known." The color is a light olive, with traces of the original mint red still adhering to the lettering and devices. The surfaces are in superb condition and the overall quality is exceptional.

The debut of this example was as Lot 2055 in the 1958 ANA Sale catalogue, where Abe Kosoff so eloquently described it, as follows: "About 18 months ago, a gentleman approached me with a cent dated 1943. It looked like copper but was in a plastic holder. Well, dealers have bothered with "1943 Copper Cents" by the score. My skepticism must have been evident."

"On several occasions, Mr. Marvin Beyer tried to get me interested. Finally, I told him I wouldn't touch it until various tests had been made. These would require time and expense. I thought I had discouraged him."

"Several months ago, at a local convention, Mr. Beyer came to me with the results of his efforts. He had established the possibility of a Copper Cent of 1943 having been minted. He had a Specific Gravity test made by Atlas Testing Laboratories, Inc., Chemists, Metallurgists and Specialists in Indulstrial X-Ray. Comparison of a 1942 Cent with the 1943 Cent indicated specific gravities of 8.54 and 8.59 respectively."

"A Norelco X-Ray Spectograph analysis made by the same company compared a 1936 Cent with the 1943 Cent. The reproduced report graphically indicates the comparative copper content. Thus far, Mr. Beyer had established that the Specific Gravity and Copper Content were in order. Now, the authenticity of the date must be checked."

"The Ferro-Spec Laboratories, Inc. Radiographed the coin and their report on the Copper Cent is that there is no evidence of a weldment. Their report is reproduced. The acutal film, cannot be reproduced but is available and no experienced eye is necessary to see that the date is genuine."

Now, I have been cautioned by many well-wishing friends and associates not to 'stick my neck out' on this coin. Remember, I was as skeptical as anyone. But in the face of all these tests, I ask, 'Is it possible to have a silver cent of 1493 (sic)? We know there are such things. Why not a copper cent? Does a copper cent require more special dispensation than one struck in silver?'"

"This catalogue features many Mint Errors, some as fantastic as this one so that the wonder of it should be no wonder at all. The fact is that the 1943 Copper Cent has captured the imagination of the whole fraternity of collectors-yes, even beyond that it has reached the general public. All sorts of rumors surround this coin. An Automobile Company would give a car-a home fully furnished would be traded for the Cent. These are rumors, of course. However, Mr Beyer has stated that he was offered $25.000.00 cash for the coin and, in fact, Mr. Beyer introduced me to the gentleman who allegedly made the offer. I say allegedly because I did not confirm this offer."

"Here you have it - The coin, the tests, the story."

"As one editor of a numismatic paper put it-it's the find of the Century."

This piece is accompanied by a letter from Donald Taxay (former Curator of the Chase Manhattan Bank Money Museum) dated May 26, 1966, where he states the following: "Having completed a study of your 1943 bronze cent, I can advise you that in my opinion the coin is authentic. The somewhat larger percentage of zinc in the 1944 cent, as shown by the comparative Norelco X-ray test graph, is of course standard for the war issues. Again, the 865 specific gravity shown by your 1943 bronze cent is about what it should be."

"A visual examination of your coin was conducted under 75 x power magnification, and the results were highly satisfactory. The surface texture and metal flow are normal, and preclude the possibility of casting. The relief is bold and the rim is "built up" as it should be on a bronze planchet struck under pressure intended for steel. The edge is also perfect. The numeral punches in the date are identical to those on the 1943 steel cant and this is diagnostic since the 4 on the 1943 is unique. For your own interest you might compare it, under a good glass, to those on the 1942 and 1944 cents. In conclusion, I would say that your coin resembles in every way the two other genuine 1943 bronze cents I have examined."

"Whether these coins are pieces de caprice, or Mint errors, can not be answered with finality. Nor do I think it matters one way value. Probably not more than a half dozen genuine specimens exist, and this fact together with the enormous publicity the coin has received, will be the prime determinates of value. I do not know of any auction records for the coin, and until one is established, the price range will be tentative. However, I feel you have a great rarity here and that the trouble you have taken to authenticate it is well worth while."

Also included with the letter are copies of the results of the X-Ray, Spectographic Analysis, and Specific Gravity tests.

Accompanied by ANACS Certificate #B 2314 (dated 12/03/75), where authenticated.

Discovered by Marvin Beyer - Lot 2055 of Abe Kosoff's 1958 ANA Sale - Fred Kassab - Milton J. Katz - Fred Weinberg - Pullen & Hanks - the present consignor through various intermediaries.

Circulated cents have done well price-wise in recent years which again points to the shrinking number of decent collectible coins. Many circulated rolls examined over the years tend to blacken and/or rust in addition to the problems cited earlier.

The following pages were furnished by Steve Benson. The letter from coin dealer Frank G. Spadone dated 10-28-87 refers to a known 1943 bronze (copper) sold by Harry Forman in 1980. A copy of the memo between Forman and John J. Ford is illustrated on the next page. By reading the letters, the catalogue descriptions, the enclosed articles, and the comments by numismatic legend, Walter Breen, the reader will have an up-to-date and clearer picture of this most intriguing of U.S. Mint errors.

FRANK G. SPADONE, DEALER (609) 652-1399

135 W. WHITE HORSE PIKE, ROUTE 30
PINEHURST, N.J. 08201
(Between Absecon-Pomona)

10/28/87

Dear Steve;

After a number of calls etc....

I spoke with Harry Forman of Phila.

He informed me he sold a BU unc. 1943 copper

cent to John Ford of N.YC. some time ago

for $10,000. I assume it might be worth 20,000.

if its for sale ?

If you do anything you can send me a small check

smile ! I will keep you posted anyway.

Why not throw a small ad in coin world! You

might get lucky.

Regards,
Frank......

A CASH $ BUYER OF COINS · STAMPS · DIAMONDS
CLOCKS · POCKET WATCHES · ACCUMULATIONS
COMPLETE COLLECTIONS AND ESTATES

(At Your Home · Bank or Our Private Office)
Parkway Exit 44 to Route #30

This is a copy of the oft-quoted memo from the U.S. Treasury denying the existence of genuine 1943 bronze cents.

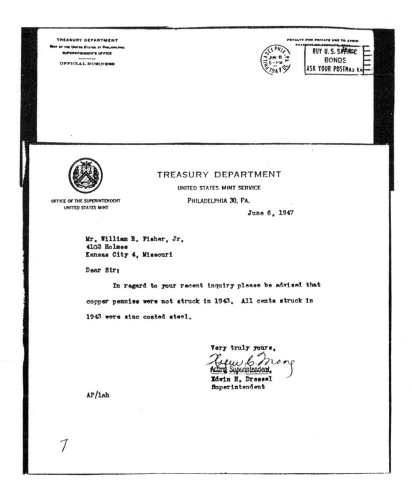

TREASURY DEPARTMENT
Mint of the United States at Philadelphia
SUPERINTENDENT'S OFFICE
OFFICIAL BUSINESS

PENALTY FOR PRIVATE USE TO AVOID
PAYMENT OF POSTAGE, $300

BUY U.S. SAVINGS
BONDS
ASK YOUR POSTMASTER

TREASURY DEPARTMENT
UNITED STATES MINT SERVICE
PHILADELPHIA 30, PA.

OFFICE OF THE SUPERINTENDENT
UNITED STATES MINT

June 6, 1947

Mr. William R. Fisher, Jr.
4102 Holmes
Kansas City 4, Missouri

Dear Sir:

In regard to your recent inquiry please be advised that copper pennies were not struck in 1943. All cents struck in 1943 were zinc coated steel.

Very truly yours,

Acting Superintendent,
Edwin H. Dressel
Superintendent

AP/lah

7

The next page is a copy of correspondence between JOHN J. FORD, Jr. and HARRY J. FORMAN dated 1980. It concerns the sale of a 1943 bronze and 1944 steel cent acquired earlier in 1961. Also courtesy of STEVE BENSON's files.

TO
Mr. Harry J. Forman
Post Office Box 5756
Philadelphia, Pa. 19120

FROM
JOHN J. FORD, JR.
Numismatist
POST OFFICE BOX #9 706
ROCKVILLE CENTRE, N. Y. 11571
(516) RO 4-8988

SUBJECT: _1943 bronze 1¢ and 1944 steel 1¢, obtained in 1961_____ DATE: _June 12, 1980_

FOLD ↓

Dear Harry:

You could do me a real favor! I just located a 1943 bronze 1¢ and a 1944 steel 1¢, which I obtained from you in May, 1961, most probably at the Metropolitan show held at the Park-Sheraton. If I remember correctly, I traded you a pair of $10,000 and $20,000 State of Georgia notes for these; you promptly traded or sold the notes to Blaise Dantone.

It was and is my recollection that both of these coins came from the estate of John R. Sinnock, or else they came from Sinnock's mistress. At least that is what I have with the two error strikes. However, in checking my files, I find that, on May 22, 1961, you sent me a package containing enlarged photos of the two coins and various X-Ray test results concerning them, the package wrapper bearing the notation "ex WILLIAM GRICHIN."

You have a helluva memory; can you tell me who this William Grichin was and what his connection was with Sinnock? I need this information, as in time I will be disposing of these pieces (most probably by auction), and would like to use your name and any other pertinent pedigree data in giving the history of the two items. Please drop me a note telling me what you know, using the lower part of this form letter.

John - Please don't fussy
blame this pussy
typing on me.
Love + xxx Rich

Best wishes,

John J. Ford, Jr.

PLEASE REPLY TO ———➤   SIGNED

REPLY Dear John   6/16/80

Grichin is a local dealer; who has always kept a low profile.

He bought the coins from Sinnocks friend, who was then an elderly woman.

He also sold me Assay medals that Sinnock had designed.

Wm Grichin has a store at 47N.11 TH.ST. Phila.Pa.

He is still active and will have a table at the Lanham Md.show next

month. Your two coins are probaslly the nicest of these existing errors.

Should bring one hell of a price. Far more than the $1200.00 we figgured

the notes, and I charged Dantone $1300.00 for the pair. Blaise is retired

in Ft. Lauderdale but calls me every so often. What can you tell me about

an A.H. Water Goblet that comes thru the courtesy of the 81st airborne and

Mint Derringer Stamped JOHN WILKES BOOTH?   Regards Harry

DATE: Derringer SIGNED

is
Oovaleo, I saw the piece
it is in Atreantic city Regency Hotel. Lets Go!
THIS COPY FOR PERSON ADDRESSED

GRAYARC CO., INC. BROOKLYN, N. Y. 11237

Vol. 4, No. 12

Second Class Permit • Dated Items Please Rush
APRIL 3, 1959

Published Monthly for the Collector of Coins, Paper Money, Tokens and Medals.

The Flying Eaglet
NUMISMATIC MAGAZINE

FLASH! SECOND BRONZE 1943 CENT TURNS UP!
The First One Sold Was Reported in Excess of $40,000

Photograph by GEORGE PACKARD

This is a photo reproduction of the genuine Cent owned by Don Lutes, of Pittsfield, Massachusetts. We are the first to examine, photograph and report the details in full. This rare Cent is for sale, offers in excess of $10,000, will be considered. This Cent was tested and verified as genuine by the noted Walter Breen and the Editor of this magazine. Story and full details are enclosed. Note the designers initials (VDB) are still legible under Lincoln's shoulder.

THE LARGEST CIRCULATING PUBLICATION IN THE EAST

$3.00 PER YEAR   REGISTERED, NEWARK, N. J.   COPY 35c

120

NUMISMATICS, LTD.
9665 Wilshire Blvd.
Suite 600
Beverly Hills, Calif.
90212 U.S.A.

Telephone: (213) 550-176∢
(800) 421-0678
Telex: 698177

September 19, 1984

Stephen M. Benson
1791 Beverly Glen Drive
Santa Ana, CA. 92705

Dear Mr. Benson,

The 1943 Copper Cent that I examined in my office Thursday August 16, 1984 is a very exciting coin. Authenticated by the American Numismatics Association Certification Service, this is the finest condition and state of preservation of any 1943 copper cent that I have seen in the past twenty years. The coin is basically uncirculated and has considerably more mint luster than any piece offered in public auction or on the open market.

The 1943 copper cent ANACS E -5960-B I value at $25,000.00 or more.

Sincerely,

Fred Weinberg
Numismatics, Ltd,
Manager of Rare Coin Department

FW:er

Part of the aura surrounding the 1943 bronze cent has been the advertising published on the subject. This small ad reflects the kind of activities dealers were conducting. Chances are this dealer did not buy any genuine 1943 bronze cents from the ad. He did probably generate quite a correspondence file. This article was most recently reproduced in LINCOLN SENSE in the March, 1992 issue.

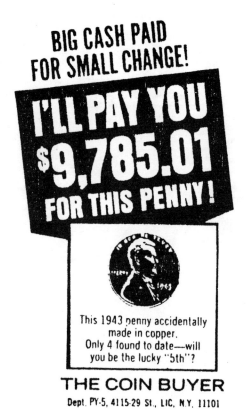

1943 COPPER

From a numismatic ad circa 1964 for a 1943 genuine copper cent. Note that for the time, four genuine specimens were reported. From recent dealer-to-dealer transaction, auction sales, and other published transactions, the actual number known in 1992 is closer to 20. Since most of the specimens have been photographed, it can be determined which specimens have been sold more than once. NO "discovery" pieces have been publicized in recent years. Any SLCC member with a recent published "discovery" piece should send that information to SLCC for future publication.

Does anyone know who ran this ad? The exact date? The publication?

(from March, 1992 issue of LINCOLN SENSE)

Researcher Steve Benson writes that this ad was run by Eugene Griffin from New York. It appeared in Photoplay magazine in 1980 as a leader to sell his coins and price lists of coins. Similar ads have appeared in the NATIONAL ENQUIRER and MIDNIGHT GLOBE.

Faked 1943 bronze cents have plagued dealers and numismatic publications since they were first publicized in the late 1940s. Most have been altered 1948 cents. Some have been cast counterfeits.

At the ANA convention in New Orleans in 1981 a genuine 1943 copper was sold at auction for $10,000. That news triggered an avalanche of "finds" and brought out a few more genuine pieces. Prices since then have been in the $15,000 range and higher.

Wednesday

Arkansan sells single Lincoln cent for record $23,250 at convention

By Jerry Dean
GAZETTE STAFF

Robert T. McIntire, owner and manager of McIntire's Rare Coins in Jacksonville, recently in Minneapolis sold a single cent ("pennies are British," numismatists insist) for a handsome $23,250.

"That's a record sale price for the [numismatic] industry for a single Lincoln cent," McIntire, who sold the coin on consignment from an Illinois coin dealer, said. The sale came at the annual convention of the Central States Numismatic Society, second largest event of its kind in the country, he said.

A casual glance at the coin would reveal nothing exceptional to the unstudied eye. It looks as it if might feel right at home among someone's pocket change. It had the standard Lincoln head and the "wheatie" impression on the reverse side that was common to pennies struck in the 1940s and 1950s.

What made this cent so valuable was its 1943 mint date, a year when the wartime need for copper was such that almost all pennies were made of steel. Copper was being diverted from coinage for use

McIntire examines steel cent.

in making ammunition shell casings.

The coin's value was enhanced, McIntire said, by its having been the "finest known specimen" of the 1943 cent. The cent was one of six wartime copper pennies struck "by accident" at the Philadelphia mint in 1943. Other 1943 copper cents were struck by accident at

the Denver and San Francisco mints. The coin had been certified by the American Numismatic Society's Authentication Service in Colorado Springs, Col., as one of the 10 of these accidentally coined cents known to exist.

The coin's buyer was Larry Parker, owner of a rare coin shop in Alexandria, La. Parker had bought the penny for a customer he'd believed would wish to own it, and he has since been offered Texas ranch land in exchange for the cent, McIntire said.

Would anyone finding a 1943 copper penny in his pocket likely become wealthy? Probably not, McIntire said.

The steel cents struck in 1943 and 1944 remain enough of a novelty among nondealers to be worth a nickel to 30 cents apiece, depending on their condition, McIntire said. A good Indianhead penny can bring up to $1.

"Someone calls me almost every day thinking they've found a 1943 copper cent," McIntire said. "I tell them to try a magnet on it."

A copper-plated steel cent will be drawn to the magnet, but not pure copper. Years ago some Arkansas promoter copper-plated

FINEST KNOWN 1943 Copper Cent

A steel version of 1943 cent is shown with pictures of the coin sold by McIntire.

about 5,000 steel cents and they surface occasionally.

The whereabouts of the other nine 1943 copper cents is generally known to dealers and collectors, as is that of nine 1944 copper cents, which could command $40,000 to $50,000 each, McIntire said.

McIntire, who opened his Jacksonville business in 1971, held the 1943 cent on consignment for three months. Fairness to buyers prohibited him from any temptation to bid on the coin for himself,
he said.

"Each coin I have on consignment becomes mostly just a lot number to me," he said. But while he held the Lincoln cent, he en-

(See CENT on Page 2B.)

This article was clipped from the American Standard of Numismatics, 1962 issue. From STEVE BENSON's files.

No recent sales data have surfaced on this unique DOUBLE ERROR. It surely would eclipse an "ordinary" 1943 bronze cent.

FIND OF A LIFETIME!
Authentic 1943 Copper Cent

One of the rarest coins in American history was found, not in a bank vault or a musty attic or cave, but rather in the pocket change of a hospital dietician of Knoxville, Tennessee!

Mrs. Gertrude D. O'Hara of 1501 Rambling Drive, Knoxville 21, Tennessee, had been in the habit of buying small change each day to bring home for examination by her husband Phil, an attorney who had recently become interested in coins while invalided home due to a heart attack. This penny, a type we all handle daily, was found in her change in April of 1963.

The coin has been properly authenticated by outstanding experts, foremost by Mr. R. A. Wilson Sr., Editor of this the AMERICAN STANDARD COIN BOOK, who has examined seven such pennies but never an oddity. (10% off center, overweight due to this, and the reverse printing is rotated 15 degrees counter clockwise).

A 1943 copper penny has sold for $32,000.00. This coin is for sale. What will it bring from some numismatist? $50,000.00?

Watch your pennies. Many 1943 steel cents have been copper coated and are worth 1c. A magnet will pick up the steel cents.

1943-S BRONZE
About 6 Known
From Walter Breen's
COMPLETE ENCYCLOPEDIA OF
U. S. AND COLONIAL COINS

Because copper had become a scarce strategic metal during WWII, efforts to find a substitute (including, among other things, plastics, ceramics, and noncuprous alloys) eventually resulted in adoption of the wretched expedient of low-carbon steel with an 0.0005" coating of zinc. Because the two metals are well apart in the electropositive series, they form a "couple" in moist atmospheres, and quickly corrode. Cents of this dross ("steelies") were coined in 1943 in enormous quantities, but they immediately proved a failure. When new they were often mistaken for dimes (numerous accidental strikings on dime planchets made matters worse!), and when corroded they looked like slugs, even to being nicknamed "lead pennies." Fortunately for some few collectors, but unfortunately for the peace of mind of Mint bureaucrats, at the end of 1942 some bronze blanks were left over in a hopper attached to one of the cent presses, and at least 40 were struck by accident early in 1943, being mixed with a normal production run of steel cents, and managed to leave the Mint undetected. Considering the enormous coinage orders that had to be filled, inspection had to be cursory.

For many years after the war, rumors persisted that the Ford Motor Company would give a new car as a prize to anyone turning in a genuine 1943 bronze cent (usually called "43 copper cent"). As one might expect, fraud artists promptly copperplated ordinary "steelies" and began attempting to sell their wares. (A magnet will instantly detect one of these; real bronze coins are nonmagnetic.) The car company vainly issued indignant denials of the rumors. Spokesmen for the Mint repeatedly denied that any such coins had been made, but the rumors refused to die - with good reason.

In early 1947, a Dr. Conrad Ottelin reported discovering a bronze 1943 cent (*NUM* 6/47, p. 434); this coin either has not become available for authentication, or else has not been connected with Ottelin's name. However, a few weeks earlier, Don Lutes, Jr., then aged 16, found one in change at his high school cafeteria (Pittsfield, Mass.), and I had the pleasure of authenticating the piece when it came to my attention in 1959. It was one of the first two (both found by youths) to achieve nationwide publicity, the other being Marvin Beyer's, also recovered from circulation (about 1958). Rumors of four- and five-figure prices followed, but the first public auction of a 1943 bronze cent did not actually result in the coin's changing hands until 1974. (Beyer's coin went into the 1958 ANA Convention auction - only to be withdrawn by the boy's father at the last moment, resulting in widespread protests as the auctioneer's book reportedly contained bids well into five figures.) In the meantime, over a dozen others have been authenticated, but there are tens of thousands of forgeries.

In the early 1960's a New York coin firm played a mean practical joke: Some member copperplated a bag lot of 5,000 "steelies" (most likely too spotted, stained, and corroded to be worth retailing), and dropped the coins singly in strategic locations where the general public would be sure to notice. For the next six months, coin dealers throughout the New York City area (including, one hopes, the perpetrator) were plagued by phone calls from finders. Counterfeit 1943 bronze cents from false dies began showing up about 1961; some were stamped on genuine cent blanks bought from coin dealers, others on homemade blanks, still others on genuine cents of other dates, notably and stupidly 1944 and later years! By 1965, the Mint Bureau was issuing press releases ignorantly denying the genuineness of any 1943 bronze cents (including, if they had only known, the one owned by Mint Engraver John R. Sinnock!), such releases in one instance including the infamous line "The Mint makes no mistakes," which has gone down in history beside "Rum, Romanism, and Rebellion."

NUMBER	YEAR	MINT	COMMENTS	CGO	CGR
EB7217	1943		Struck on Copper Planchet	50	50
B 2314	1943		Struck on Copper Planchet	58	58
B 5199	1943		Struck on Copper Planchet	40	40
EB5960	1943		Struck on Bronze Blank - Polished	50	50
FA9644	1943		Struck on Copper Planchet	45	45
FD0251	1943		Struck on Bronze Planchet	45	45
GH3356	1943		Struck on Copper Planchet	NA	
EC9117	1943	S	Struck on Bronze Planchet	40	40
SA1436	1943	S	Struck on Copper Planchet	40	40
SB4685	1943	S	Struck on Copper Planchet	45	45
B 1272	1944		Struck Zinc - Coated Steel Blank	NA	
EA4288	1944		Struck on Steel Planchet	40	40
EB1575	1944		Struck 1943 Zinc - CTD Steel Planchet	50	50
EI7144	1944		Struck on Steel Planchet	NA	
EI7852	1944		Struck on Steel Planchet - Cleaned	50	50
EL5085	1944		Struck on Steel Planchet - Cleaned	40	40
EI0759	1944		Struck on Leftover Steel Planchet - Cleaned	NA	
EX0313	1944		Struck on 1943 Steel Planchet - Corroded	20	20
EZ2458	1944		Struck on Steel Planchet - Polished	50	50
FA6294	1944		Struck on Steel Cent Planchet	NA	
FY6740	1944		Struck on Steel Planchet	NA	
GB1761	1944		Struck on Steel Planchet	NA	
GE1401	1944		Struck on Steel Planchet	50	50
GG8900	1944		Struck on Steel Planchet	50	50
GK2041	1944		Struck on Steel Planchet	NA	
GL0776	1944		Struck on Steel Planchet	63	63
GL1073	1944		Struck on Steel Planchet - Polished	NA	
GL1996	1944		Struck on Steel Planchet - Cleaned	NA	
TWJ019	1944		Struck on Steel Planchet	NA	
TWJ020	1944		Struck on Steel Planchet	NA	
UED065	1944		Struck on Steel Planchet	NA	
GL2568	1944		Struck on Steel Planchet	NA	
WF6415	1944		Struck on Steel Planchet - Cleaned	50	50
MJ6619	1944		Struck on Steel Planchet - Corroded		
WF5880	1944	D	Struck on Steel Planched	62	62
WF5881	1944	D	Struck on Steel Planchet	62	62
WF5882	1944	D	Struck on Steel Planchet	62	62
XA7378	1944	D	Steel Planchet	55	55
TS2612	1944	D	Steel Planchet	50	50
0436	1944	D	Struck on Steel Planchet - Damaged	40	40
A 3708	1944	D	Struck on Steel Planchet	50	50
EG3659	1944		Struck on Steel Planchet	30	30
EC0225	1944		Struck on Steel Planchet	40	40
EA1989	1944	S	Struck on Steel Planchet	40	40
UED065	1944		Struck on Steel Planchet	40	40

Sales Report
Of
1943 Copper Cents

Sold	Sale Type	Mint	Certificate	Condition	Seller	Price Realized
1958	Private Sale	1943P	(B-2314)	A.U.58	Marvin Beyer	40,000
1960	Private Sale	1943P		V.G.8	Caro Martin	10,000
1965	Private Sale	1943P	(F-9644-A)	E.F.45	Frank Spadone	15,000
1973	Private Sale	1943S		E.F.45	Jan Bronson	9,000
1974	Superior Auction	1943S		A.U.50	Charles Ruby, Part 1	12,000
1979	Superior Auction '79	1943S	(E-9300-B)	E.F.40	Fred Weinberg	10,750
1981	Bowers-Ruddy A.N.A.. Auction	1943P	(G-3356-H)	E.F.45	John Ford	10,000
1982	Private Sale	1943P		Fine12-Damaged	Dave Berg	8,000
1984	Private Sale	1943S	(E-9300-B)	E.F.40	Dwight Berger	35,000
1984	Private Sale	1943P	(F-5960-B)	A.U.50	Steve Benson	18,500
1985	Central State Auction	1943P	(F-9644-A)	E.F.45	McIntire	23,250
1986	F.U.N. Auction	1943P	(B-2314)	A.U.58	Mid-America	15,400
1989	Heritage St. Louis Auction	1943S	(S-1436-A)	E.F.40	Dwight Berger	14,500
1989	Kurt Krueger Auction	1943S	(E-9117-C)	E.F.40	Dave Berg (Lot 979)	22,750
1992	Bowers - Merena Auction	1943P	(G-3356-H)	E.F. 45	Somerset Sale	12,700

Benson also reports after many years of extensive searching, no authenticated 1943D copper cent has been located. He recently (March, 1992) wrote that calls and meetings with ANA, Tom Delorey, John Ford, Harry Forman and others has failed to trace any 1943D bronze cent. Thus any earlier reference to such coins is in error. The 1943D has long been rumored,but never confirmed. Benson also traced exactly five 1943S cents, a few of which have sold more than once.

This author is grateful for the many pages of materials related to both the 1943 bronze cents and the 1944 steel cents contained on these pages furnished by Steve Benson.

Under 1944, a similar chart tracks the known public and private sales of the 1944 steel cents.

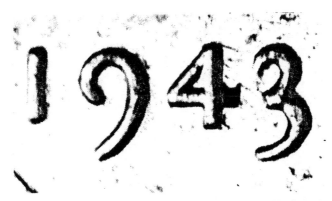

Here we show a normal 1943 cent. Note how the tail of the 3 swoops down like the tail of the 9. Also note how the top of the 3 curls down tightly to end in a point above the center tine of the digit. Check any possible altered 1943 bronze cent to see if the shape of the 3 matches this. From Bill Fivaz of Georgia.

The 1943 date shown is a genuine steel cent dated 1943. It is shown to avoid considering an altered 1948 cent as a 1943 bronze. The "3" is quite different in 1943 than other years except 1934. According to FORD, there may be 20-30 genuine 1943 bronze cents in existence, however, fewer than that number have been traced so far by numismatic scholars such as FORD and BENSON.

—1944—

The cents of 1944 and 1945 were made from brass and bronze strips derived mainly from spent shell casings from the U.S. Navy. They tend to show more colors and streaking than other bronze coins.

MINTAGES:

1944 — 1,435,400,000 The first billion plus issue.
1944D — 430,578,000
1944S — 181,770,000
1944D/D — Unknown, estimated at 100,000
1944D/S — Unknown, estimated at 20,000 or less. Two
    distinct types. No proofs were struck this year.

AVAILABILITY:

1944 Steel Planchet Lincoln Cent

1050   **1944 Lincoln cent struck on a zinc-coated steel planchet intended for 1943. EF-45,** lightly brushed. Brilliant. Certified by ANACS for authenticity. Fairly sharply struck, although not as well defined as the same impression would be in bronze. Breen-2170, noted as ''very rare.'' On page 227 of his *Encyclopedia* Walter Breen notes that the 1944 steel cents are rarer than the famous 1943 bronze cent. (Reserve or starting bid on this lot: $3,500).

The cents of 1944 were a first just as the 1943 cents. The so-called "wartime" cents were made from spent shell casings which also were brass. However, regardless of the processing methods used, some of the impurities of the explosives managed to invade the alloy and most 1944 cents (as well as 1945 cents) show streaks of iridescence in the bright BU red coins. Some coins have pale greenish streaks--most likely due to the combination of traces of manganese, phosphorus, and other explosive ingredients mixed in with the brass alloy. The coins also tend to be a bit paler than pre-war bronze coins. The 1944 cent has been widely hoarded and until the mid-1960s was readily available in bag (5,000 coins) quantities. Recent Trends values a BU 1944P roll at $27. Choice early die strikes are not hard to find, but most tend to be medium to later die states and colors range from bright (but pale) red to dull red and reddish brown. Streaks are common. Spotting is common.

The 1944D cent is also found in roll quantities and most tend to be average die state red coins. Due to the high mintage of 430 million, rolls have always been available and at price levels of 1988--$11-12. Because of the popularity of the D/S over-mintmark, many rolls (if not most) have been carefully culled over for these very scarce over-mintmarks. In addition, a very distinct D/D RPM is known and these coins bring $5-10 each in choice BU. Thus one can expect to find neither the RPM not the OMMs in existing rolls--especially in plastic tubes. If one found a hoard of red paper wrapped rolls, then there is a chance some of these varieties might still be found. The OMM #1,S to the north of the D, choice BU coins have sold recently for $500 and more. The price for the OMM #2 where the S lies to the west of the D runs about $125 for a choice BU red coin.

The 1944S roll also shows the same features of the 1944D. The current Trends shows a value of $10.50. The price has remained virtually unchanged for five years. Most BU coins have a weaker finish in the bust and date and the color tends to be more red, but as before, some streaky colors are common. Some actually enhance the overall eye appeal. Streaks of gold color also are common. But as with many rolls, so are the spots, tarnish, and fingermarks.

Fantastic Set of 1944 Steel Cents

See Color Photo

785 **1944 steel cent** (struck on a 1943 blank in error). Weight 42.9 grains, or close to standard for the zinc plated steel blanks used in 1943 (regular copper 1944 cents weigh close to 48 grains). **AU-50** or so, but processed, just like the popular 1943 cents sold in jewelry stores. Large lamination type depression on lower reverse. Very weak about the rims; this is diagnostic as the steel planchets were thinner than the regular bronze ones intended for 1944. Detailed X-ray diffraction and X-ray flourescence data supplied by the consignor indicate strong spectral peaks at frequencies characteristic of zinc and iron, and only minor peaks at frequencies corresponding to copper; the graphs match exactly runs done on a 1943 steel cent for comparison, and prove conclusively that the present 1944 cent was struck on a planchet of the type used for the 1943 cents. Just about as rare as the corresponding 1943 cent in copper, but not quite as well publicized. Judd, appendix B states eight or nine pieces known of each; Taxay (*Scott's Encyclopedia*, pg. 352) lists the 1943 copper as R-7 and the 1944 steel as R-6, but does not break down these estimates by mint. We have handled two of these in the past five years, one comparable to the present specimen in our Bartlett sale (November, 1979), Lot 2199 at $3700 and an Uncirculated directly from the Sinnock estate in our 1981 ANA sale at $3500.

Note: The 1944 cent is also known struck in silver on a dime planchet, in aluminum-bronze and in brass, both of these being meant for foreign coins which were being struck at the same time at the Philadelphia Mint. The large number of off-planchet errors during the period 1942-1944 compared to earlier years was a direct effect of the emergency coinage conditions during the War years. The same type of off-planchet errors occur in the Jefferson nickels (pre-war types struck on war-time planchets and vice-versa), but these have not received anywhere near the popularity of the cents, probably because the difference in color between the copper and zinc plated steel blanks is so dramatic.

Copy of the page from the Bowers & Merena Roy Harte Sale, 1983. This is only set of three (1944P,D,S) ever offered for sale at one time. Since the 1944S in steel in UNIQUE, chances of this occurring again are minimal.

See Color Photo

786 **1944-D Steel cent. 42.3 grains. Brilliant Uncirculated,** mostly choice, though displays signs of a cleaning. Not quite as nice as the piece in our 1981 ANA sale, though this mintmark is considerably rarer in error form. Also weak at the rims (an alleged 1944 steel cent would be immediately suspect of being a forgery were it sharp at the rims, as explained above). This particular piece can be identified by a slight diagonal tarnish streak running across the reverse, bisecting C in CENT, and touching top point of left wheat stalk and bottom point of right one. Listed in Judd, Appendix B as "two known." The fact that this same error occurred at all three mints is quite remarkable.

See Color Photo

787 **1944-S Steel cent. 41.5 grains. EF,** cleaned, very weak about the rims. With ANACS certification No. E-1089-A. Rarest of the three mints and **completely unlisted in both Judd and Taxay** (Judd only lists the 1943-S cent struck on a silver dime planchet). As far as we know, this is the first time in auction history that all three of these have been offered at once; an extraordinary opportunity.

The catalogue description of the 1944 steel cent was furnished by Mike Batkin from the Bowers & Merena Frontenac Sale held in November, 1991.

Most catalogues and numismatic books gloss over the 1944 cents because of the notoriety of the 1943 cent and especially the 1943 bronze cents. The 1944 is equally interesting with its share of equally rare 1944 steel cents. The excellent up-to-date summary by Steve Benson is shown below. Though prices are not nearly as strong as for 1943 bronze cents, the 1944 steel cent ranks as high in scarcity and value. Perhaps as publicity grows, the value gap will narrow.

1944-D/S Cent; Overmintmark: Var. I

Sales Report
Of
1944 Steel Cents

Sold	Sale Type	Mint	Certificate	Condition	Seller	Price Realized
1975	Superior Auction	1944P		Unc.M.S.60	Charles Ruby Part 3	10,2
1979	Error Catalog #10	1944P		E.F.40	Numismatics Ltd.	1,0
1979	Bowers-Ruddy Auction	1944P		E.F.45	Bartlett Sale	3,7
1980	Paramount, Auction '80	1944P		A.U.50		4,6
1981	Bowers-Ruddy A.N.A . Auction	1944P		Unc.M.S.63	John Ford	3,5
1981	N.E.R.C.A. (Lot 173)	1944P		V.F.20	New England Rare Coins	2,3
1981	Mass.State Rare Coin Auction	1944P		E.F.45		2,0
1983	Bowers-Merena Auction	1944P		E.F.45	Roy Harte Sale	3,3
1983	Bowers-Merena Auction	1944S	(E-1989-A)	E.F.40	Roy Harte Sale	5,3
1983	Bowers-Merena Auction	1944D		A.U.50	Roy Harte Sale	3,3
1984	Private Sale	1944P		Unc.M.S.60	Steve Benson	4,2
1985	Heritage A.N.A. Auction	1944P	(E-3659-G)	V.F.30	Ernest Grimm Sale	1,6
1985	Kurt Kruger Auction	1944P	(E-0225-C)	E.F.40	Cherry Hill Sale	5,3
1986	Central States Auction	1944D	(A-3708)	A.U.50	McIntire	2,3
1986	Private Sale	1944D	(A-3708)	A.U.50	Steve Benson	3,8
1987	Private Sale	1944P	(G-0776-L)	Unc.M.S.63	Steve Benson	4,9
1987	Coin World Ad	1944P		E.F.40	Devonshire	3,9
1989	Heritage St. Louis Auction	1944D	(0436)	E.F.40-Damaged	Dwight Berger	3,1
1989	Heritage Dallas Auction	1944D		E.F.45	Market Hall (Lot 92)	4,8
1989	Private Sale	1944P	(E-0225-C)	E.F.40	Larry Parker	4,0
1989	Private Sale	1944P	(G-0776-L)	UNC.M.S.63	Larry Parker	6,0
1991	Bowers-Merena Auction	1944P		E.F.45	Frontenac Sale	4,4
1992	Bowers-Merena Auction	1944P		UNC.M.S.63	Somerset Sale	5,7

—1945—

MINTAGES:
1945 — 1,040,515,000
1945D — 226,268,000
1945S — 181,770,000

Also shell-case bronze as in 1944.

No proofs struck this year.

AVAILABILITY:

The 1945 cents topped the one billion mintage mark. Many were hoarded by the roll and even Mint sewn bags of 5,000 coins. By the late 1960s and early 1970s many were sold and culled over for the choicest coins. Made of shellcase brass (or bronze), many BU red coins show golden and iridescent streaks. Also, some yellowing in the red makes this issue a little paler than pre-war issues. Die states tend to be early but medium die state coins are also seen. The current Trends value of $19.50 is about 60% of the prices in 1988.

The 1945D cent is also shellcase alloy and shows the streaks of the 1944 and 1945 cents. The current Trends value of $13 is about 60% off the 1988 prices and about half the prices of ten years ago.

The 1945S is also shellcase alloy and with a huge mintage of over 181 million, it is still available in BU rolls. The current Trends value of $14.50 is similar to 1988 values.

SLCC has sold BU matched 1945P, D, and S sets for more than $5 in MS65. Choice, spot-free coins are available in early die state, but finding a matched trio takes some looking. Most of the 1945S coins tend toward average die state and off colors are common.

—1946—

Bronze pre-war composition of 95% copper: 4% zinc and 1% tin restored. However, some shell-case alloy probably also used since the coins often show all the features of shell-case 1944-45 coins.

MINTAGES:
1946 — 991,655,000
1946D — 315,690,000
1946S — 198,100,000

AVAILABILITY:
The 1946 cent is still available in roll quantities and many are still quality mint reed and early die state. The Trends value of $15 has almost doubled since 1988, perhaps as testament to the number of quality rolls still offered for sale. Since single coins have so little premium, apparently many rolls have not been culled over. Some of the BU rolls exhibit the same impurities of the shellcase cents and thus probably were also made form shellcase stock. Breen comments on this as well. The majority appear to be pre-war bronze stock.

The 1946D cent is also still available in large roll quantities. At current Trends of $6.50 it is just about 10% less than its 1988 price levels. Most appear to be average to late die state, but come with full mint red.

The 1946S also still is available in large roll quantities. The die state varies from average to late with some nice mint red coins struck from almost worn out dies. The S comes in two styles according to Breen. The blunt serifs and the sharp serifs. No distinction is made as to relative value. The Trends value of $13.50 is about 10% less and 1988 values.

—1947—

MINTAGES:
1947 — 190,555,000
1947D — 194,750,000
1947S — 99,000,000

No proofs were struck this year, however, U.S. Mint packaged sets were sold containing two of each coin minted that year. The cents almost always are heavily toned or tarnished. They have no premium outside the set holders.

AVAILABILITY:

The 1947 cent dropped off to a fraction of the 1946 levels. Only 190.5 million were minted. Not as many hoards were put away and the current Trends value of $52.50 may be a reflection of that fact. This is one of the few dates which has risen sharply in the past four years. Choice rolls are not common. Most singles are average die state and deeper red than usual. Choice singles are not easy to find. Apparently most early rolls have been will culled over.

The 1947D cent is also available in rolls and at $7 one can assume the low quality of existing stock. Most singles are average to late die state and soft red colors. The price has remained static for the past five years.

The 1947S is available in rolls and at the same price level for the past five years. As with the 1947D, rolls have been pretty well culled over. As with the 1946S there are two types of S mintmark, one with blunt serifs and one with sharp serifs. Most pieces tend to be average die state with a fair number of late and even very late die state BU coins seen.

—1948—

MINTAGES:
1948 — 317,570,000
1948D — 172,637,000
1948S — 81,735,000

As with the 1947, the U.S. Mint packaged double mint sets this year. The cents are found heavily toned or tarnished and have no premium outside the original set holder.

AVAILABILITY:

The 1948 production of cents rose over the past year and the stock of rolls seen recently indicate many choice coins still exist, both in rolls and singles. The roll price in Trends is $20 about 1/3rd higher than in 1988. Many come in early die state and later and weaker die states are also seen.

The 1948D seen in BU rolls is a less sharply struck version of the 1948, with average to late die state the rule. Colors tend also to be off the true mint red. Roll prices have held the same level for the past five years at $14. Red paper wrapped rolls still can be found, and tend to be spotty.

The 1948S is generally a late die state coin and the existing rolls apparently have been well culled over. Breen describes a blunt serif S which is described as "very rare". No prices available on this variety. The more common sharp serifs S is still found in BU rolls at 1/3rd less than the 1988 price levels. Current Trends is $23.50.

SLCC has sold several matched 1948P,D,S sets for $5 in recent mail bid sales.

There are over five hundred repunched mintmarks known in the Lincoln Cent series. Only a few are included in the date analysis (Chapter 5). Many are very minor and hard to find. Some are questionable. Those that are most significant or well-known are included under the proper date heading. Thus, if you have RPMs of dates not shown in Chapter 5, do not conclude it is a new discovery. The ERROR INDEX lists all published RPMs and OMMs as of 1990. In addition, all known pieces up to 1983 are featured in THE RPM BOOK. In addition, THE RPM BOOK shows the various types of mintmark doubling, some of which is not a RPM. This book does not attempt to duplicate the materials in THE RPM BOOK.

From 1947 through 1958, the U.S. Mint issued double mint sets in cardboard holders with one coin from each mint. No sets were issued in 1950. These sets are traded only complete in the Mint holders and often bring a premium over the quoted prices if the original mailer is also included. The coins are almost always heavily toned, tarnished, even spotted. but the complete package represents a Mint issue and they are traded accordingly. From a May 1992 price list prices for some of these annual sets are:

1948 with mailer envelope $295., 1951 $395., 1952 $295., 1953 $295., and 1954 $195.

Actual mintage figures are not known, but based on supplies, the numbers are probably equal to or less than proof set mintages of comparable years (except 1947-1949 which had no proof sets).

No doubt many if not most such sets were destroyed when the coins were removed and the holders discarded.

—1949—

MINTAGES:
1949 — 217,490,000
1949D — 154,370,000
1949S — 64,290,000

No proofs were minted this year. The double mint sets are the most valuable of the U.S. Mint sets issued 1947-date, currently trading at $850-950. Again, the toned coins have no premium outside the entire set in the holder.

AVAILABILITY:

The 1949 cent can still be located in gem BU singles and in selected BU rolls. The current Trends value of $20 is a little less than in 1988. This date comes in various die states including early and usually in full mint red. It is not hard to locate a few gems at any major coin show or from dealers who specialize in Lincoln Cents.

The 1949D is also readily available in choice to gem mint singles. Uncirculated rolls Trends at $22.50 and that is steady with 1988 prices. The coins often come in average die state and full to subtle mint red.

The 1949S cent also comes in BU rolls and at $52 current Trends it is about 40% lower than in 1988. It is fairly scarce in gem BU singles and SLCC has sold gem singles for up to $10 a coin, though $5 is more often the sales price. PCGS has encapsulated 3 MS66 Red and 6 MS65 Red. Most roll specimens rate MS64 and lower. Spotting is common. Circulated rolls have always commanded a premium and roll prices have held steady and even risen over the years.

—1950—

MINTAGES:

1950 — 272,686,000
1950D — 334,950,000
1950S — 118,505,000
1950 - Brilliant proofs — 51,386
Proof sets were made this year but no mint sets were prepared.

AVAILABILITY:

The Philadelphia Mint resumed minting brilliant proof coins in 1950 after an eight year hiatus. Unlike the 1936-1942 sets, the 1950-1955 sets were packaged and sold as complete sets containing the cent, nickel, dime, quarter and half dollar. Each coin was placed by hand into a small poly bag and the five bags connected together with a small staple. The coins were wrapped in tissue and sealed in a small square box. These sets are still traded in the box and referred to as "boxed sets". Most have been broken down as the coins do not hold up well in this type of packaging. In 1955, two types of proof set packaging were used. See -1955- for more details.

The 1950 cent was traded by the roll and even bag up to the late 1960s, now rolls are still traded at current Trends levels of $22 per roll. This is slightly higher than the 1988 prices. The 1950 cent tends to be dull red, average die state, and average luster. True gems are seen, but many fewer than other "P" mint dates of the same era.

The 1950D cent is also actively traded by the BU roll and current Trends value is $9.50, about the same as in 1988. Most are average red color, less than full luster, and medium die state. Again, gems are known, but not in any great numbers.

The 1950S cent is currently trading at Trends value of $20 which is about the same as four to five years ago. The coin typically is average to late die state, nice mint red to pale golden red, and comes in full to average luster.

Matched choice BU red sets of 1950P,D,S cents have brought $3 to $5 at SLCC mail bid sales.

The 1950 proof cent is a scarce coin, based on mintage as well as those that have been well-preserved Many have been submitted for encapsulation since the coin has traded at price over $100 for choice specimens. The current PCGS data show: 4 - Pf67, 93 - Pf66, 235 - Pf65, 100 - Pf64, and 30 lesser graded proofs. Based upon examinations of many raw coins, the 1950 proof tends to be toned, hairlined, and wine red. Many other problems exist, including spotting, fingermarks, and various surface defects—perhaps the most commonly seen are thin streaks made by the staple holding the poly bags together. The early die state and earliest struck pieces tend to have a wire rim, flashy mirrored surfaces, and medium red color. Those pieces which have been in the box sets for more than ten years tend to have small black spots. Late die struck pieces tend to show thinner lettering in the mottoes as a result of die polishing. Also, some hair details and coat folds fade away with die polishing. The earlier released pieces have a satiny surface (not full mirror-like), and most of the remaining 51,000 sets have full mirror-like brilliant surfaces. Prices quoted always seem to be for the second version. Unlike the 1936, the certification services do not classify the two types separately.

—1951—

MINTAGES:
1951 — 294,633,500
1951D — 625,355,000
1951S — 100,890,000
1951 - Brilliant proofs — 57,500

Double mint sets were resumed after a one year layoff.

The 1951 cent is readily available in BU rolls, and some quality rolls still exist. Current Trends shows a quote of $24 a bit higher than in 1988 but lower than peak value of 1978-79 of $40. Most BU coins are early to medium die state, nice mint red to orange red, and usually highly lustrous.

The 1951D is also available by the BU roll and currently quoted at $10 in Trends. That is about the same price level of five years ago and up from $5 in 1980. Apparently the discovery of the very scarce over mintmark D/S has depleted many rolls. The OMM#1 is listed in Wexler as very scarce.

The 1951S is traded by the roll at Trends value of $27. This roll has risen in the past four years form 1988 prices of $23-25. However, it has slipped greatly from the peak price of $65 a roll in 1979-80. Gem singles are available, but more often than not, the usual BU coins is a late die state coin.

The 1951 proof cent is available in gem proof condition, in sets, singles, and certified (slabbed). The late 1991 PCGS data show: Pf67 - 7, Pf66 - 52, Pf65 - 107, Pf64 - 75, and Pf63 - 21. A check of recent price lists show a Pf64 Red for $24 and a Pf65 Red for $30 and a Pf66 Red for $40 (LS Jan. 1991 P.6 et al).

Wexler reports (LINCOLN CENT DOUBLED DIE) a minor obverse doubled die (also listed as Breen #2199). It is considered rare.

In the Lincoln Cent series there are dozens of reported doubled dies. Only a few selected ones are reported in Chapter 5. Many are very minor and hard to determine. The more popular ones are included in the appropriate date heading. The types of doubled dies are described in Wexler's THE LINCOLN CENT DOUBLED DIE and in a handbook furnished by SPLIT IMAGE. The third character in a doubled die description refers to the type of doubling. For example, 1909 VDB 1-0-IV, refers to the first doubled die of 1909 VDB (as discovered and reported), the "0" represents the obverse, and the IV represent the type of die doubling. Where the letter used is "R" it refers to reverse.

—1952—

MINTAGES:
1952 — 186,856,000
1952D — 746,130,000
1952S — 137,800,000
1952 - Brilliant Proofs — 81,980

AVAILABILITY:

The 1952 cent is readily available in BU rolls at current Trends value of $27. This is up from 1988 prices of $15-19. Prices had remained steady at that level for some ten to twelve years. Apparently as remaining roll quality has dropped (spotting is very common), the few "clean" rolls have risen in price. Most 1952 cents are bright mint red, average die state and usually fully lustrous.

The 1952D cent is also available in BU rolls at present Trends level of $7.50. This is up about 10% over the 1988 prices, but down considerably from the peak of $32 in 1979-80. Since the discovery of the 1952D/S (two varieties) and D/D RPMs, apparently many rolls have been cherrypicked. The low price is due more to the low quality of rolls examined recently. Spotting is common and the late die state coins are also the majority. Red-brown BU coins are more often found than full red. In recent SLCC mail bid sales, BU matched MS65 red 1952P,D, and S sets have fetched prices from $7.50 to $10 (March, 1992 results).

The 1952S is also available in average condition BU rolls at current Trends levels of $22. This price is roughly the same for the past four to five years and down from the high of $32 in 1979-80. Many are late die state, nice mint red, and lustrous.

Time has made many of the shotgun (red wrapper) rolls undesirable due to darkening, spotting, and tarnishing. This is true of most of the shotgun rolled coins of the 1940s, 1950s, and 1960s.

The 1952 proof cent is available in original mint boxes, plastic sets (3-piece holders), raw singles, and encapsulated. The nicer ones are submitted regularly to the certification services as noted by monthly gains in the population data. Late 1991 data from PCGS show: Pf67 - 8, Pf66 - 65, Pf65 - 125, Pf64 - 75, Pf63 - 22 and 3 of lesser grades. These numbers grow by four to five coins per month. Since proof coins will more than likely hold up better in the long run in a slab, more collectors are submitting the better quality coins for protection-- and of course hopefully of a super high grading value.

—1953—

MINTAGES:
1953 — 256,883,000
1953D — 700,515,000
1953S — 181,835,000
1953 Brilliant proof — 128,000, the first issue of proofs to exceed 100,000.

Double mint sets were issued this year through 1958. As before, the coins have no premium outside the original sets in the holders.

AVAILABILITY:

The 1953 cent is readily available by the roll as well as choice to gem singles. They often come well struck and full mint red. The BU rolls seem recently still have enough MS65 Red coins to meet collector needs. The current Trends for a BU roll is $6. This is slightly higher than 1988 prices and about the same as 1979-80 price levels. Even shotgun rolls have been as recently as 1991.

The 1953D cent is also readily available in BU rolls and recent Trends shows a value of $5.50. Many come well struck along with some medium die state coins. Colors run from bright mint red to dull red and reddish brown. Price levels have been steady for almost ten years--supply always seems to be there.

The 1953S is a bit harder to find as many of the BU rolls were late die state and off-color coins. The current Trends of $12 is about the same as 1988 and even the same as 1979-80. Supply is adequate, but quality varies a great deal from roll to roll.

The 1953 proof cent is a fairly common proof inasmuch as it was the first proof cent minted in over 100,000 quantity. Some still are being offered for sale in the original mint boxes. Most have been bought and sold in custom three-piece plastic proof set holders for all five coins dated 1953.

And there are many singles available uncertified. The few that have been submitted have been high end, nice looking, bright coins in the hopes of getting the highest possible Pf-grades. PCGS has certified 21 - Pf67, 91 - Pf66, 85 - Pf65, 44 - Pf63, and 9 lesser grades. With the 1953 proof set retailing at $115 the major portion of which is the value of the half dollar, the cent has relatively little value--singles sell for $25 and less in gem red. Certified Pf65s are offered at $35 or so and Pf66s would bring upwards of $45-50. No recent price quote is available on the Pf67.

—1954—

MINTAGES:

1954 — 71,873,000, the lowest Philadelphia issue since 1933.
1954D — 251,552,000
1954S — 96,190,000
1954 - Brilliant proof — 233,300

AVAILABILITY:

The 1954 cent ranks as perhaps the lowest quality minted cent in the 1950s. In fact, its scarcity became very evident only in the past decade as dealers and collectors were assembling BU "short sets" dated from 1934-1958. The inability to locate early die state full mint red 1954 cents was apparent. Despite relatively low roll prices for BU rolls, sharp BU red 1954 cents remained very elusive. SLCC sold a few MS65 Red cents in recent mail bid sales for up to $5 a coin. This illustrates the scarcity of such coins--and they were average die state. The BU rolls listed in price lists and Trends tend to be very well culled over with few coins better than MS63 RB.

The 1954S is a very interesting coin because of numerous collectible varieties. There are several RPMs (S/S) described in Wexler as well as several die breaks. The most popular is the so-called "San Jose" die break where a small J-shaped die break lies to the right of the S looking somewhat like "SJ". It is mentioned in Breen. SLCC had sold at least one such variant in a recent mail bid sale in BU for $4.50. The other popular die breaks errors include LIBIERTY (die break in between B and E in LIBERTY). These bring $0.50 to $1.00 each in BU. Numerous other die breaks have been described in the head, coat, and reverse.

Most BU rolls examined in recent years are medium to late die state, full mint red, and often contain one or more die break varieties.

Though the 1954D can be found in choice even gem rolls, the majority of rolls in 1992 are culled over late die state less than MS64 quality and mostly red brown. At Trends value of $6 it is up about 50% over 1988 and peaked in 1983 at $8. Since bags are probably still available, the availability of BU rolls well into the future is assured.

The 1954 proof was minted in a record number of sets, over 233,000. Many are still available in choice to gem condition. Since the market value is low (under $12), relatively few have been encapsulated. PCGS had certified: Pf68 - 3, Pf67 - 30, Pf66 - 47, Pf65 - 34, Pf64 - 29 and 6 lesser graded coins. Plenty of gem fiery red coins exist raw and in five coin sets. Many sets however, focus on the silver coins and in these the cent often is tarnished, spotted, and otherwise impaired. Pieces sold singly tend to be the nicer looking coins.

LINCOLN CENT
1954-S/S (N)
RPM #4 Unc.
$8.00 ppd.

—1955—

MINTAGES:
1955 — 330,958,000
1955 Doubled die — estimated 20,000
1955D — 563,257,000
1955S — 44,610,000
1955 - Brilliant proof — 378,200

AVAILABILITY:

The 1955 cent has many reasons for prominence. Perhaps the most popular is the distinctive 1955 doubled die cent which has soared in value since its discovery. According to Breen (p. 227) Mint coiner Sydney C. Engel released a batch of cents containing some 20,000 to 24,000 of the doubled die cents in a total of 10 million coins. Most started appearing in change in the Boston and New York areas. Early finders were able to sell them to dealers for up to $50 a coin creating a major stir among coin hunters. No rolls or bags of 1955 doubled die cents were ever found--only single finds by lucky lookers. Because of their popularity and strong market value, many have been counterfeited and many genuine pieces have been cleaned, toned, and artificially colored to look BU. From recent PCGS data, the totals certified are: MS Red - 65 - 5, 64 - 35, 63 - 14, 62 - 3, 61 - 1, 60 - 1, and in Red brown: 65 - 1, 64 - 54, 63 - 60, 62 - 16, 61 - 2, 60 - 2, and brown: 65 - 1, 64 - 54, 63 - 66, 62 - 20, 61 - 5, 60 - 3. Many others have been certified in lesser grades. At the Heritage Sale in February, 1992, an uncertified 1955/55 EF-45 was sold for $429. In the same sale a NGC MS64 RB went for $1210. Sales of $3500 have been known for MS65 Red pieces. Reports of finds were made well into the 1970s. At the 1991 Stacks New York Mail Bid Sale an AU (lot 2917) went for $440. In a recent fixed price list (LS 1/91) a PCGS MS62 BN was listed for $665.

Less well-known than the popular 1955/55 are the doubled die 1955 proof cents with doubling in the revere motto. These have been sold for over $100 each for the more prominently doubled dies. Since most sets have not been inspected (as of 1991), finds are reported by collectors recently. This author bought a set from a dealer and it contained a 1955 DDR. 1955 was a transitional year for proof sets, with the first run in boxes and the majority of the 378,000 sets in pliofilm (flat pack) sets. Over the years, it has been shown that neither type of packaging was suited for long term storage of any of the coins. Thus most of the proof cents are found singly or in five coin plastic custom holders.

Choice to gem 1955 proof singles are available and due to the large mintage, are not hard to find. Prices for nice red Pf65 coins run from a low of $12 to close to $20. Only a few have been certified due to the relatively low market value of the 1955 proof. PCGS data show: 15 - Pf67, 48 - Pf66, 25 - Pf65, and 20 others in lesser grades. With 1955 flat pack proof sets listed at $55-58, the majority of the value is in the silver coins, the cent often is the lowly coin in the set. Spots are common. So is toning. Owners of 1955 proof sets should take a closer look at the cents and compare with illustrations in Wexler's LINCOLN CENT DOUBLED DIE.

The 1955 cent is available in BU rolls at about $5. This is slightly up form 1988. Supplies seem to always be available. Choice BU gems are available, and many rolls are also medium to late die state which account for many of the rolls offered for sale. Shotgun rolls have sold recently at major shows. There is a strike doubling variant which is popular since it shows the date 19555, also called by many as the "Poor Man's Doubled Die". Sales are known at the $1 to $2 level. This is a late die state coin and found in almost every bag of 1955 cents.

FEATURES OF 1955 CENTS

On the reverse of the 1955 double die, there is a pair of thin lines from a die scratch running down from under the left crossbar of the T. See photo.

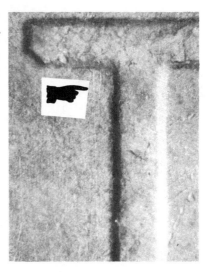

1955 Cent—Doubled Die Obverse: Two vertical die scratches downward from the crossbar of the T of CENT, just left of the vertical, form a tall "X."

1955 1¢ Pr 3-R-II

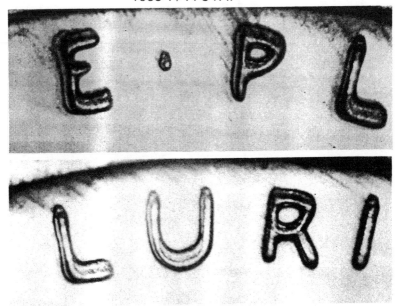

155

—1956—

MINTAGES:
1956 — 421,414,384
1956D — 1,098,201,100
1956 - Brilliant proof — 669,384

AVAILABILITY:

The 1956 cent is still available in huge quantities including mint-sealed bags. The lack of major discoveries or varieties has probably made it impractical to scour through the tons of unsearched 1956 cents. They come in early and average die state, sharp mint color, and bright red. Gems are common. Roll prices have remained steady at under $4 for most of the last decade. The chances of becoming scarce are small as the supply is large.

The 1956D was a record-breaker for a Denver Mint issue of over one billion cents. The discovery of a few distinctive RPMs has broken down many hoarded bags and rolls in search of these popular D/D coins. Of the several RPMs which range in value form $1 to $4, the widely separated RPM can bring considerably more. The huge stock of BU rolls and bags has kept prices under $3 for most of the past decade. Many are well struck and full mint red.

The 1956 proof cent at a mintage of 869,000 is still readily available in mint sealed flat packs and five piece custom plastic holders. Many others are in singles. Due to low market value of under $3 very few have been submitted for certification. They come full mirrored, sharp strikes, and wire edges. Spotting seems to be the common problem of many of the sets--both Mint sealed and custom plastic holders.

—1957—

MINTAGES:
1957 — 283,787,952
1957D — 1,051,342,000
1957 Brilliant proof — 1,247,952 First million plus proof
  issue.

AVAILABILITY:
As with 1956, the 1957 cent is available in large hoards, both in rolls and bags. They come in choice and gem quality and can easily be located to satisfy and collector's needs. At under $3 a BU roll, the price has remained steady over the decade. the lack of any major variations has kept many rolls "original" shotgun wrapped rolls.

The 1957D is another billion plus mintage coin. Thus it is also very available. However, some very interesting varieties have been found and thus, many rolls have been culled over in searching for the several RPMs and three minor obverse doubled dies. Retail values for these varieties run upwards of $5, not much more even for choice BU coins. The 1957D is also found with various die breaks, cuds, and strike doubling, all of minor value. Gem 1957D coins are also fairly easy to locate. Roll values of under $3 have been steady for most of the past decade.

The 1957 proof cent is still readily available in flat packs and singles. Many others come in three piece custom plastic holders. The choicest coins usually are found as singles. Since over a million proof sets were made, the 1957 proof cent can be located in almost any state--from circulated to Pf68. The vast majority of the 80 pieces certified by PCGS are Pf66 and higher. Lesser pieces are worth $1 or so. As with other flat pack years, spotting is common as well as toning.

—1958—

The last of the Wheat reverse.

MINTAGES:

1958 — 253,400,600
1958D — 800,953,000
1958 - Brilliant proof — 875,652

AVAILABILITY:

Though slightly lower mintage than 1957, as the last year of the wheat stalk cent, large hoards were put away. With the discovery of the 1958/7 and 1958/7D first described by Alan Herbert in 1978, many bags and rolls have been scanned closely for these--the only over-dates in the entire Lincoln Cent series. Prices for late die state coins have been advertised as low as $2 and choice early die state pieces have brought close to $100. The illustration in Breen is the example one would expect for a premium overdate. Considered a doubled die (modified hub) the 1958/7 is also listed as MH 1-0-VII and the 1958/7D is known as MH-1-0-VII. (Breen, p. 232)

The 1958P is available in large hoards and as the word of the overdate spreads, more rolls will be searched and broken down to singles. They come in all die states and bright mint golden red. Gems are easy to come by at low prices.

The 1958 doubled die has been seen and shown at several coin shows. Apparently the same coin has been making the rounds, but has not been sold at a public sale. (See story next pages).

The 1958D is readily available in choice to gem grades even by the roll. There are several interesting RPMs and at a few dollars value each, more rolls are being scoured to find them.

The 1958 proof set production dropped from 1957 and thus the value for the set is consistently higher than the 1957. The proof cent is available in all grades and a few high end certified pieces are available. Many uncertified singles are available at under $5 a coin. Those found in sets tend to be the imperfect cents with spots, stains, or other surface defects.

1958...

Here we show close-up photos of a 1958 Doubled Die cent that was brought to light at Errorama '84. Photos courtesy of John A. Wexler

MORE ON 1958 DOUBLED DIE

According to specialist John Wexler in the current issue of EVN NEWS, the photos of the 1958 doubled die cent show it is genuine. He goes on to report that this coin (possibly the same one) showed up before. He is told by the unnamed owner that it was found in a mint sealed bag. And it was the only one. The owner also stated he took the coin to the (Phila) mint where Mint officials said such a die was destroyed after a few coins were struck and the coin was genuine.

Being naturally suspicious, this editor and others, feel that the coin never left the Mint in a sealed bag, but rather was snapped off the production line and smuggled out of the Mint. The owner, may well be a former Mint employee waiting for the time factor to lean in his favor as far as the government trying to reclaim the coin. We also feel that there are others in this same unnamed person's possession. The owner if fishing for a top price on this super rarity—and then offering the balance to other dealers at a discount and make a good haul. Of course, this is pure speculation and may not be true at all—it may be some lucky stiff found this UNIQUE doubled die in a Mint sealed bag and NO ONE has found another since! The odds say NO. Had the coin been found by any common person, he or she could have checked it out at a coin shop or coin show and taken an offer comparable to the 1955/55—which back in 1959 would still have been a real find—$50 or so for a single CENT! But no, the owner knew something we don't know. He knew it was imprudent to show off the coin too soon—at least not before ten or more years had passed. He must also know that if no one at the Mint is around who can recall the events regarding the finding of the doubled die and its destruction, there is little that can be done if such a coin suddenly showed up let us say in 1983 or 1984. We suspect that the 1958 doubled die cent may well be a "mini Watergate" or another 1913 Liberty nickel story in the making. Only time will tell—or will the owner tell us first?

—1959—

MINTAGES:
1959 — 610,864,291 The first of the Memorial type reverse.
1959D — 1,279,760,000
1959 Brilliant proof — 1,149,291

Single mint sets started this year and ran through 1964. The single coins have no premium outside the set.

As the first year of the Memorial reverse, the 1959 cent is readily available in roll and bag quantities. The roll price has remained fairly steady at about $1 for many years now. Due to a lack of known major varieties, there seems little incentive to cherry-pick over the large number of rolls. Most are well struck, bright mint red, and very lustrous.

The 1959D was a large production and it too is available in large numbers from various sources. Shotgun rolls are common. The popular RPM (actually a triple D) is available in several positions and another RPM, the D/D exists also in several forms. These RPMs have been found in recent fixed price lists from $1.50 to $8.50 in BU. Refer to Wexler for illustrations and prices for each RPM variety. Despite the presence of RPMs in this date, many original rolls and even bags exist "unpicked".

A remarkable 1959D with a wheat back reverse has been shown to a number of collectors.A photo of this coin was made by ANACS but the coin has not been certified. It is a circulated specimen and according to SLCC member Steve Benson it has been authenticated by none other than the U.S. Treasury. Thus far,this is the only known specimen of a "mule" --a mismatch of obverse and reverse in the Lincoln Cent series.

The 1959 proof cent exists in large numbers and is available in the choicest grades either as a single "raw" or certified. A small number has been certified by PCGS due to the relatively low value per coin--seen in price lists as low as $2 for Pf65. The PCGS data show: Pf68 - 3, Pf67 - 29, Pf66 - 19, Pf65 - 3, and Pf64 - 4.

The 1959 proof set in original mint sealed holders is listed for $14.95 in one recent ad and that price is mainly for the silver coins. Most sets offered for sale are in three piece custom hard plastic holders. From personal examination of many such sets, the cent is often less than gem quality in such sets. Collectors can do well by searching for gems in dealer's stock as singles.

—1960—

MINTAGES:

1960 Large Date — estimated 500,000,000
1960 Small date — estimated 25,000,000
1960D Large date — estimated 1,500,000,000
1960D Small date — estimated 80,000,000

Total mintages reported
1960 — 588,096,602
1960D — 1,580,884,000
1960 Large Date Brilliant proof — 90-92% total
1960 — Small Date Brilliant Proof — 8-10% total
Proof totals 1,691,602

AVAILABILITY:

Early in 1960, stories were circulating that there were two distinct varieties of the 1960 date on the cent and the small date cent was very scarce. That was the beginning of a most interesting year in the series. Many variants have been identified and the year 1960 represents a real challenge to a serious collector.

The first cents minted, the 1960 small date apparently created many die breaks and clogs in the date. Shortly after the first 20 million or so were released, the design was modified to a larger version of the date. The entire mintage of small date cents for 1960 may have occurred entirely in January, 1960 (Breen, p. 234). Thus, the 1960 small date is relatively scarce as compared with the large date version which was minted for the remainder of the year and about 500 million total. The price of the 1960 small date cent ranged wildly over the years with several peaks of $500 a roll and several troughs of under $100. Recent fixed price lists show prices of $80 and thereabouts. The number of rolls and bags set aside in 1960 have been surfacing each year and until major hoards were uncovered in the late 1960s, prices in 1964 were around $500 a roll. More hoards were released in the mid-1980s. In fact circulated specimens of the small date are less common than the BU coins.

The 1960D cent also comes in both small and large date versions. The small date was hoarded and roll prices gyrated wildly as supplies disappeared and then new hoards appeared. Prices peaked at about $25 a roll in the mid 1960s and fell to about $1 today.

An exciting doubled die is described by SLCC member, Carole Kelsey. In choice BU, SLCC has sold several over $100 each.

LINCOLN SENSE   Vol. VI. No. 4 P. 8
1960D SMALL over LARGE
The doubled die 1960D 1-0-111 in the last mail bid sale generated not only many bids, but also this article from SLCC member LM6 Carole Kelsey.

THE 1960D 1c RPM #1 DD 1-0-111
by Carole Kelsey

Hello, perhaps some of you know this coin to be my pet project. This beauty truly has something for everyone. Multiple error collectors just have to have one!

It is an obvious RPM to the north with some thoughts that there are as many as 5 other-though minor or overlapping-RPMs. It is also listed as a doubled die, a small over a large date hubbing. It has several die scratches and die breaks which identify its different die stages. (John Wexler describes these, with photographs, in *The Lincoln Cent Doubled Die.*) It is found in four known circulation strike stages as small/large and one in proof. In addition, there are two verified proof dies as large/small.

The following is a value/rarity chart based upon my correspondence with some of those 'in the know', and my own research:

	EF	AU	UNC	BU	RARITY
Stage 1	30	40	60	100	rare
Stage 2	15	20	30	50	scarce
Stage 3	10	15	25	30	very rare
Stage 4	3.50-5	6.50-10	12-20	17-25	available
Proofs	125	150	175	225	very scarce

Well, have I wet your appetite any? If you have any other tidbits on this coin or any stage 1 or stage 3 specimens that you would be willing to part with, write me: P.O. Box 826, Cheshire, CT. 06410.

References: *The Lincoln Cent Doubled Die,* John Wexler, 1984.

The RPM Book, John A. Wesler and Tom Miller, 1983.

Special Thanks: Lou Coles, Ronn Fern, Allan R. Levy, Mike Niespodzinski, Neil Osina, Henry Oulman, Ken Potter, Rich Schemmer, and John Wexler.

A few of the RPMs of 1960D.
Courtesy of Harry Ellis.

Sm1960D 1¢ RPM #2
D/D North
Cohen Sm60D-DM1 and DM3.
CONE E-04

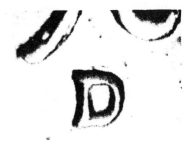

Sm1960D 1¢ RPM #5
D/D Northeast

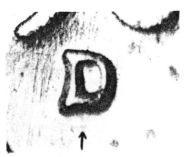

Sm1960D 1¢ RPM #3
D/D South

Sm/Lg 1960D 1¢ RPM #1
D/D North
Kramer 60N12, CONE E-07
The obverse is also a doubled die listed as 1-O III by
Wexler. It has a Small Date/Large Date.

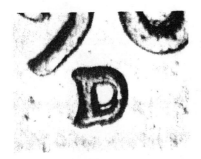

Sm1960D 1¢ RPM #4
D/D North
Cohen Sm60D-DM3, CONE E-14

Lg1960D 1¢ RPM #1
D/D West
RPM #1c
#1a and #1b do not show these
heavy die scratches.

The 1960D cent represents a unique coin in the series. No less than 73 different RPMs are identified as 1960D/D. There may be more. Prices in recent price lists (Error Nibble #16) run from $1 in XF to $4 for several varieties in BU. Many are early die state, some medium and some late die state. In addition to the many RPMs, there are die breaks, and other minor varieties described in fixed price lists and catalogues (Coles, Cohen, Fivaz).

The 1960 proof sets contained several varieties. The small date proof cent represents about 10% of the total of 1.69 million sets. In addition to the small date, three overdate varieties have been described. The photo by Chris Lane shows the large over small proof. It is currently rare and recent prices have been in the $150 level. There is also a small over large proof. Most 1960 proof sets have been broken down and examined for these valuable varieties. Original mint-sealed flat packs are rarely encountered in 1992. Up to a few years ago, they were still traded in quantities until news of the overdates was spread and sets were carefully examined by collectors and dealers alike.

1960 large over small proof

—1961—

MINTAGES:
1961 — 756,373,000
1961D — 1,753,266,000
1961 - Brilliant proof — 3,028,244

AVAILABILITY:

The high mintage of the 1961 cent has made it readily available by the roll and even in bag lots at under one dollar a roll for most of its existence. The coins usually come full mint red, well struck, and relatively free from blemishes. Choice singles are readily available.

The 1961D is also readily available by the BU roll or bag. The number of repunched mintmarks in this date is up to 47 as shown in Wexler. The most popular, RPM#1 the D over horizontal D has been seen in fixed price lists at $15 for a BU specimen. It comes in several die states and prices vary. VF and XF specimens have been noted at $2.50 and $5 respectively. (ERROR NIBBLE #16 p.29).

With a mintage of 1.75 billion, there are many decades of supply available. However, if searching for RPMs is a challenge, there are many unsearched bags and shotgun rolls available at under one dollar a roll.

The 1961 proof is the largest proof production to date with over 3 million sets produced. The price of single gem coins has never gone much over one dollar and thus very few have been submitted for encapsulation. Of the 80 pieces submitted to PCGS, 63 graded Pf66 or higher. And at retail prices of $15 for a Pf66, versus the cost of more than $20 for the service, it gives one pause before submitting even the sharpest brightest 1961 proofs.

There are two minor doubled dies in the 1961 proof shown in Wexler. The obverse Pf 1-O-II shows minor doubling in the motto, and the reverse Pf 1-R-II shows minor doubling in CENT and AMERICA. Both are shown on fixed price lists at under $5.

—1962—

The small percentage of tin in the bronze alloy was dropped and the composition reverted to brass with 95% copper and 5% zinc. This continued into 1982 when the alloy was changed to a copper-plated zinc coin.

MINTAGES:

1962 — 609,263,000
1962D — 1,793,148,000
1962 - Brilliant proof — 3,218,019

AVAILABILITY:

As with the 1961 and high mintages, the 1962 cent is readily available by the roll, bag or singles. Most come well struck and full mint red. Some of the recently opened shotgun rolls show spotting and thus are reduced to face value. The roll price levels have remained steady since the date of issuance to the present at under one dollar a roll with a few peak years (1983 $1.70) at slightly higher prices.

There are several minor doubled dies to look for in this date. Wexler describes three obverse and four reverse doubled dies. All require close examination with magnification to identify. Though scarce, those identified in recent price lists are listed under $10 in BU. (Note the number of proof doubled dies below).

The 1962D is another huge mintage of 1.7 billion. Many original rolls and mint sealed bags still remain. Prices here too remained low throughout the years and today are still under one dollar a roll. Wexler describes 9 different RPMs. Recent price lists show several at under $2 each in BU. In the back of Wexler's (1983) all nine are shown as $2 or less in BU.

The 1962 proof is another 3 million plus issue and as such is readily available by the set, single, or by the roll. Gem coins are readily available at under $2 a coin. Encapsulated Pf66 and Pf67 coins are available at under $15. Pf68 and Pf69 coins are known, but no price data are known.

Five different minor doubled dies are reported by Wexler in proof. They range from a value of $1 to $35. For illustrations consult Wexler (pp. 118-125). Each one requires close examination of that portion of the coin which shows the doubling.

—1963—

MINTAGES:
1963 — 757,185,600
1963 — 1,774,000,000
1963 Brilliant proof — 3,075,645

AVAILABILITY:
As with the two preceding years, the 1963 mint output was very high and the rolls and bags of 1963 cents still unopened attest to that fact. Most shotgun rolls recently examined tend to be spotty, but at under a dollar a roll, not much is lost. Inert plastic tubes are recommended for long term roll storage.

There are two minor reverse doubled dies known for the 1963. Both are illustrated in Wexler (pp. 124-125) and are both listed at under $3.

The 1963D is another billion plus mintage and it too comes in original rolls, square tubes, bags, and singles. The interest in the doubled die obverse 3/3 is fairly strong and as such many bags have been scanned for this variety which has been advertised for up to $15 in BU. In 1987 SLCC had a full roll in its mail bid sale which went for $83. The 1-O-VII in early die state shows a different styled 3 under the 3 in the date. Later die stages show only a portion of the under numeral and sells for much less. Since the mintage of this variety is unknown, probably more will be discovered as the original bags and rolls are searched. There are three other minor doubled dies in this date and they command a premium of $1 to $5 in BU. They require magnification to identify. Refer to Wexler (pp. 127-129).

The 1963 proof cent tapered off from the 1962 mintage levels to 3.075 million. Many still remain in mint sealed flat packs. Many others are traded by the roll. And many gem singles are available. As before, those few that have been submitted for slabbing (encapsulation) have been almost entirely Pf66-Pf68 level coins. Only a very few are encapsulated Pf65 and Pf64 Red. Single gem proofs have been sold for under one dollar a coin. Slabbed Pf65 Red coins have been listed for as little as $8 and Pf66 Reds have been seen at $15.

Two minor doubled die reverses are described in Wexler. Both require close examination under magnification to see. Catalogue values are $15 and $20 respectively.

—1964—

MINTAGES:
1964 — 2,652,525,000
1964D — 3,799,071,000
1964 Brilliant Proof — 3,950,762

Due to the popular demand for the 1964 proof sets (the Kennedy half dollar primarily), the U.S. Mint increased its proof set production beyond its original 3 million projection.

AVAILABILITY:

The 1964 cent passed the 2 billion mintage mark and as such is readily available in original rolls, mint sealed bags, and singles. Due to over polishing and longer die use, many if not most are average to late die state and show less detail than previous years' issues. The roll price has remained steady at under one dollar since its issuance with minor ups and downs.

A fairly easy to spot doubled die, 1-R-V shows good separation in most of the letters of UNITED STATES OF AMERICA. This scarce and popular doubled die sells for over $100 in BU. It is also featured in the Cherrypickers Guide. With so many unsearched rolls and bags still out there, more are sure to be discovered. A minor doubled die, 6-R-II, is less obvious and brings $5 in BU.

The 1964D is another very abundant issue. Available still in mint-sealed bags and shotgun rolls, the price has been steady at under a dollar for most of the years since it was issued. The interesting facet of the 1964D is that Wexler had described 12 different RPMs. Though most are less than spectacular, they catalogue in BU for $1.50 to $2.50 each. With more collectors becoming active in collecting RPMs, this field has great growth potential. No doubt many are yet to be found--including new varieties. Several new RPMs have been added to Wexler's book since it was released in 1983.

The 1964 proof cent is readily available in mint-sealed flat packs, rolls, and singles. Many of the proof sets have been placed into three-piece plastic holders since the pliofilm holders tend to crack and cause spotting. Gem proof singles are easy to come by at under a dollar each. Almost all of the 212 pieces submitted to PCGS graded Pf66 and higher including a record number of 31 in Pf69. No other Lincoln has that many in Pf69. No price is available for such a coin.

Four minor proof doubled dies are known and they require close scrutiny for identification. Wexler catalogues them from $2.50 up to $35 each. Current price lists show several pieces in this price range. No doubt many sets have yet to be examined for these varieties.

The 1964 doubled die (actually multi-struck cent) is a counterfeit. It was heavily promoted by the counterfeiters and allies in 1964 for $50 each. The separation is far more dramatic than the 1955 doubled die and was made by fake dies impressing genuine 1964 cents. The counterfeiters were arrested and convicted and most of the coins destroyed. A few pieces have been seen by SLCC.

FEATURES of 1-R-V

—1965—

Due to a shortage of cents the U.S. Mint halted the use of mintmarks in 1965 (through 1967). Also, no proof sets were minted 1965-1967. Selected polished coins were packaged in plastic for collectors and known as "special mint sets." The packaging was similar to the regular mint sets packaged in 1959-1964. Many of the coins in these sets were no better quality than regular mint production coins.

MINTAGES:
1965 — 1,497,224,000
1965 - Special Mint Set — 2,360,000

AVAILABILITY:

The 1965 cent is remarkable in the sense it has no special varieties reported in the error publications and is has no proof issue for the year. Most of the mint 1965 cents appear to be average die state quality, full mint red, and average luster. They have always been available in roll quantities (though rarely seen in bag lots) and a BU roll prices at about $2.50 level. Prices have remained steady most of the time since issued.

The 1965 proof-like or special mint set (SMS) issue is often a barely better quality than the business strikes. Few true proof-likes are seen and even is the original mint-sealed sets, the cent appears to be a regular business strike.

A few gem singles have been seen at under $2 a coin. PCGS has certified at few pieces--1 - MS67 Red and 3 MS66 Red.

No mintmarked 1965 cents are known--a first since 1908.

—1966—

As with 1965, no mintmarks were used. For the Special Mint Sets, the U.S. Mint switched to hard plastic set holders and used higher quality polished planchets and generally the sets are of a proof-like nature including frosted coins.

MINTAGES:
1966 — 2,188,147,000
1966 SMS — 2,261,583

AVAILABILITY:

The 1966 cent is available by the roll at about $3. Due to the high mintage of over two billion, the supply always seems adequate to meet any demand. The coins come well struck, nice flashy mint red and fully lustrous. Lesser known BU coins are seen and may represent the larger hoards of shotgun wrapped rolls. A minor doubled die, 1-O-V is listed by Wexler at $15 in BU.

The 1966 SMS coins are much more proof-like than the 1965 and for many singles, they match the proofs struck for years prior to 1965. Fully mirrored surfaces are common. Even frosted relief coins are known and bring a substantial premium. Many still reside in the blue boxed mint packages. PCGS has certified only a very few as the market value of MS65 coins is still under one dollar. The PCGS data show: MS68 Red - 2, MS67 Red - 7, MS66 Red - 9, and only 1 - MS65 Red.

These were offered by the roll until recently. Recent price lists are notably lacking in SMS rolls for sale.

—1967—

This was the last year of no mint marks. The coin shortage eased off and in 1968 the D and S mintmarks were returned to our coins. It was also the last year of the Special Mint Set in lieu of the regularly-issued proof sets.

The SMS were generally of superior proof-like quality including frosted coins.

MINTAGES:
1967 — 3,048,667,000
1967 SMS — 1,863,000

AVAILABILITY:

The 1967 cent was minted in huge numbers--over 3 billion. Yet, BU rolls are not that available and bags are unknown--at least from price lists from the dealers who handle rolls and bags. The current price of $2.50 a roll has been up and down but steady at this average price for many years. The coins generally are well struck though medium die state coins are known. The color and luster tend to be good quality. Finding a gem single is not much of a task as most dealers have some in stock.

The 1967 SMS was made in similar manner to the 1966 cent and in similar packaging. Many still are traded in the original mint box and plastic holder. Most appear to be of similar quality to earlier fully mirrored proof sets.

Though traded by the roll until the mid-1980s, price lists are notably lacking in SMS rolls. As with the 1966 SMS, a very few 1967 SMS have been encapsulated by PCGS: 1-MS68 Red, 14 - MS67 Red, 4 - MS66 Red and none lower. No prices are available on these slabbed coins. Gem singles with frosted relief have been seen advertised at under $3 a coin and the last roll prices for SMS 1967 was seen in 1990 at $15.

In the shortage era, many banks paid a 5% premium for full bags (or even partial bags) of circulated cents. This author received a certificate from the Director of the Mint for bringing in more than 5,000 circulated cents to a local bank.

Since the 1967 cent was not minted with a mintmark, any reports of the 1967D or 1967S are referring to counterfeits or coins of other dates. The coin shortage of 1965 and 1966 had abated, and after the Treasury Department had provided all sorts of enticements to circulate existing cents, the Mint went back to regular mint-mark and proof set production in 1968.

—1968—

The U.S. Mint resumed the use of mint marks and the return of proof sets. Since the sets were minted in San Francisco, it was the first time that a branch mint used its mint mark on proof production coins. The sets were housed in rigid plastic holders for long term storage and safety.

MINTAGES:
1968 — 1,707,880,000
1968D — 2,886,296,600
1968S — 261,311,500
1968S - Brilliant proof — 3,041,506

AVAILABILITY:

The coins minted in 1968 mostly lack the details of earlier years and for the most part, they are classified as late die state. The 1968 cent with over one billion minted is readily available by the roll or even bag. They come full red and quite lustrous, but the die quality is lacking. Thus MS65 Red coins are not comparable to earlier dates. Lincoln's bust and beard are almost smooth and the coat details are largely lacking. Minor die breaks are common.

The 1968D also is notably late die state quality, with some average die state coins noted. Available by the roll at current Trends of $2.50, the prices have gone up and down in recent years.

There is a minor doubled die reported in Wexler as 1-O-II with a catalogue value of $5. It requires close scrutiny to identify. One RPM is reported for this date with a catalogue value of $2.25.

The 1968S is also hard to find gem early die state single. Most issued pieces were late die state. There is one RPM shown in Wexler. Two minor doubled dies are known and described in Wexler.

Only a dozen have been encapsulated by PCGS and all but one are Pf66 and higher. Even then, the market value of such coins is relatively low--under $15 for a Pf66 Red. Perhaps a Pf67 would go for $20. No price listed for a Pf68.

A minor doubled die 1968S proof exists and is listed as Pf 2-O-II in Wexler with a catalogue value of $15.

Most of the proof sets issued since 1968 tend to hold up well in terms of coin stability and security (rigid holders) and with few exceptions of minor staining and toning, the majority of rigid proof set holders appear to be doing well after twenty or more years for some issues. In time, those holders with the greatest stability will stand out and the rest will be replaced by other forms of containers.

The use of the San Francisco Assay Office (Mint) to make proof sets required adding the S mintmark to U.S. proof sets for the first time. The 1968S proof cent is available in original sets, rolls, and singles. Gems are readily available in the highest grades.

—1969—

Reacting to the disintegrating features of the 1968 cents, Mint Director, Mary Brooks, ordered new dies prepared which sharpened up Lincoln's bust and the Memorial reverse. Most newly minted 1969 coins look very sharp and easily make MS65 grade.

MINTAGES:
1969 — 1,136,910,000
1969D — 4,002,832,000
1969S — 547,309,630
1969S Brilliant proof — 2,934,631

AVAILABILITY:

A spectacular doubled die 1969 cent made the rounds in 1969 and found several dealers, distributors, and collectors eagerly paying $50 to hundreds of dollars each. The counterfeiter, a Southern Californian, Mort Goodman was tried and convicted on counterfeiting charges and sentenced to prison. The confusion over the 1969 doubled die fakes caught up with the genuine U.S. Mint-made 1969S doubled die cent. Several of these were confiscated by the Treasury Department and destroyed. Dealer Lonesome John lost one such coin. In Wexler's book on DOUBLED DIES, 3 1/2 pages are devoted (pp. 140-142) to this story. He points out that 3,000 of these fakes were found at the home of collector Roy Gray in 1969. The extreme rotation of the two dies alone was subject to suspicion. Perhaps a few of these still reside in personal collections. Ownership is subject to confiscation. Breen also cites this fake in his ENCYCLOPEDIA.

1969S Doubled die estimated $7,500.

182

This story is not unlike a similar case in 1964 where a group of New York counterfeiters struck several thousand multiple struck 1964 cents and had the gall to advertise them for $50 each in various numismatic publications. They were tried and convicted and the coins were destroyed. One specimen was sent to SLCC in 1990 for examination. Others no doubt reside in private collections. These coins also are subject to confiscation.

The 1969S cent was extensively hoarded and BU rolls and even bags can be located today--though far fewer each year. The discovery of the 1969S doubled die and the prices realized for some of these coins has sent dealers and hoarders into their bags to scan each coin carefully. This prominently doubled die has brought $3500 for a well used EF specimen owned by Jeff Oxman found in change in 1988 in Los Angeles to a BU specimen sold via SLCC to a private collector in New York for $7500. A well-publicized sale was reported in COIN WORLD in 1989 of a collector who recycled several tons of aluminum cans to raise the $7500 for a circulated specimen advertised by an eastern dealer. To date, some 15-20 1969S doubled dies have been identified. Most have been found in change versus being "cherried" in BU rolls or bags. PCGS has certified only 3 1969S doubled die cents as of late 1991. Several more have been certified by ANACS.

There are two RPMs listed under 1969S and both catalogue under $2.50.

The 1969D cent is readily available by the roll. Current Trends shows a value of about $1. This price has been steady for some years. There are six different RPMs known for this date and according to Wexler, they catalogue from $2 to $3.50 each.

The 1969S proof cent is readily available in the original mint holder, in rolls, and in singles. Gem coins are fairly easy to locate. Because of the large numbers, the 1969S proof still sells for under a dollar a coin.

Rolls have traded for $35-$40 recently. PCGS has encapsulated 21 pieces, 20 of which are Pf66 Red and higher. Prices for a Pf66 Red have been seen at $15-$17.50. Prices for the Pf67 and Pf68 are not known at this time.

The 1969P cent dropped off considerably in production from the previous year but still was a billion plus mintage. For some reason, fewer hoards of the 1969P were put away and prices for this date in BU rolls (very rarely by the bag) rose to strong prices in the peak period 1983 to $17 a roll. Even at 1992 prices levels of almost $10 a roll, this is high as compared to mintage and comparable coins of the era. Nonetheless, the 1969P is fairly elusive in BU rolls and also in circulation. Perhaps some major hoards exist and are still off the market. This newly remodeled Lincoln bust and lettering make the coin appear much sharper than 1968 and is easily found in gem conditions.

THE 1969 1¢ COUNTERFEIT DOUBLED DIE

—1970—

MINTAGES:

1970 — 1,898,315,000
1970D — 2,891,438,900
1970S — 693,192,800
1970S Brilliant proof — 2,632,810
1970S Small date — included above
1970S Brilliant proof small date — included above

AVAILABILITY:

This year is replete with interesting as well as valuable varieties. The 1970 cent has always been a premium roll with current Trends value of $4. This is despite its high mintage of 1.9 billion. The sharp dies and bright luster make finding a choice or gem fairly easy.

The 1970D is readily available by the BU roll ar current Trends value of $1.25. Mostly sharp and bright, the 1970D includes three described RPMs in Wexler. They range form $1.25 to $2.50 in BU condition.

The 1970S comes in two distinct varieties. Sometimes called "large date" and "small date", the photos show the "large date" is actually the low 7 and thin 0 in the date. The small date is actually the 7 and 0 level in the date and thick 0. The level 7 is the scarce variety. These have been listed for $10 and up in recent ads in BU. Of the 38 pieces encapsulated by PCGS, 28 are graded MS66 to MS68. Lesser graded pieces have nominal value.

The 1970S proof (large date or Type I) is quite common and sold by the roll, in sets, and singles. Usually priced under a dollar for even choice proofs, this is a common coin.

The 1970S (Type II or small date) is scarce and is listed up to $100 for early die state bright Pf65 or nicer pieces.

There are six different known doubled dies of the 1970. Most are minor and hard to detect without magnification.

There are three different doubled dies of the 1970D and they are listed in Wexler at prices from $5 to $25.

In addition, there are three different RPMs of the 1970D and they are priced in Wexler at $2.50 each.

There are four RPMs of the 1970S and they are listed at $1.50 to $3 each.

A dramatic doubled die of the 1970S is quite rare and listed in Wexler as 1-O-I and listed in BU as $1000. The CHERRYPICKERS GUIDE shows a BU value of $500+. It is as clearly doubled as the popular 1972/72 and easily seen with low magnification. In addition there are three other doubled die 1970S which are minor and listed at $5.50 to $10 each.

There are two known 1970S proof doubled dies. The 1970S Pf 3-O-VI shows a clearly doubled and thickened date. It is quite scarce and listed at $100 in the CHERRYPICKERS GUIDE and $300 in Wexler. The second type is 1970S Pf 6-O-I. It is listed in Wexler with a value of $250.

Dramatic doubled die 1970S.
Courtesy of Harry Ellis.

1970S 1¢ 1-0-I

DOUBLING: A strong CW spread shows on IN GOD WE TRUST, the date and LIBERTY.

MARKERS: A die scratch runs Southwest through the 0 and lower 7 to the mint mark. Several die scratches run Southeast through WE.

—1971—

MINTAGES:
1971 — 1,919,490,000
1971D — 3,911,045,600
1971S — 528,354,190
1971S - Brilliant proof — 3,220,733

AVAILABILITY:

The 1971 cent was not heavily hoarded and present Trends value of $7 indicates a relative scarcity in BU rolls. This is despite a high mintage of 1.9 billion. The coins come well defined, early die state, and full mint red. Choice singles are easy to come by.

Four different obverse doubled dies are known. They catalogue from $35 to $100 in BU and all require magnification to identify.

The 1971D is also relatively hard to locate in BU rolls and current Trends of $8 so indicates. They come early die state and very sharp. Singles are easy to find.

Three distinct 1971D RPMs are known and they all catalogue for $1.50 in Wexler.

The 1971S Trends for $5.50 a roll--also despite a high mintage of 528 million. They come in early to medium die state and full red. Two RPMs are known and they catalogue at $3 and $3.50 respectively.

The 1971S proof is a common proof coin and is available in sealed sets, rolls, and singles. Even choice coins sell for under one dollar. However, two very scarce doubled dies exist and they are catalogued in Wexler at $1,000 for the Pr 2-O-II+V and $750 for the Pr 1-O-II.

This author has searched several thousand 1971S sets and not found either doubled die. Other collectors have also searched in vain for twenty years for one of these scarce to rare doubled dies.

The relatively high prices for BU rolls of these dates is not clear since nearly 2.8 billion were minted. However, over the years BU rolls have always been scarce and bags almost unknown. Even circulated rolls for these dates seem to be less than common. Whether hoards exist or large quantities were never released is unknown. Several companies regularly advertise to buy these three rolls (1971P,D,S) at $3 a roll (or higher) and up to 100 rolls wanted.

Rare 1971S Proof doubled die.
Courtesy of Harry Ellis.

1971S Pr 1¢ 2-O-II+V

DOUBLING: The second hubbing is spread to the rim of the die and shows a strong spread on LIBERTY. The doubling is spread in a CW direction on IN GOD WE TRUST from a strong pivot at K-6.

MARKERS: None significant.

—1972—

MINTAGES:
1972 — 2,933,255,000
1972D — 2,665,071,000
1972S — 380,200,000
1972 Doubled die — estimated 20,000
1972S Brilliant proof — 3,260,996

AVAILABILITY:

The year 1972 is best known in the Lincoln Cent series for the dramatic and popular doubled die (1-O-I) which was discovered by Michael Bauer shortly after being released early in August. Early publicity traces to Harry Forman of Philadelphia. The distinctive doubling reminded many collectors of the earlier 1955 doubled die. At the ANA convention in New Orleans in August of 1972 this find was the focus of much of the floor activity. This author bought two BU 1972 doubled dies for $75 each on behalf of a dealer in California who was offering them to a client at $100 each. One lucky person brought five rolls (250 coins) to the show and all were bought by one dealer for a reported $3500 a roll.

The prices have remained fairly stable since 1972 in the $100 to $300 range depending on quality. Most 1972/72 are known in BU. Wexler estimates as many as 75,000 may have been minted and released. Dealer Robert Brock actively promoted this doubled die in his ads and submitted hundreds to ANACS for grading--essentially creating a market for this date in buy-sell ads he ran up until the late 1980s. He also specialized in two other doubled dies, the 1983 doubled die reverse, and the 1984 doubled die obverse.

PCGS has encapsulated close to 1,000 of the 1972 doubled die cents. The other services have certified almost an equal number making this the highest population of Lincoln Cents other than the 1909 VDB. Most of the PCGS pieces (555) are graded MS65 Red. Only 83 are graded higher by PCGS.

190

In addition to the 1-O-I doubled die, there are no less than eight other minor doubled dies of the 1972 cent and they range in value from under a dollar to $35.

The regular 1972P coins are readily available in rolls, though most have been culled over. The same is true of any bags they may have remained after the discovery in 1972. The current Trends value of $1.75 reflects the adequate supply of rolls. The coins tend to be early to average die state, full mint red, and lustrous.

The 1972D is also available in original rolls at $8 a roll, it reflects a relatively strong demand and a short supply. This roll appears regularly on a major advertiser's "buy" ad. With a mintage of over 2 billion, it should not be that hard to find.

One interesting variety, with no V.D.B. on the shoulder is described by Breen as "rare". Discovered in 1973, it was caused by either overpolishing of the die or foreign matter in the die. No current prices are available.

Three different RPMs are described by Wexler for the 1972D and they each catalogue for $3 in BU. Four minor doubled dies are described in Wexler and they catalogue from $15 to $35 each.

The 1972S is still available by the roll, though bag lots have been dissipated long ago. At Trends value of $2.65 it is a premium roll perhaps due to lower mintage figures of 380 million. It comes well struck early die state and full mint red. Singles in choice condition are not hard to locate. One RPM is described in Wexler and it catalogues for $3.

The 1972S proof is available in original proof sets, in rolls, in custom sets, and singles. A relatively common proof, it can be found for under a dollar in choice condition.

There are two doubled dies known of this proof. The first clearly shows a doubled motto on the obverse and this rarity has been listed at $300. It is listed as "rare" in Breen and CHERRYPICKERS GUIDE. Very few sales are known.

Counterfeit 1972 Doubled Die Cent Discovered

The appearance of a counterfeit 1972 Doubled Die cent came as no surprise to the ANACS staff. With the ever increasing values placed on varieties, it was just a matter of time before a counterfeiter decided to fill the demand. While this new counterfeit is not one of the better attempts at duplicating coins, it could fool newcomers to coin collecting.

See closeup
details

Genuine

Counterfeit

—1973—

MINTAGES:
1973 — 3,728,245,000
1973D — 3,549,576,000
1973S — 319,937,000
1973 Brilliant proof — 2,760,339

AVAILABILITY:

The 1973 cent is still readily found in BU rolls. At current Trends of $1.45 its availability is high as compared to its demand. With recent discoveries of two obverse and one reverse doubled die, these figures may change. The two obverse doubled dies catalogue for $10 and $15 and the reverse doubled die for $5. Apparently the cherrrypickers have not scoured this date yet. They come well defined, early die state, and fully mint red. Average die states also seen.

The 1973D is a plentiful issue with over 3.5 billion minted. Rolls are listed for $1.20 in Trends and by the bag prices drop to under a dollar a roll. There are three RPMs described in Wexler and they catalogue for $1.50 to $3 each. This appears to be a choice date for cherrypickers since the supply is so large.

The 1973S is currently quoted at $1.35 per BU roll. No special varieties are described in the catalogues. The details found in this date are sharp and mint red is typical.

This date had the initials "FG" (Frank Gasparro) enlarged on the reverse, and minor details were strengthened on the bust and the reverse.

—1974—

Due to the increased output of cents at the Philadelphia and Denver mints, the San Francisco mint discontinued circulation strikes of cents in 1974. The S mint coins thereafter were only proof productions.

MINTAGES:
1974 — 4,232,140,000
1974D — 4,235,098,000
1974S — 412,039,000
1974S Brilliant proof — 2,612,568

AVAILABILITY:
The 1974 LIncoln Cent is best known for the coin that isn't. In an attempt to solve the rising copper price crisis, the Director of the Mint Mary Brooks recalled her experiences with this coin is an interview in 1990. Early in 1974, the Mint was ordered to strike 1.5 million of the aluminum cents. About 25 were distributed to the 1974 Annual Assay Commission which met in Philadelphia in February of that year. Commission member, Charles Colver recalled examining the new cent and indicated it looked very nice and felt a bit light. It had a good ring and would not easily be mistaken for a dime (a problem the 1943 steel cent had). These 25 (or so) pieces were returned after the two day commission meeting and Miss Brooks had them sent to various members of Congress for their opinions. In the intervening months, ten of the coins failed to be returned to the Mint. An internal investigation failed to recover all the missing coins. A few congressmen did not even recall seeing the coins. Once congressman who left office discovered two of the coins taped to an office memo he had filed some years earlier. He returned the coins to the Treasury Department explaining he did not know he had them. That leaves about 8-10 aluminum cents unaccounted for. One specimen was sent to the Smithsonian Institute for its numismatic collection. No other official 1974 aluminum cent is known. The Treasury indicates that to own or sell this coin is a violation of federal law.

THIS 1974 aluminum cent from the Smithsonian Institute collection is the only verifiable example of the controversial metallurgical trial piece. The dozen other examples suspected of escaping the melting pot are illegal to own or to sell.

THE PROBLEMS aluminum cents could pose to vending machine mechanisms is explained by G. Richard Schreiber, president of the National Automatic Merchandising Association, as he testifies before Congress in early in 1974.

Many nations use aluminum coins. They are durable, lightweight, and much cheaper than copper or copper alloys. They are easy to mint as they require much less impact to strike up a well defined coin.

The 1974 cent was struck in record numbers--over 4 billion. Rolls are available today at $1 or less. One doubled die is described in Wexler as 1-O-II and catalogues at $3.50.

The 1974D also was record-breaker for a branch mint at over 4 billion. It too is available in roll and bag quantities. Most 1974 coins appear to be well defined, early die state and bright mint red. A minor obverse doubled die is described in Wexler.

The 1974S was reported to be the last of the S-mint cents made for circulation. The future S-mint cents would appear only in proof sets. As such, the 1974S cent was gobbled up early and set aside. At today's Trends of $2.85 it indicates still a good demand versus supply. Prices were once much higher. Circulated rolls bring almost as much as BU rolls--a phenomenon seen in other hoarded issues.

The 1974S proof is a common coin available in original sets, rolls, singles, and custom holders. Gems are easy to locate at under a dollar each. PCGS has certified only six--4 - Pf66, 1 - Pf67, and 1 - Pf68. No doubt many others can match these grades as the supply is out there. The value per coin however is too low to warrant the fee.

—1975—

Starting with the 1975 issue, no circulation strikes were prepared with the S mintmark.

MINTAGES:
1975 — 5,451,476,000
1975D — 4,505,275,000
1975S - Brilliant proof — 2,845,450

AVAILABILITY:

The 1975 cent was also minted for the first time at the Philadelphia branch mint at West Point (U.S. Military Academy site). No mint mark distinguishes West Point coins. More than 1.5 billion cents were struck at West Point in addition to the 5.4 billion in Philadelphia. BU rolls Trends at $1.25. Choice and gem cents are readily available.

The 1975D cent is readily available in large quantities. Although Trends at $2.75 and on many buy lists at about half that, BU rolls are available. Prices have fluctuated over the years, but large supplies must still be available when market demands rise. Nice specimens readily available at a few cents each.

The 1975S is traded singly and in original sets. Rolls were actively traded, however, with higher proof grades (Pf67 and higher) commanding large premiums, no rolls have been offered in recent price lists. Singles have been traded for $5.50.

Two minor obverse doubled dies are known of the 1975 and both are listed in Wexler at $15 each.

No RPMs are reported in this year.

—1976—

MINTAGES:
1976 — 4,674,292,000
1976D — 4,221,592,000
1976S Brilliant proof — 4,149,730

AVAILABILITY:
The 1976 cent is another 4+ billion issue and thus very common in all grades. Current Trends is $1.60 a roll. There are two minor doubled dies of this date and the catalogue at $10 and $15 respectively in Wexler.

The 1976D is a popular roll appearing on various wanted lists and currently Trends at $4.50 a roll. There are no reported RPMs on this date and gem quality singles are readily available.

The 1976S proof is a huge production coin and gems are available at current fixed prices of $2.75 or so. Up to a few years ago, they were traded by the roll. The few certified pieces are the high end Pf66 and Pf67 coins. Frosted relief proof bring a premium of up to 50%.

—1977—

MINTAGES:
1977 — 4,469,930,000
1977D — 4,194,062,000
1977S Brilliant proof — 3,251,152

AVAILABILITY:

The 1977 issue also exceeded 4 billion resulting in large supplies of rolls and BU bags. At current Trends of $1.35 prices have been steady for several years moving only slightly downward in the past two years. They come average to late die state. Select BUs are readily available by searching one or two rolls.

Breen reports a deceptive counterfeit which alleges to be a 1977/6. These were traced to a Stephen Von Zimmer (CW 7/13/77). Apparently few got out into collectors' hands and most if not all have been retrieved and destroyed.

The 1977D is another mega-issue and supplies are always available to meet the demand. At current Trends of $1.25, they have fluctuated little since 1977. No RPMs reported on this date.

The 1977S proof is readily available in high grades and flawless gems can be bought for under $2. Prices have dipped in recent years as most 1977S proof sets have been broken down and sold off coin-by-coin. Rolls of 1977S proofs trade for about $100. Frosted relief singles bring about double the regular price.

—1978—

MINTAGES:
1978 — 5,558,605,000
1978D — 4,280,233,000
1978S Brilliant proof — 3,127,781

AVAILABILITY:

The year 1978 saw new high in mintage figures--over 5 billion from a single mint. The 1978 rolls are $1.80 in the current Trends and have been at that level most of the time since 1978. Most rolls are nice quality, early to medium die state and full mint red. Choice singles are easy to find.

The 1978D is also readily available by the roll or even by the bag. Since no RPMs or major varieties have been reported, most rolls have gone unsearched. The quality is good overall and choice BUs can be easily found.

The 1978S proof with a mintage over 3 million is a common coin. Singles are advertised at under $2 for gem quality. Frosted proofs bring about $3.

—1979—

MINTAGES:
1979 — 6,018,515,000 A single mint record.
1979D — 4,139,357,250
1979S Brilliant proof — 3,677,175

AVAILABILITY:
The 1979 cent was another record-breaker with over 6 billion minted. It is readily available by the roll or bag. Since no major varieties have been discovered, most hoards have been unsearched. Nice quality coins are easy to find. Roll prices of $1.50 are up a bit over the last few years, but steady over the years since mintage. Supply always seems ready to meet demand.

The 1979D is also a hoarded coin with bags available at about double face. Again, with no major varieties reported, most hoards have gone unsearched.

The 1979S proof has two distinct varieties. The mintmark shows two (actually gradations) distinct varieties--an early Type II fully formed S and a late Type I filled S which looks indistinct. See photos next page. The Type II is more valuable and brings about $1.50 a coin. For frosted versions each brings about fifty percent more. Gem quality coins are easily located. Prices have slipped in recent years for both varieties as many of the 3 million proof sets have been broken down and the cent has been trading by the roll.

As a note, it is not advised to store proof cents in tubes. First of all, 50 coins do not fit a standard tube--proof cents are a little thicker and only 48 will fit properly.

Next, proof coins should not touch each other as their surfaces are highly polished and any contact will leave a mark. Finally, handling proof coins should only be done with gloves or tongs. Fingerprints show up (latently) on proof coins--including the edges.

—1980—

MINTAGES:

1980 — 7,414,705,000
1980D — 5,140,098,600
1980S Brilliant proof — 3,554,806

AVAILABILITY:

The 1980 cent has leaped into prominence when Dwight Stucky reported finding a doubled die obverse (Wexler 1-O-V, Breen 2292). Breen reports (1987) only 28 found. Several dozen more have been identified and SLCC had one for sale in 1991. Prices for BU coins have been over $100.

The regular mintage at over 7 billion has resulted in high quantities of BU rolls and bags. With the doubled die becoming better known, these supplies will shrink. At $1 a roll, the price has been at this level since 1980.

The 1980D is also receiving special attention due to the discovery of two over-mintmarks. Described in Wexler as OMM#1 and OMM#2 these two D over S catalogue for $25 each. Both are faint and require close examination.

The regular 1980D cent Trends at $1.60 a roll and is readily available in rolls and bags. Choice singles are easy to find.

In addition to the two OMMs, there are six different RPMs described for this date. They catalogue form $2.50 to $10 in BU in Wexler. Most are faint and require close examination. As these RPMs become more popular, the population of original rolls and mint-sealed bags will drop sharply.

The 1980S proof is readily available in original sets, custom cased sets, rolls, and singles. Gems are easy to find as are fully frosted relief pieces. At a retail value of $1.10 for Pf65, this date is fairly easy to locate.

1980 1¢ 1-O-V
DOUBLING: Very nice CW spread shows on date and LIBERTY.
MARKERS: None significant.

TYPE I AND TYPE II MINTMARKS

These COIN WORLD photos clearly show the variations in S mintmarks for the years 1979-1982.

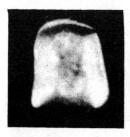

1979-S Variety I (filled stage) S Mint mark.

1980-S Mint mark (also used for the 1979-S Variety II coins).

1982-S Mint mark with serifs. The bottom serif juts out from the lower curve of the S.

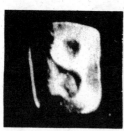
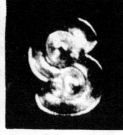

1979-S Variety I (aging, defective stage) S Mint mark.

1981-S Variety I (aging, defective stage). Also used for the 1979 Variety II and 1980 coins.

This 1982-S Mint mark shows wear and filled loops as compared to the 1982-S Mint mark pictured above.

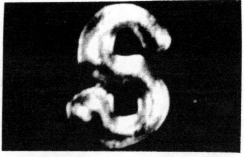

1979-S Variety II (more distinct) S Mint mark.

The 1981-S Variety II Mint mark pictured above has clean top and bottom loops.

—1981—

Due to the cost of copper moving up toward the dollar level (but trading mostly in 1981-82 at 65-75 cents), the U.S. Mint switched in 1982 to copper-plated zinc planchets with only 2% copper by weight saving in cost some 80% of the raw material used in coinage of our cents. 1981 was the last year of all bronze (actually brass) cents. Some 1982 issues were also brass but the bulk of cents minted in 1982 and thereafter are copper-plated zinc.

MINTAGES:
1981 7,491,750,000
1981D — 5,373,235,000
1981S Brilliant proof — Type I and Type II — 4,063,083
  (combined)

AVAILABILITY:

The 1981 cent is readily available by the roll and bag. Prices have remained at about one dollar a roll since 1981. Nice choice specimens are readily available.

The 1981D is a huge branch mint mintage and is available by the roll and bag. There is one RPM in Wexler and it catalogues $4.50 in BU. That fact does not seem to cut into the supply. Other RPMs may be yet discovered.

The 1981S proof comes with two distinctive mint marks- -refer to photographs on preceding pages. The clear Type II is the more distinctive mintmark and is considerably scarcer than the Type I which is the less distinct "blob" type of mintmark used earlier in 1979 proof sets. The Type I shows up on current price lists at under a dollar while the Type II is listed for $18.95 on a recent price list. The 1981S proof is available in original mint sealed sets, by the roll, and singles. Choice Pf65 or better coins are readily available. Chances are the Type II can be cherrypicked from any large selection.

—1982—

Due to the switchover to zinc cents in 1982 and due to the change in the master hubs and dies, a total of seven varieties were created.

They are described under availability since the actual breakdown of mintages is unknown.

MINTAGES:

1982 Zinc Large Date
1982 Zinc Small Date
1982 Brass Large Date
1982 Brass Small Date
1982D Zinc Small Date
1982D Zinc Large Date
1982 10,712,525,000 (all types)
1982D 6,012,979,368 (all types)
1982S Proof 3,857,479

Refer to the photos for the differences in the Large and Small types. As for the zinc versus brass, there are several easy ways to tell - the brass cent weighs 3.1 grams and the zinc cent weights 2.5 grams. The zinc cent has a dull ring as compared with the brass cent when dropped on a smooth hard surface. The zinc cent has a paler color than the brass cent. But the best test is the weight test.

1982-P Variety 1—copper-plated, zinc

1982-S Type I proof obverse die. All 1982-S proof cents were struck on brass planchets (95 percent copper, 5 percent zinc; described as gilding metal by the Mint) with the old cent die in use since 1969.

1982 Type I circulation strike obverse die. Again, the old cent die in use since 1969 and used to strike cents on brass without mint marks at Philadelphia, and on zinc at West Point and San Francisco.

Denver: Type I die used for all brass strikes, Type I and II dies used to strike zinc cents beginning Oct. 27, 1982.

1982-P Variety 2—copper-plated zinc

1982 Type II circulation strike obverse die. A new, modified die with chamfered edges on the date and lettering, and slightly lower relief on the Lincoln bust. "Liberty" reworked so that all letters are evenly lined up and the same height. The "8" in the date repositioned slightly higher, and both the "8" and the "2" thinned down, appearing slightly smaller than the Type I date. Placed in service in early September 1982. Used at Philadelphia to strike brass and zinc cents, and at West Point and San Francisco to strike zinc.

1982 VARIETIES

COIN WORLD has done several fine detailed articles on the subject of the different 1982 cents. The chart below and the photos clearly point out the seven known varieties. It is however, the first time this many types are known for a given year of the Lincoln Cent since 1909.

Variety I —	1982P brass	Variety II —	1982P brass
	1982P zinc		1982P zinc
	1982D brass		1982D zinc
	1982D zinc		

Close-up photos under our microscope compare dates on the 1982 Variety I (top photo) and Variety 2 cents (bottom photo).

The word LIBERTY on the Variety 2 (bottom photo) is straight, sharp and clear as compared to the LIBERTY on Variety I shown in the top photo.

As explained in the story, the motto on the 1982 Variety 2 cent (bottom photo) is further from the rim than Variety 1 pictured in the photo above it.

Transition years tend to create interest in collectors. The seven recognized varieties of the 1982 cent make this year more interesting for collectors. The major problem has been with the bonding of the copper coat to the zinc core. The majority of 1982 copper-coated zinc cents are discolored, have raised pits, and other surface blemishes which make them less than attractive. Grading such coins is a problem-- true MS65 coins are not "nice" coins. A roll set of fifty (all seven varieties) was sold at an SLCC mail bid sale in 1992 for $51 (just over $1 per set). Retail advertised prices have been seen at $2 to $3 recently.

Two doubled dies have been reported for this date. The 1982 1-O-VI occurs on the large date bronze cent and catalogues for $7.50 and the 2-O-V occurs also on the large date bronze and catalogues for $25. It is much easier to identify the doubling in the motto and LIBERTY.

The 1982S proof comes in bronze only and is readily available in original mint sealed sets, rolls, or high grade proof singles. Current retail is $1.35 for Pf65.

-1983-

MINTAGES:

1983 - 7,571,590,000
1983D - 6,476,199,428
1983S - 3,228,648 Proofs Only
1983 - DOUBLED DIE REVERSE - estimated 20,000

The 1983 cent was best noted for both its inferior quality coins and the famous doubled die reverse. Although Breen attributes the discovery to John Barkanic, this author had seven for sale at the Long Beach Convention in February, 1983 which were received from a SLCC member in Florida who found them at his local bank. All seven were sold at prices ranging from $75 to $115. They were the only ones at the show and they changed hands several times before the show was over. The 1983 DDR became an instant celebrity and several dealers promptly bought all they could find from sources mainly in western Pennsylvania and northern Florida.

The zinc-coating on the 1982 and 1983 cents was a problem. Many (if not the majority) of coins had bubbles, pitting, and discoloration. Examination of many rolls revealed similar problems. Most of the 1983 DDR cents have raised bubbles indicating a lack of uniform bonding between the copper coating and the zinc core. This problem has been addressed and later year cents (after 1983) appear to have fewer problems.

The 1983 roll price according to recent Trends and fixed price lists is under $2. There are three minor doubled dies described in Wexler they are quite scarce and catalogue from $35 to $75 each in BU.

The 1983D cent is plagued with similar problems as the 1983P. With the huge mintage, rolls are easy to find, though choices may be limited. At Trends value of $1.70 per BU roll prices have been steady in this range since 1983.

The 1983S proof cent is available in singles and in mint-sealed sets. Twenty-five have been slabbed by PCGS and they all grade from Pf66 to Pf69. Though traded by the roll, most are sold singly as Pf65 Red.

Popular 1983 DDR.
Courtesy Joja Jemz.

-1984-

MINTAGES:

1984 - 8,151,079,000
1984D - 5,569,238,906
1984S - Proofs Only - 3,198,999
1984 - Doubled die obverse - estimated 2,000

The discovery of the 1984 doubled die obverse (doubled ear) right on the heels of the 1983 DDR, created a stir to scour over the bags and rolls of the 1984 dated coins. Still according to dealer Robert Brock, fewer than 2,000 have been found. PCGS has certified over 500 pieces, mostly MS64 and MS65 with 39 MS66 Red. Very few have been found after 1984 according to Brock and other collectors. Because of the lack of obvious doubling (seen mainly in the two ear lobes), many perhaps are yet to be found.

Many original rolls and even bags exist. Thus finding a nice BU 1984 is relatively easy. And perhaps a lucky find will include the doubled die variety. Current prices range from $1.00 to $1.75 a roll. A less obvious doubled die, 2-O-II, shows doubling in 19 of the date and ERTY in LIBERTY. Fivaz shows a value of $25 in MS65 in THE CHERRYPICKERS GUIDE.

The 1984D exists in large quantities in rolls and bags and finding a choice BU coin is fairly easy. Prices are just over $3.00 a roll.

The 1984S is retailing for $5.75 a coin according to recent price lists. Available in original mint-sealed sets, by the roll, and singles, prices have varied in the past few years as singles are broken out of the sets.

Gems are fairly common, with Pf66 and higher coins for sale at under $10.

Breen describes a 1984 variety with no FG on the reverse due to overpolishing of the die. No value is placed on this variety.

DOUBLING:

1984 1¢ 1-O-IV
Very strong spread to North shows as strongly doubled ear and beard.

From a recent issue of Joja Jemz.

-1985-

MINTAGES:

1985 - 4,951,904,887
1985D - 5,287,399,926
1985S Proof Only - 3,348,814

Up to 1985 Philadelphia Mint production numbers did not include coins minted at West Point. Due to restriction in the Gramm-Rudman Act of 1986, coinage at the West Point facility was suspended. In 1985 that included 696 million cents (with no mintmarks).

The 1985 cent is available in rolls and mint-sealed bags. Choice quality singles are available for a few cents each. Trends quotes BU rolls at $4. The doubled die 1-O-II is listed at $37.50.

The 1985D cent is also available in BU quantities. Prices are just over face value. Trends value for BU rolls is $1.40.

The 1985S proof comes in original proof sets, rolls, and choice singles. Trends value of $2.75 for Pf65 is indicative of the quantities available. These coins are also found with full frosted cameo finishes which bring a premium of 50-100%. At this point, certification services do not usually distinguish that variation. ANACS has indicated "cameo" as a feature of Lincoln proofs. The other services have not.

-1986-

MINTAGES:

1986 - 4,491,395,493
1986D - 4,442,866,689
1986S (Proofs only) - 3,010,497

The 1986 cent is readily available by the roll or bag and generally can be found in high quality early die states. The peeling problems as well the bubbles and spotting of the 1982 and 1983 issues are not noted in this issue. Perhaps time will tell. The BU rolls seen are high quality. Prices are in the $2.50 range with buying ads offering $2 a roll.

The 1986D cent is also readily available by the roll and by the bag. There are several known RPMs and prices are modest at this time. Culling through the rolls may not have caught on with most collectors., Finds are being reported regularly.

The 1986S can be readily found in pristine Pf68 quality and several slabbed pieces are known. Full cameo relief pieces are also fairly common and command a premium over the full mirror relief pieces.

-1987-

MINTAGES:

1987 - 4,682,466,931
1987D - 4,879,389.5M
1987S - (Proofs Only) - 3,792,233

Due to the large mintage, the 1987 is readily available in roll or bag quantities. Prices are two to three times face value on most lists.

The 1987D has several reported (confirmed as well as pending) RPMs. This factor may cause more cherrypickers to cull over the existing roll stock. The quality of the 1987D rolls examined seem to indicate a high quality, early die state as the rule. Average or mid-die state is also common. Most coins appear to be free from bonding problems seen in 1982 and 1983.

The 1987S can be found in all gem grades up to Pf68 in slabs. Many also are found as full frosted relief (cameos). These command a premium over the Trends values found in current publications.

-1988-

MINTAGES:

1988 - 6,092,810,000
1988D - 5,253,740,443
1988s (Proofs Only) - 3,262,948

The high mintage 1988 cent is available by the roll and bag. Prices are marginally above face value. Gem quality is readily available for singles. The surface problems seen in 1982-1984 is not apparent.

The 1988D is similar to the 1988. Several RPMs have been listed and in Error Index, three additional not yet numbered RPMs are described including a large over normal D. According to Harry Ellis it is a triple D, not a large over normal D.

Roll Prices for the 1988D are marginally over face value.

The 1988S proof is available in the highest grades up to Pf68. Cameo relief pieces are also common. The 1988S is also traded by the roll as well as singles and complete five piece sets.

-1989-

MINTAGES:

1989 - 7,261,535,000
1989D - 5,345,467,111
1989S (Proofs Only) - 3,215,728

The 1989 is available by the roll and bag. No major varieties have been reported and prices are marginally above face value. Quality pieces are common and though few pieces show problems evident in 1982-1984 issues, they seem to be the exception. Time will tell.

The 1989D is also available as the 1989. Several RPMs have been listed and a few others are shown in the Error Index.

The 1989S is available as gem singles, by the roll, in original sets, and in custom plastic holders. PCGS Pf68s are known and in recent sales, late date proofs (Pf68) have bought $15-25 each. Gem cameos are also known.

-1990-

MINTAGES:

1990 - 6,851,765,000
1990D - 4,922,894,533
1990S (Proofs only) -
1990 Proof "No S" - Mint estimate 3,700

The highlight of 1990 is the discovery of a small number (so far in 1992 under 200) of proof sets with the 1990 "No S" proof cent. See Chris Lane's analysis on the following pages.

The 1990 cent has become a collector's hope since many collectors read about the 1990 "No S" proof and incorrectly assumed all the 1990 "P" cents they have found are worth thousands of dollars each. SLCC received dozens of letters asking where one can sell these "rare finds". One letter accompanied by a 5x7 color photo arrived from the Philippines with a dozen 1990 "P" cents. The writer wanted to offer them for a bargain price of only "a few hundred US dollars each".

The 1990 P is available by the roll from many dealers and even by the bag. They tend to come nicely struck, fully mint red and free of most surface problems. Time will tell. The copper bonding (1982 to date) has a tendency not to hold up well in time whether handled or not.

The 1990D also is readily available by the roll or bag and price marginally above face value. They also tend to be found in early die state, full mint red. Though the Error Index goes up to 1990, any RPMs are not yet published.

The 1990S is also readily found in high grades (only a few have been slabbed). One 1992 price list offered the Pf68 Red at $35. Thus one can assume the Pf67 and Pf66 prices to be close to the cost of the service itself.

Cameo proofs are also seen and they command a premium of 20-33% over the comparable fully mirrored proofs. The V.D.B. on the bust was enlarged about 20% and is more legible than on earlier issues.

4 March, 1992

Greetings to all,

I've finally gotten around to writing about one of my favorite coins, the 1990 no "S" Proof Cent. The below is a quick review of known information, speculation, and ideas I have arrived at over the past eighteen months.

Numismatic News broke the story to the numismatic world about the discovery of the no "S" Proof Set in their August 7th, 1990 edition. Mr. Alan Herbert, a variety/error specialist on the News staff examined three of the sets and felt they could eventually reach a five-figure value. The first set discovered from sets mailed was reported by Jim Cullen of New York on the 18th of July, 1990.

The United States Mint issued a statement on the 27th of July, 1990 acknowledging that a Philadelphia circulation die without a mintmark was inadvertently shipped to the San Francisco Mint with a shipment of normal "S" mintmarked proof dies. The Mint went on to state that the offending die was found and was determined to have produced 3700 proof cents without the "S" mintmark. Out of this 3700, the Mint located 145 "S" less proof sets which had not been shipped, these were destroyed.

David L. Karmol, assistant to Mint Director Donna Pope said the number 3700 was just a calculation based on the life of proof dies. With this being an estimate, the possibility exists that much less than 3700 sets were produced.

It's interesting to note, with all the exposure this error has gained, both national and international, Philadelphia coin dealer Harry J. Forman was only able to purchase 21 sets as of 27 September, 1990. During October 1990, less than 50 sets had been confirmed. I spoke with Harry on the 19 of March, 1991 and he felt there were less than 100 sets extant. He also stated he had handled only 35 sets so far!

I ran an advertisement in both Coin World and Numismatic News for 8 weeks trying to purchase the no "S" 90 proof sets, yet didn't receive one offer. The ads ran from September through October 1990.

In his letter date 17 April, 1991, Alan Herbert of Numismatic News states he has no reason to doubt the Mint's figure of 3700, and feels about 200 sets have turned up so far.

Andy Muller advertised to purchase the sets in late 1990 until mid 1991, with buy prices ranging from a low $1050 to a high of $1350. I spoke with him last week and he advised he hadn't bought any of the no "S" sets .

The "Gray sheet" started to list the 90 no "S" proof set with their August 17th, 1990 edition, with a bid price of $1300. Since August of 1990 until now, bid prices in the "Gray sheet" have gone from a low of $1100 (Dec 90, Jan, Mar, Apr 91) to a high of $1600 (Sept 91).

Staff writer, Paul A. Gilkes, of Coin World stated that roughly 50 sets are known to be in the hands of collectors and dealers, his estimate was made in an article dated 2 October, 1991.

Eighteen months have passed since the discovery of the no "S" 90 proof set, very few have turned up indicating the possible rarity is much more than previously thought. Checking dealers at major conventions such as the 1991 Dallas, Texas early Spring convention, very few are to be found. (Two sets at the Dallas convention). Also, only 1 set was for sale at the 1992 Dallas ANA convention. The following observations are made:

a. Sets known and or sold at this time total 93, this total includes 35 sets handled by Mr. Harry J. Forman, Forman Enterprises, Philadelphia, 10 or 12 handled by Mr. Leon E. Hendrickson, Silver Towne Coin, Winchester, Inc., and 10 sets handled by Mr. F.J. Vollmer and Company, Bloomington, Illinois.

Some of these sets may possibly have been counted twice and maybe even 3 times before reaching their final strong hands destination. The real question remains as to the actual mintage and how many are still out there undiscovered???

   b. During the discovery phase, I was stationed in Europe where there is a large contingent of foreigners who collect coinage from the United States. U.S. proof sets were a common sight at most of the conventions I attended which gave me the opportunity to check for the no "S" cent well before the general public and overseas dealers became knowledgeable. Not one set was encountered . . .

   c. Very few sets were offered, if any, to willing purchasers who advertised in the numismatic press over the past eighteen month.

In closing, I believe the 1990 no "S" proof set will increase in price substantially over the next few years. I believe the set is VERY, VERY rare, and less than approximately 100 sets are out there . . . .If any are still hiding, how many and where are they???

Another reason I believe this set is so special: All of the previous "S" less proof sets which the mint produced were of other denominations, nickels, and dimes. I would make an uneducated guess there are more Lincoln Cent collectors out there than nickel and dime collectors combined. In the coming years some of there Lincoln Cent collectors will want to include one of these unique coins in their collections, however, once the true rarity becomes known they will almost be impossible to obtain. Price? If these coins are as rare as I believe, Alan Herbert's estimate of a five-figure value is not far off. . .

One last thing; during the last 30 days, the set has jumped $150.00 on the Gray Sheet . . . . .

Chris

Enjoy!

Chapter 6 — FIDOs

In the mid 1960s, error coin collecting got its headway with booklets, articles, exhibits, and lectures on the subject appearing everywhere. The term, FIDO, may have been invented at that time. It is an acronym for: freaks, irregulars, defects, and oddities. Lincoln cents contain probably more such FIDOs than any other series by weight of their sheer numbers. There are several books on the subject listed in the bibliography. This chapter is only a cursory look at the major types of FIDOs which attract collector interest and where figures are available, what prices they bring. This is still one area of Lincoln cent collecting where searching through circulated coinage can yield good results.

The major subsections are of the author's design and do not necessarily conform to the NECA (Numismatic Error Collectors of America) or any other organization. They are set forth as a guide to the collector.

The types of errors can be divided into three major categories:

The striking errors can result in clipped coins, double struck coins, off center coins, blanks (not struck), and variations of these occurrences.

The die error results from striking coins in which the dies or dies break, clog, or when the dies contain anything that detracts from their intended purpose—such as striking a coin with some metal filings or staples or striking a coin with clashed dies.

The planchet errors result from having a coin struck on the wrong planchet or on a defective—undersized or oversized planchet.

Refer to "JOJA JEMZ" (Georgia Gems) by Bill Fivaz and J.T. Stanton, a fixed price list of error coins, P.O. Box 932, Savannah, GA 31402.

Chart I. Prices for Off Center and Clipped Planchet Cents
Premiums for Scarcer Dates and for Full Dates Showing

Percent of Offcentering	VG	Fine	VF	EF	Unc
5%	$ 2.00	$ 2.50	$ 3.00	$ 4.00	$ 5.00
10%	3.00	4.00	6.00	7.50	10.00
25%	5.00	6.00	8.00	10.00	12.50
50%	7.50	9.00	10.00	12.00	15.00
75%	10.00	12.00	15.00	18.00	22.50
90%	12.50	15.00	17.50	20.00	25.00
Clipped Planchet Cents					
Rim Clip	.15	.25	.40	.50	1.00
10%	.25	.40	.60	.75	1.25
20%	.50	.75	1.25	2.50	4.00
30%	.75	1.25	2.00	3.00	6.00

50% or more—RARELY SEEN

Chart II. Die Varieties - LIBERTY Die Breaks

Date & Mint	Grade		
	VF	XF	Unc
Pre-1940	.50	1.75	12.00 and up
1942P	7.50	10.00	40.00
1944D	7.50	10.00	40.00
1950P	.25	1.00	2.50
1950D	.50	1.50	3.00
1951P	1.00	2.50	7.00
1951D	.30	1.00	2.50
1952P	2.00	3.00	7.50
1953P	.50	1.00	3.50
1954D	3.00	4.50	12.00
1954S	.10	.15	.50
1955D	.10	.15	.25
1955S	.75	1.50	5.00
1956P	.10	.15	.25
1958P	4.50	10.00	20.00
1959P	9.00	12.50	40.00

D D	**D**	**D D**
NORTHWEST	NORTH	NORTHEAST
D D	NW | N | NE W **D** E SW | S | SE	**D D**
WEST		EAST
D D	**D**	**D D**
SOUTHWEST	SOUTH	SOUTHEAST

D	**D**
D/L	D/I
D	**D**
OVERLAPPING D NORTH	LIGHT D NORTH

MORE ON DOUBLED MINT MARKS

These illustrations were selected from Spadone's early work in 1961 on Coin varieties. They are clear illustrations that can be helpful in identifying RPMs (doubled or multiple mint marks).

With the press working at a speed of close to 120 strikes per minute, many malformed coins may result. The Lincoln cent in the above photo was improperly fed into the collar and received only five percent of the strike.

This interesting 1981-P cent from Bete Bishal of Massachusetts, is struck off center on a straight clip that was punched from the end of the planchet strip.

226

Chart III. Planchet Errors

Type of Error	Valuation
Cent on dime planchet	$25-50
Cent on silver 10¢	100-150
Cent on foreign coin	25-50
Cent on partial planchet	5-10
1943 copper planchet	7,500-20,000
1944 zinc-steel planchet	2,500-5,000
Cent with struck fragment	2-5

Error collecting has grown to where there are conventions, clubs, newsletters, and several publications which deal with the subject. The bibliography cites several references.

Some error collectors focus on a single typed—such as the "cud" a filled in area caused by a die break near the rim of the coin. Often a cud will blot out part of a coin's motto resulting in some interesting variations such as the "Godless cent," or "dateless cent." These variants bring $10-20 in BU condition.

Another variant is the die crack—which can result in endless patterns on coins—connecting devices normally that are separate.

One such popular die crack is a J shaped crack on the 1954S cent that resembles a mint mark of "SJ," referred to by collectors as the "San Jose" mint 1954 cent. Other die cracks resemble letters in legends on the coin also creating interesting spellings such as "LIBIERTY," "IIBERTY," "LIBEIRTY," and dates such as 19411, and filled in mint marks and letters.

Doubled letters especially mint marks are very popular collector items. Several very distinctive doubled mint mark cents include: 1936D/D, 1944D/S, 1945D/D, 1960D/D, 1960D triple D, 1957D/D several variations, and others. These can be found in rolls and even in unsorted bags of coins.

The potential in this area is great—perhaps not from the investment viewpoint, but from the collector viewpoint. See Chapter 8 for references.

With the publication by John A. Wexler and Tom Miller in 1983 of THE RPM BOOK, the popularity of repunched mintmarks soared. Regular display ads featuring one or more RPMs appear regularly in COIN WORLD. Several dealers have expanded their price lists to include one or more pages of RPMs. With over 500 Lincoln Cent RPMs already known and some very scarce ones as well, the trend is clearly to the upside. Many remain to be discovered. Many unsearched rolls, albums, bags, and dealers' stock boxes remain to be searched (also called "cherrypicking"). Since the Red Book only lists a very few RPMs or OMMs for all coinage series,they are not that well known to the general collecting public. But from sales records, mail bid sales activity, and prices realized, the trend is clear.

The coins featured on the next 13 pages are <u>not for sale</u>. They are taken from various error publications with permission of the authors. Prices may vary as some items are sold. Most prices are dated 1991.

The coins shown here are from the price lists of Lonesome John of Newbury Park, CA, Bill Fivaz and J.T. Stanton of Dunwoody, GA., and Lou Coles of Carson City, NV.

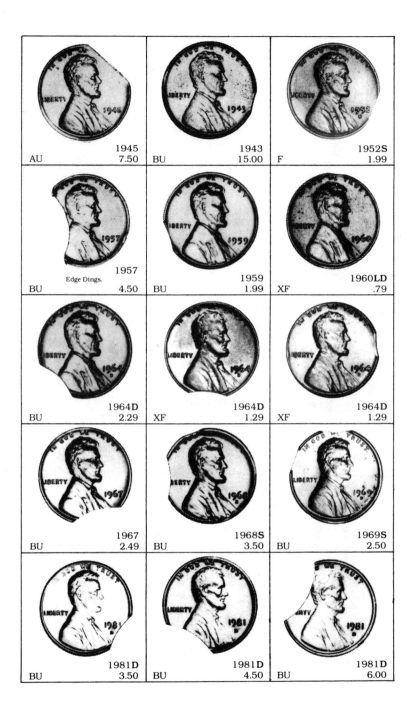

1945	1943	1952S
AU 7.50	BU 15.00	F 1.99
1957 Edge Dings.	1959	1960LD
BU 4.50	BU 1.99	XF .79
1964D	1964D	1964D
BU 2.29	XF 1.29	XF 1.29
1967	1968S	1969S
BU 2.49	BU 3.50	BU 2.50
1981D	1981D	1981D
BU 3.50	BU 4.50	BU 6.00

1918S F 14.95	1919S G 9.95	1935 VF 5.50
1937 VF 10.50	1944S VF 4.50	1951D BU 12.50
1947 Nickel-sized broadstrike. Ch. BU 11.95	1968S Broadstruck; hairline scratches, reverse ding. BU 1.50	1947 Broadstruck, near nickel size. XF 7.50

N.D.
Immense broadstruck cent with full 50% brockage o obverse. Multi-struck on center, nearly quarter dollar size!
BU   29.50

1968**D**

Double struck, unifaced second strike.
BU 18.50

N.D.

"Mickey Mouse" saddle strike. Larger strike uniface.
BU 26.50

1973

Off-center, partial brockage.
BU 14.95

N.D.

Off-center with indent.
BU 14.95

N.D.

Mirror brockaged cent.
BU 34.95

1966

Cent struck on clad dime blank.
BU 115.0G

1979**D**

Off-center, major straight clip.
BU 29.95

1981**D**

Off-center with a large pair of curved clips. BU 34.95

1925**S**

Lincoln cent RPM with widely separated S over S south.

VG   3.50

1944**D**

Lincoln cent RPM with widely separated D over D north.

BU   4.95

1945
Expanded
double
struck
cent.
AU
44.50

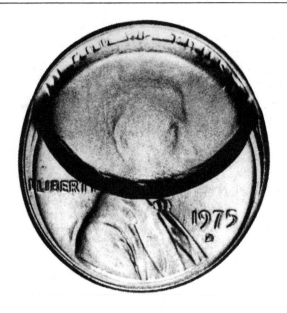

1975**D**

Double struck *(see extra "L" in Liberty)*. Reverse is even nicer. The *big* news is that this is the only coin of its type that I know of that is proveably brockaged through an elliptical clip. The entire motto, "In God We Trust," is untouched. When such coins are struck through off-center blanks, the motto is flattened as Lincoln is on this specimen.

BU   *UNIQUE*   175.00

The next three pages include illustrations from JOJA JEMZ (George Gems) by Will Fivaz and J.T. Stanton (1990-1991) issues.

DOUBLE DIES

1960	1ᶜ	PR-63
	6-0-II & IV	
	(Lg/Lg/Lg/Sm)	

$175.00

1960-D/D	1ᶜ	BU
	SD/LD (1-0-III) & RPM	

$25.00

1964-P	1ᶜ	BU
	1-R-V	

$95.00

1970-S	1ᶜ	Proof
	3-0-VI	

$125.00

STRIKING ERRORS

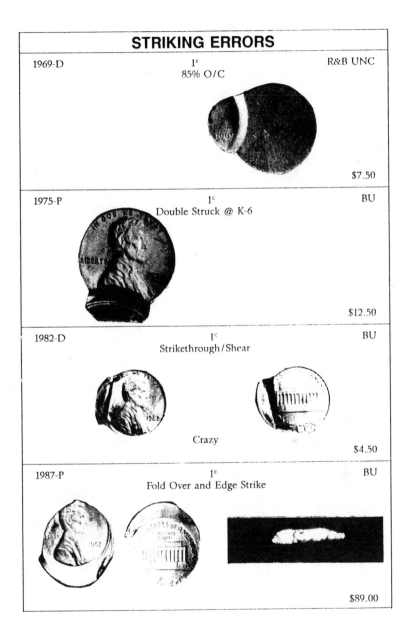

1969-D   1ᶜ   R&B UNC
85% O/C

$7.50

1975-P   1ᶜ   BU
Double Struck @ K-6

$12.50

1982-D   1ᶜ   BU
Strikethrough/Shear

Crazy

$4.50

1987-P   1ᶜ   BU
Fold Over and Edge Strike

$89.00

DOUBLED DIES

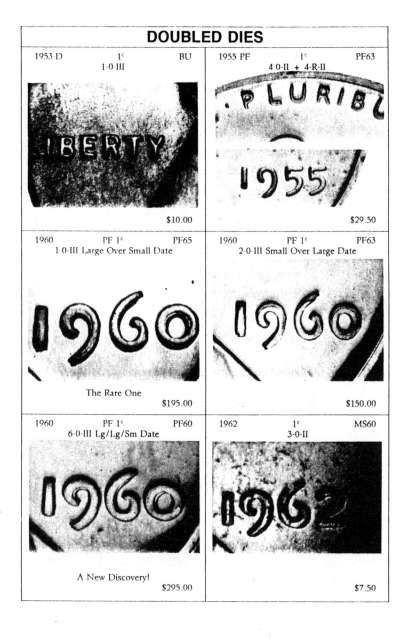

1953-D	1ᶜ	BU
	1-0-III	

$10.00

1955 PF	1ᶜ	PF63
	4-0-II + 4-R-II	

$29.50

1960	PF 1ᶜ	PF65
	1-0-III Large Over Small Date	

The Rare One

$195.00

1960	PF 1ᶜ	PF63
	2-0-III Small Over Large Date	

$150.00

1960	PF 1ᶜ	PF60
	6-0-III Lg/Lg/Sm Date	

A New Discovery!

$295.00

1962	1ᶜ	MS60
	3-0-II	

$7.50

236

Repunched Mintmarks

```
...1c....1910-S....RPM # 2...S/S.....North...........................VF 27.50
...1c....1911-S....RPM # 1...S/S.....West................cleaned..XF45 37.50
...1c....1935-S....RPM # 1...S/S.....East............................GD  3.50
...1c....1938-D....RPM # 1...D/D.....West.................EDS/MDS.MS63 17.50
...1c....1938-S....RPM # 2...S/S/S...West & Northwest..............VG  2.50
...1c....1938-S....RPM # 2...S/S/S...West & Northwest..............XF  7.50
...1c....1938-S....RPM # 2...S/S/S...West & Northwest.............UNC 10.00
...1c....1938-S....RPM # 2...S/S/S...West & Northwest.......Brn...MS60 12.50
...1c....1938-S....RPM # 2...S/S/S...West & Northwest....MDS/EDS.MS63 17.50
...1c....1939-D....RPM # 1...D/D.....North...........................AU  5.50
...1c....1941-S....RPM # 3...S/S.....Southwest......................FN  1.50
...1c....1941-S....RPM # 7...S/S.....East............................FN  1.50
...1c....1941-S....RPM # 8...S/S.....East............................VF  2.00
...1c....1941-S....RPM # 9...S/S.....North...........................VF  2.00
...1c....1941-S....RPM # 9...S/S.....North...........................XF  2.50
...1c....1942-D....RPM # 3...D/D.....South...............EDS/MDS..MS65 12,50
...1c....1944-D....RPM # 1...D/D.....North...........................VF  1.50
...1c....1944-D....RPM # 1...D/D.....North...........................AU  2.50
...1c....1944-D....RPM # 1...D/D.....North...............MDS/MDS..MS63  7.50
...1c....1944-D....RPM # 2...D/D.....North........................MS60  4.50
...1c....1944-D....RPM # 2...D/D.....North...............EDS/MDS..MS62  6.50
...1c....1944-D....RPM # 2...D/D.....North...............MDS/MDS..MS63  7.50
...1c....1944-D....RPM # 4...D/D.....North...............LDS/VLDS.MS60  5.00
...1c....1946-D....RPM # 6...D/D.....North...........................XF  2.25
...1c....1947-S....RPM # 2...S/S.....North...........................XF  2.00
...1c....1947-S....RPM # 3...S/S.....South...............MDS/MDS..MS63  4.00
...1c....1948-D....RPM # 2...D/D.....West............................AU  2.00
...1c....1949-S....RPM # 1...S/S.....West............................XF  2.00
...1c....1949-S....RPM # 4...S/S.....East............................XF  2.00
...1c....1949-S....RPM # 4...S/S.....East...........................UNC  3.00
...1c....1949-S....RPM # 4...S/S.....East...............EDS/EDS..MS63  5.00
...1c....1949-S....RPM # 5...S/S.....West............................XF  2.00
...1c....1949-S....RPM # 5...S/S.....West............................AU  2.25
...1c....1949-S....RPM # 5...S/S.....West...........................UNC  2.50
...1c....1949-S....RPM # 6...S/S.....East............................VG   .50
...1c....1949-S....RPM # 6...S/S.....East............................VF  1.00
...1c....1949-S....RPM # 6...S/S.....East............................XF  1.75
...1c....1949-S....RPM # 6...S/S.....East...............LDS/MDS..MS63  5.00
...1c....1950-D....RPM # 7...D/D.....North ( I think Horiz) MDS...MS63  7.50
...1c....1950-S....RPM # 4...S/S.....North.................MDS...MS63  5.00
```

Repunched Mintmark Cents from Lou Coles . . .

```
..1c....1951-D....RPM # 2...D/D.....West..........................VF    1.50
..1c....1951-D....RPM # 10b.D/D.....East..........................XF    2.00
..1c....1951-D....RPM # 18.D/D/D...North & South..........MDS.MS60     5.00
..1c....1952-D....RPM # 2...D/D.....West..........MDS.MS63           3.50
..1c....1952-D....RPM # 3...D/D.....West..........................FN    1.00
..1c....1952-D....RPM # 3...D/D.....West..........................VF    1.50
...1c....1952-D....RPM # 3...D/D.....West..........................XF    1.75
...1c....1952-D....RPM # 3...D/D.....West..........................UNC   2.25
...1c....1952-D....RPM # 3...D/D.....West..........MDS/LDS.MS63      4.00
...1c....1952-D....RPM # 11.D/D.....West..........MDS/LDS.MS62      3.50
...1c....1952-S....RPM # 2...S/S.....Northwest..........LDS/LDS.MS60  5.00
...1c....1952-S....RPM # 7...S/S.....West..........................VF    1.25
...1c....1952-S....RPM # 14.S/S.....East..........................XF    2.00
...1c....1953-D....RPM # 1...D/D.....West..........................FN    1.25
...1c....1953-D....RPM # 1...D/D.....West..........................VF    1.75
...1c....1953-D....RPM # 1...D/D.....West..........................XF    2.25
...1c....1953-D....RPM # 8...D/D.....West..........LDS..MS63         3.50
...1c....1953-S....RPM # 3...S/S.....South..........................FN    1.00
...1c....1953-S....RPM # 3...S/S.....South..........................UNC   2.25
...1c....1953-S....RPM # 6...S/S.....North.& Choen DM2.............VF    1.75
...1c....1953-S....RPM # 13.S/S/S...East & West..................AU    3.00
...1c....1954-D....RPM # 1a..D/D/D...North & South................VF    2.00
...1c....1954-D....RPM # 3...D/D.....South..........................XF    2.00
...1c....1954-S....RPM # 2...S/S.....West..........................FN    1.00
..1c....1954-S....RPM # 2...S/S.....West..........MDS/MDS.MS60     3.25
...1c....1954-S....RPM # 2...S/S.....West..........EDS/EDS.MS63     5.00
...1c....1954-S....RPM # 4b..S/S.....North.........................XF    2.00
...1c....1954-S....RPM # 4d..S/S.....North.........................UNC   3.00
...1c....1954-S....RPM # 6...S/S.....West..........LDS.MS60         4.00
...1c....1954-S....RPM # 7...S/S.....West..........................UNC   3.00
..1c....1955-D....RPM # 2...D/D.....South..........................VF    1.25
...1c....1955-D....RPM # 2...D/D.....South..........................XF    1.75
...1c....1955-D....RPM # 11.D/D.....West..........LDS.MS60         3.25
...1c....1955-S....RPM # 2...S/S.....East.Cohen.L5..stg 8 of 10.....VF  1.00
...1c....1955-S....RPM # 2...S/S.....East Cohen.L5..stg.8 of 10.....XF  1.50
...1c....1955-S....RPM # 2...S/S.....East.Cohen.N58.stg.5 of 10..MS60  3.00
...1c....1955-S....RPM # 2...S/S.....East.Cohen N/L too early EDS.MS60  4.00
...1c....1956-D....RPM # 3...D/D.....North.........................VF    1.00
...1c....1956-D....RPM # 4...D/D.....North..........MDS/LDS.MS63    3.00
...1c....1957-D....RPM # 1...D/D.....South..........................VF    1.00
...1c....1957-D....RPM # 5c..D/D.....South..........................VF    1.00
...1c....1958-D....RPM # 15.D/D.....West..........................XF    1.50
...1c....1959-D....RPM # 1a.D/D/D...Southeast & West..........MS63   8.50
...1c....1959-D....RPM # 1b..D/D/D...Southeast & West..........XF    3.00
...1c....1959-D....RPM # 1b..D/D/D...Southeast & West..........UNC   5.00
...1c....1959-D....RPM # 1b..D/D/D...Southeast & West..........MS63   7.50
...1c....1959-D....RPM # 1c.D/D/D...Southeast & West..........MS60   6.00
...1c....1959-D....RPM # 3...D/D/D...North & Over..............XF    2.25
...1c....1959-D....RPM # 3...D/D/D...North & Over..............MS60   4.00
...1c....1959-D....RPM # 5...D/D/D...Southwest & Over..........MS60   4.00
```

Additional Repunched Mintmark Cents from Lou Coles.

cent	19.05	5 cents	21.21	25 cents	24.26
Suzie	26.50	50 cents	30.61		

```
..1c....1968.........................19.98.....................XF  1.75.
..1c....1968.........................20.35.....................UNC 3.00
..1c....1980.........................20.47.....................BU  3.00
..1c....1981.........................20.58.....................UNC 3.00
..1c....1982.........................20.60.....................BU  3.00
..1c....1983.........................20.31.....................BU  1.50
..1c....1983.........................19.69.....................BU  1.25
..1c....1984.........................19.93.....................BU  1.50
..1c....1984.........................19.33.....................BU  1.15
..1c....1984.........................20.42..fingerprint........BU  1.25
..1c....1985.........................20.43.....................BU  1.75
..1c....1985.........................19.70.....................BU  1.15
..1c....1987.........................21.27.....................BU  7.50
..1c....1987.........................20.61.....................UNC 1.00
..1c....1988.........................20.64.....................BU  3.00
..1c....1988.........................19.92.....................BU  2.00
..1c....1990.........................19.95..obv scratch........BU  2.00
```

From Error Nibble #16 listing of Broadstruck Lincoln Cents for sale.

Broadstruck

Broadstrike, remember E/V's only rule everyone agrees upon, that is it is not a uncentered broadstrike if <u>any</u> detail, even denticles are missing, it's off center I believe we could improve this definition because not all coins have denticles. If a coin is missing any of its normally struck diameter, it's off-center. I've been seeing many coins labeled uncentered broadstruck that are really off-centers. Instead of using descriptions like nickel size I've put the exact measurements

Lincoln Cent Doubled Dies for sale by Lou Coles . . .

Doubled Dies

```
...1c....1957-D..3-0-III............................................UNC  2.00
...1c....1957-D..3-0-III............................................MS65  4.50
...1c....1957-D..6-0-III+V..........................................MS63 10.00
...1c....1958..Md-1-0-VII...........................................BU  1.00
...1c....1958-D.Md-1-0-VII...........................................BU  1.00
...1c....1960....2-R-VI..................................early...BU 12.50
...1c....1960-D..1-0-III + RPM # 1.........................stg 4..VF 15.00
...1c....1960-D..1-0-III + RPM # 1.........................stg 4..XF 20.00
...1c....1961..Pr-1-0-II............................................PRF  4.50
...1c....1961......2-0-II............................................BU  4.50
...1c....1961..Pr-1-R-II............................................PRF  4.50
...1c....1962......3-0-II............................................BU  7.50
...1c....1962..Pr-5-0-V.............................................PRF 22.50
...1c....1962..Pr-2-R-II............................................PRF  4.50
...1c....1962..Pr-4-R-V.............................................PRF  4.50
...1c....1963..Pr-7-R-II + V........................................PRF 12.50
...1c....1963-D....1-0-VII..mid stage ( some of lower 3 showing )...AU  4.50
...1c....1963-D....1-0-VII..late stage..............................BU  4.00
...1c....1964..Pr-2-R-V.............................................PRF 17.50
...1c....1964..Pr-3-R-V.............................................PRF  4.50
...1c....1964..Pr-4-R-I.............................................PRF  4.50
...1c....1964......6-R-II...........................................MS63  4.50
...1c....1964..Pr-7-R-II+V+VI.......................................PRF 22.50
...1c....1968-S....1-0-II..................................MDS..MS63  5.50
...1c....1968-S.Pr-4-0-II+V..........................................PRF  7.50
..1c....1971......1-0-II............................................XF 27.50
..1c....1971......2-0-I.............................................XF 10.00
..1c....1971......3-0-I.............................................XF 10.00
..1c....1972......2-0-I..............................EDS....XF 10.00
..1c....1972......2-0-I.............................................BU 35.00
..1c....1972......3-0-I..stage 3....................................XF  3.00
..1c....1972......3-0-I..stage 6....................................XF  3.00
..1c....1972......3-0-I..stage 6...................................UNC  4.00
..1c....1972......3-0-I..stage 7....................................AU  3.50
..1c....1972......3-0-I..stage 7....................................BU  5.00
..1c....1972......4-0-I..this DD must have rim cuds to be 4-0-I....AU 35.00
..1c....1972......4-0-I.............................................BU 75.00
..1c....1972......6-0-I.............................................XF  3.00
..1c....1972......6-0-I.............................................BU  6.00
..1c....1972......7-0-I..early stage................................XF  3.00
..1c....1972......8-0-I..early stage.....................2 spots..XF  3.00
..1c....1972......8-0-I..late stage......................2 spots..XF  2.00
..1c....1972......8-0-I..early stage................................AU  5.00
..1c....1972......9-0-II+III early stage........................XF45 15.00
..1c....1972-D....1-0-I..stage 2....................................BU 30.00
..1c....1972-D....3-0-I..early stage...............................UNC 20.00
..1c....1972-D....4-0-I..stage 2...................................UNC 12.50
..1c....1972-D....4-0-I..stage 3.......................cleaned...XF  3.00
..1c....1972-D....4-0-I..stage 3....................................AU 15.00
..1c....1973......2-0-VI...........................................UNC  4.00
```

From Lou Coles ERROR NIBBLE (1991 edition), another sample of U.S. cent errors. Thee publication includes many other types of errors, and all denominations. The prices listed are the retail values.

```
...1c....1955......C # BA104   obv. BIE type die break...............FN   .20
...1c....1955......C # B653    obv. BIE type die break...............VG   .15
...1c....1955......C # B653    obv. BIE type die break...............FN   .20
...1c....1955......C # B653    obv. BIE type die break...............VF   .25
...1c....1955......C # B653    obv. BIE type die break...............XF   .35
...1c....1955......C # B656    obv. BIE type die break...............VG   .15
...1c....1955......C # B656    obv. BIE type die break...............XF   .35
...1c....1955......C # B704    obv. BIE type die break...............VF   .25
...1c....1955......C # B704    obv. BIE type die break...............BU   .75
...1c....1955-D....C # B431    obv. BIE type die break...............BU   .75
...1c....1955-D....C # C23     obv. die break connecting #'s date....BU  1.00
...1c....1955-S....C # B603    obv. BIE type die break...............BU  1.50
...1c....1956......C # B515    obv. BIE type die break...............VF   .20
...1c....1957-D....C # B355    obv. BIE type die break...............VF   .20
...1c....1957-D....C # BR4     obv. BIE type die break...............VF   .35
...1c....1957-D....C # R40     obv. DIE CHIP ON 1 & 9 IN DATE........XF   .25
...1c....1957-D....C # R42     obv. DIE CHIP ON 1 IN DATE............FN   .10
...1c....1957-D....C # R42     obv. DIE CHIP ON 1 IN DATE............XF   .25
...1c....1957-D....C # R61     obv. DIE CHIP ON 1 IN DATE............FN   .10
...1c....1957-D....C # R103    obv. DIE CHIP ON 1 IN DATE............VF   .20
...1c....1958-D....C # R24     obv. DIE CHIP ON 1 IN DATE............VF   .20
...1c....1958-D....C # R26     obv. DIE CHIP ON 1 IN DATE............XF   .25
..1c....1958-D....C # R26a    obv. DIE CHIP ON 1 IN DATE............VF   .20
..1c....1958-D....C # R29     obv. DIE CHIP ON 1 IN DATE............FN   .10
..1c....1958-D....C # R29     obv. DIE CHIP ON 1 IN DATE............VF   .20
..1c....1958-D....C # R45     obv. DIE CHIP ON 1 IN DATE............VF   .20
..1c....1958-D....C # R45     obv. DIE CHIP ON 1 IN DATE............XF   .25
..1c....1959-D....C # N/L     obv. CRACKED SKULL & REV DIE BREAK....BU   .75
..1c....1961-D....C # R3      obv. "PENCIL BEHIMD EAR" type diebreakXF   .55
..1c....1961-D....C # R3      obv. "PENCIL BEHIND EAR" type.........AU   .75
..1c....1961-D....early stage of Cohen RE13.......................BU   .20
..1c....1961-D....C # TA1     obv. "PEN IN POCKET" type diebreak....BU  1.00
..1c....1968-D....C # 56C     obv. SPIKED HEAD type diebreak........BU  1.00
..1c....1968-D....obverse rim cuds K7-K10.........................BU   .50
..1c....1968-S....C # 57      obv. SPIKED HEAD type diebreak........BU  1.00
..1c....1968-S....C # N/L     rev. clashed dies.....................BU   .25
..1c....1968-S....C # N/L     rev. clashed dies.....................BU   .20
..1c....1968-S....C # N/L     obv. die gouge rev broken hub.........BU   .30
...1c....1969-D....C # 57     obv. SPIKED HEAD type die crack.......BU   .85
...1c....1980......Laminated die reverse thru one..................BU  3.00
...1c....1983......Spiked Head CONECA F-20.........................BU  1.00
...1c....1986......Spiked Head CONECA F-02.........................BU   .85
```

Chapter 7 — Grading and Storage

No other issue in modern day numismatics gets as much attention as the issue of grading—or the apparent lack of standards in grading coins. This was not much of an issue thirty, forty, or more years ago since a mint state coin was hardly going to set new price records just for its superb qualities—except perhaps for the early American coppers. But that's another story. Looking at many old catalogues, we note that mint state coins are often referred to as: "1909 Indian head cent uncirculated $1.50, 1909 indian head cent uncirculated, full mint red $1.75." This was taken from a 1944 retail coin price list from a major midwest coin company.

It was not until the late 1960s that the subtle differences in grades began to mean large differences in dollar prices. Up to 1940 hardly any coin warranted a price of $1,000. In 1970, fairly recent coins were bringing over $1,000 due to the "gem" quality of the coin. Dealers often were besieged by investors and collectors who insisted on the top or gem quality coins and were offering large premiums to get them.

The late Dr. William Sheldon had developed a numerical grading scale in the 1940s that was suited to and used for the grading of early American coppers—half cents and large cents, 1793-1857. This system was used by the serious collectors of these coins and in essence was a tie-in to the condition and relative value of a coin based upon a scale of 1-70, with 70 being perfection. It was not that a scale of 1-100 was not thought of, it was just that in many cases a coin with a basal state of 1 (worn almost smooth) would be worth about 65-70 times that amount in gem mint condition.

The overall scale as now used and modified slightly from Sheldon is as follows:

Basal state — 1
Good — 4
Very good — 8
Fine — 12
Very fine — 20
Extra fine — 40 — Also extremely fine, XF
About uncirculated — 50 — Also, AU, MS50
Uncirculated — 60 — Typical or average Unc
Uncirculated — 63 — Selected uncirculated, MS63
Uncirculated — 65 — Choice uncirculated, MS65
Gem Uncirculated — 67 — MS67
Perfect uncirculated — 70 — MS70

For proof coins, the grading is shown as:

PF50 — About uncirculated proof
PF55 — About uncirculated, choice proof
PF60 — Typical unc proof
PF63 — Select unc proof
PF65 — Choice unc proof
PF67 — Gem unc proof
PF70 — Perfect unc proof

Proof coins that have been circulated to any grade below AU50 or PF50 are usually described as "circulated proofs" and assigned the proper grade based upon wear.

There are intermediate grades to fit those coins which are not exactly matching the features of one grade or the nearest higher grade. They are shown as: VF30, XF45, and even on rare occasion, AU58. Split grades are also used to indicate that the two sides of a coin are not the exact same grade—not too unusual when two die pairs were used to mint coins. Such grades as MS60/63 indicate that the obverse is typical unc and the reverse is select unc.

Again, the numerical system was designed over 40 years ago to meet the conditions of the early coppers and the pricing structure of the time. Thus today, most MS70 coins are valued at thousands of times the value of a basal state coin. Yet, in 1975 when the American Numismatic Association named the late Abe Kosoff and Ken Bressett to head up a blue ribbon committee to formulate and write a standard guide to grading United States Coins, the aim was to standardize the grading criteria and made them universal in the hobby. The Official Guide to Grading U.S. Coins by the ANA adopted the modified Sheldon scale of 1-70 and established some guidelines for the grading of each series of U.S. coins. However, in the past few years, dealers and collectors alike have disagreed often with some of these guidelines and have lobbied for changes and specifics in some of the criteria. In 1976 the ANA established the ANA Certification Service, ANACS, to render grading opinions of U.S. coins. In the past few years, with changeover of staff and input from many corners of the hobby, the criteria for each series have become more clear and the specialists in each area are coming to closer consensus on what constitutes each grade—especially as they relate to the more expensive mint state grades.

This chapter is an expansion of the grading thesis proposed by the author in his article in the Spring issue of LINCOLN SENSE, the Journal of Lincoln Cent Collectors, April, 1983.

The greatest amount of detail will be devoted to the higher grades. This is a close proximation of the grading criteria as used by ANA, Photograde, and Brown & Dunn—the three widely used grading guides to U.S. coins.

GRADING THE LINCOLN CENT

AG-3 — The obverse rim will be worn into the field at some points. The last digit in the date will be weak, but readable. The mint mark (if any) will be flat, but readable. L in LIBERTY may be gone.

The reverse will be worn into the letters at the top of the coin and the wheat ears will be merged with the rim.

G-4 — The rims will be intact but the lettering may touch the rims. All letters are visible. The reverse rims will be intact but the letters on the motto may be touching at some or all points. The wheat ears will be worn smooth, but separate from the rim.

VG-8 — The fold in Lincoln's coat will show, but no separation between coat and shirt collar. All lettering clear of the rim. The top of Lincoln's hair will show some hair detail.

The reverse will show two ro three stalk lines in each wheat ear—at least in the left one.

F-12 — Lincoln's coat collar will be shown separate from the coat. The knot in the bow tie will show. At least half of Lincoln's ear will show. All mottos and letters clear and free from the rims.

The reverse will show 4-6 wheat stalk lines in each wheat ear, and evidence of separate kernels in the lower 2/3 of the stalk.

VF-20 — Most of the ear will show except the top. The bow tie will show two or three ends. Hair detail should be evident above and behind the ear. The cheek should be evident. A brow ridge should show.

The stalk lines should all be visible, though there may be some wear in them. Also, most kernels should also show, even though some may be flattened.

XF-40 — All of the ear should show, as should the cheekbone, eyebrow ridge, beard detail, sideburns, and separation of coat and shirt collar at the back of the neck. For certain dates 1918-1930, extra fine coins are shallow and may lack some of these fine details on the obverse, but have sharp letters and digits.

The reverse should show all ten wheat lines in each stalk and all the kernels should be directly connected to a respective wheat line. All letters should be sharp—no rounded ends, fuzzy stems, and weakly defined letters.

AU-50 — Hair details should be evident above and behind the ear. The ear should be fully evident. Coat and shirt collar must be separate.

The coin must show SOME MINT LUSTER. This grade as well as all MS (mint state) grades MUST SHOW MINT LUSTER—the colors may range from brilliant orange gold to black—but the luster—actually a surface corruscation resulting from the minting process must show over some portion of the coin surface to rate an MS grade.

All wheat lines and kernels must show. The difference between AU and BU is seen in the criss-crossing of lines on the high points of the coin and random marks in the field showing some level of circulation. Bag marks or marks made by bagging mint coins are quite different looking from circulation marks. Newly minted coins are bagged and hit each other. Circulated coins strike all sorts of objects and surfaces and have many kinds of surface abrasions other than "bag marks."

MS-60 — Typical or average uncirculated. These coins are struck from worn or used dies and dies prepared from often-used master hubs that have lost some surface details. MS60 coins can have less detail than XF coins—but strictly speaking can be BU coins.

Lincoln will shown an undefined beard looking more like a large chin than a beard, no sideburns, no hair detail, one-half or less of the outer ear, and merging coat and shirt collars at the neck. The bow tie will show three or less corners. The edges often are beveled and there are stress marks, flow lines, clash marks, and other softening or ill-defined features in the coin. The color often tends to be on the reddish-brown or multicolored side. For certain years of issue notably the mintmarked coins dating from 1919-1930, the vast majority of coins leaving the Mint left as MS60 coins.

The reverses often show flattened stalk line and flattened wheat kernels, soft letters in the motto and often one or more flat letters in ONE CENT.

MS-63 — Select uncirculated. These coins were struck from new or nearly new dies with the following details present.

Lincoln's hairdo shows incused lines above and behind the ear. The ear rim is 2/3-3/4 complete—rarely 100%. The bow tie should show 3 or 4 corners—the left triangular corner tends to be lacking in many coins. The eyebrow ridge must be clearly showing as should the cheekbone, and the temporal indentation. All mottos should have sharp letters save perhaps one soft letter in each, including L in LIBERTY. Bag marks visible to the naked eye are acceptable, but must be minimal. Mint luster must be fully evident and could be almost any color. (See section on colors after MS70.)

246

MS-65 — Choice uncirculated. These coins must first of all be fully brilliant—either red, reddish-gold, irridescent red and gold, or overall brilliant hues of red. Dark or dull coins MAY BE classified as MS65, but would be priced more like MS63 coins.

The bow tie should show all four corners. The beard should have incused details and be connected to the sideburns. Any softness must be limited to a small area such as a single letter in a motto.

MS-67 — Gem uncirculated. For all practical purposes, this grade actually can be found in only a few years of issue—based upon a search of catalogues and interviews with collectors and dealers alike. The most often found "gems" are 1909 coins—P and S, VDB, SVDB, 1910P and S, 1926, 1927, 1928, and then many P mint coins from 1930-1949.

In fact, the grade MS67 in Lincolns is even scarce to come by in issues minted in the past 10-20 years.

For MS67, Lincoln must show incused hair details in the hair, beard, and sideburns. The Adam's apple is actually a part of the beard, and except for a gem coin cannot be so discerned. All coat lines are continuous. All lettering is squared off at the ends. Date and mintmarks are squared off and bold. No evidence of bagging, softness, edge beveling, die stress, flow lines, die clashes, or other marks can be included on any coin rated MS67.

Thus VERY, VERY FEW Lincolns ever are graded MS67.

MS-70 — This term is reserved for late date proofs only. Business strike Lincolns have not been identified as "perfect."

This grading scale is not the official ANA Grading Guide of the Lincoln Cent, but has been offered to standardize and objectify those criteria in use for grading mint state Lincoln cents.

Since the reverse dies tend to hold up better than many obverse dies, it is not uncommon to see many MS Lincolns grades as: MS60/63, or even MS60/65. Do not try to "average" the two to determine the coin's grade. The value most often tends to be much closer to the lower grade, not the mean grade. For example, a 1921S MS63/65 would probably sell for $220-$240, rather than the mean value between MS63 and MS65 which is $650.

Grading the Lincoln Memorial Cents is basically the same as the 1909-1958 Wheatback series, as far as the obverse is concerned. However, for certain years, namely 1955, 1965, 1968, 1973, and 1975, the details in the master dies lost much of Lincoln's facial features, his coat and the lettering. Thus few, if any business strikes of these years would even quality as MS65, no less MS67.

The key feature on the Memorial reverse is the Memorial itself. It has 22 steps—a fact that is hard to determine since so few coins seem to show it—including proof issues.

On the lower four steps to the left and right are some hedges—they too tend to be barely visible on most issues. And you should be able to see that Lincoln has two legs in the tiny statue visible in the center of the Memorial. There are other features of the building that are key points for sharpness, but the steps and statue seem to cover them for now. Since so few 1959-1983 Lincolns (except for the 1972 double die and the 1970S small date proof) rate prices in the hundreds of dollars (at this time), little attention is being focused on the Memorial reverse cents. But time will tell—and the current prices, these sharply struck gems may well be the scarcities of the 21st century.

A WORD ABOUT COLORS

Color alone does not make a grade. However, color is often a crucial factor in the PRICE of a Lincoln Cent. We devised a color chart, which shows whether the colors ENHANCE, DETRACT or HAVE NO EFFECT on VALUE.

ENHANCING COLORS: Bright colors generally, gold, red, copper, irridescent, reddish-gold.

DETRACTING COLORS: Dull colors generally, black, brown, streaky colors, spots, spotty colors, brassy colors, blues, purples, greens, glossy colors (usually indicate processing), oily colors or surfaces (indicate treatments), and combinations of any of these. Brassy color usually indicates cleaning. Blues and purples usually indicate heating or chemical tampering.

NO EFFECT COLOR: Brownish red, reddish brown, halo effects, dark edges but bright interior, bright chocolate or sepia, toning reds.

SURFACE FEATURES

These photos from the April 25, 1983 issue of COIN WORLD show a common feature of some new coins, die polish marks. Unlike scratches or hairlines, these marks are raised in the field and usually only in the field and not on the raised devices, note that the date is unaffected.

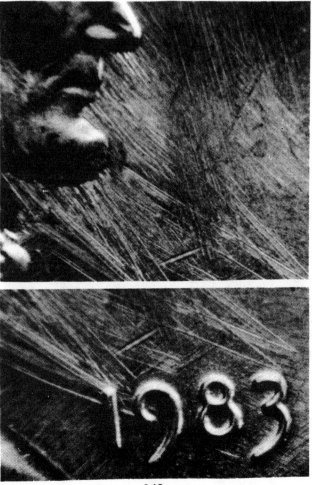

Such features detract somewhat from the coin's value and often appear to be scratches made outside the Mint.

STORAGE AND CARE FOR LINCOLNS:

Many older collections have been housed in coin folders, coin albums, and coin envelopes and thus it is safe to say that NONE of the products made before 1940 seem to be safe for long term storage of BU Lincoln Cents.

The Mint holders issued from 1936-1942 and from 1950-1955 (so-called box sets) also seem poorly qualified for long-term storage. The coins often tend to spot and even show rusting—due to the use of staples in the box sets. The cardboard holders for Mint sets from 1947-1958 also cause rapid tarnishing of all the coins in the sets.

The three-piece plastic display holders as seen from Capitol Plastics and other manufacturers appear to hold up fairly well for long-term storage of BU coins, but here too unless the plaques were stored in a dry cool environment, they too show spots, stains, and tarnishing.

Most modern albums are probably ill-suited for long-term storage of BU Lincolns, though they may do well for circulated coins.

To assure long-term safe tarnish-free care for Lincolns and other copper or bronze alloy coins, the atmosphere must be freed from tarnishing agents. There are several products on the market today and holders to house coins that will probably accomplish this goal. Kointains and similar holders offer chemically treated holders which have anti-tarnish agents. In the past, PDB, paradichlorobenzene has been a very effective anti-tarnish agent for silverware, silver-plate, and coins. In addition to using such agents, the coins should be stored in a safe metal or plastic box—vault, cabinet, locker, etc. and a packet of dessicant such as silica gel should be added to the container—not to touch the coins—so all moisture would be drawn away from the coins. Collections should NOT be stored in garages, bathrooms, kitchens, wooden boxes (other than oak), cigar boxes, iron (tin) boxes, leather cases, cardboard files, softwood closets (such as cedar), under floors, in attics, outdoors, near water, near a heater, near an air-conditioner, or in close contact with rubber bands, paper clips, staples, newspaper, matches, medicines, liquids of any kind, or gas producing substances or equipment. That's a long list of no-nos but your coins need all the care they can get.

The safest places for the life of your coins includes: bank vaults, home safes (above floor), acrylic boxes, stainless cabinets, mylar holders, hard plastic holders, polyurethane holders and boxes, styrofoam boxes or holders, glass boxes or holders, or modern-made coin cabinets. The old cabinets made beofre 1920 were made of resinous woods and often lined with felt or velvet which hairlines the coins. The resinous woods caused the coins to tarnish excessively.

In addition, smoking near coins can be harmful to the coins. So can smog, cooking aromas, plant products, foods, and even fingerprints. They do not come off and become darker with time.

An excellent article in the April, 1983 issue of THE NUMISMATIST by John C. Loperfido, pp. 706-709 clearly identifies the nature of airborne particles and their relationship to coin surface problems. The particles named and measured range from atmospheric dust 0.01 to 50+ microns, tobacco smoke .01-1.0 microns, household dust .02-5.0 microns, sea salt nuclei .03-.05 microns, bacteria .03-40 microns, human skin cells 2.0-30 microns., pollens 10-100 microns and lints 11-1,000+ microns. These small particles can and will attach to coin surfaces and create spots, etching, discoloration, and other surface problems if allowed to make contact with the coin.

CLEANING AND RESTORING LINCOLN CENTS

In general, cleaning a coin will not enhance its value and in many cases not enhance its appearance. But, skillfully done restorations can remove tarnish, spots (certain kinds), and in cases of very dirty coins can remove much of the surface materials and restore the coin to some degree of respectability.

Toned and tarnished coins are darkened by oxides, sulfides, and carbonates (amongst the more common chemical combinants of copper). In many cases, these surface chemicals are one layer (monomolecular) thick and thus if removed, the surface features of the coin are undisturbed. In the Mint sets prepared from 1947-1958, many of the coins have tarnished badly—especially the reverses since they were in direct contact with sulphur-treated paper. If the tarnish is especially unattractive, it can be dissolved away in a solution of buffered acid such as Nic-A-Lene, Coin Dip, Jeweluster, and a number of other commercial products designed to dissolve away surface oxides and sulfides.

The end result of such "dipping" can be a much improved looking coin, or in some cases a coin that looks worse than before. The undersurface which is hidden by the tarnish may be etched, pitted, or otherwise permanently damaged. By removing the surface contaminants, the undersurface problems may stand out. Further, the resulting colors may be unnatural and thus make the coin look "dipped."

For Lincoln Cents, the commonly used dips are buffered solutions of phosphoric acid and they are effective in restoring some coins. In cases where the coin is not restorable, the end result often is a brassy-looking surface, or a streaky surface, or unusual colors such as orange, rust, bluish toned, purples, and rarely greens. In the section on COLORS, these are all listed as DETRACTING colors.

If a Lincoln Cent is a candidate for a dip, it should be dipped into the solution for a second or two and removed promptly then dipped into alcohol to remove the dip and to aid in prompt drying which will avoid spotting. If the coin was lightly tarnished, the tarnish will have dissolved in the dip and the coin will look much improved. This is the case when one has a roll of cents in which the two end coins are tarnished on one side while the other 48 coins are bright mint red or gold in color. The dip MAY restore the two end coins to their "normal" uncirculated mint color.

If the coin in question is well-worn but coated with some foreign materials such as calcium carbonate (sea immersion), or rust (from contact with iron), or copper carbonate (from acid contact) these substances can be removed by lightly brushing the coin with the dip and wiping it with a light oil such as mineral oil. This often will remove the surface materials and enhance the appearance of the coin.

In neither case mentioned thus far will the treatment raise the grade of a coin. A coin which is graded XF40 cannot be elevated to AU50 by dipping, cleaning, brushing, or replating. Its surface appearance can be improved essentially by cleaning—or restoring. The process of restoration is a legitimate and often used practice in museums for works of art that have been neglected, mistreated, or simply aged badly. Likewise, coins can be restored. The process is best left to experts just as with works of art. The end result can be a disaster if handled poorly or if the coin is not a good candidate for restoration.

Many coins have been harshly cleaned and improperly restored. The date analysis indicates many of the 1909-1925 date coins are brighter than natural due to various cleaning processes used by many collectors to enhance their appearance. The presence of myriads of hairlines often will indicate the process of cleaning. Some cleaning attempts were so crude as to use abrasives such as rubber erasers or cleanser. In both cases the surfaces will show numerous criss-crossing hairlines and the surface colors will look unnatural.

In more recent years, the process of "whizzing" had become widespread. It involved the use of a lathe or similar turning device to rotate the coin rapidly while applying a copper brush (or fiber brush or even jeweler's rouge) to the surface. This removes the old surface and reveals the new undersurface of virgin metal which in the light looks as bright as newly minted coinage—to the untrained eye. To the trained eye, whizzed coins are fairly easy to spot due to the manner in which they reflect light, their coppery red or brassy colors, and the circular pattern of hairlines in the field. Unfortunately, many whizzed coins have found their way into many collections and investment portfolios over the years and they are worth a fraction of their alleged grade—in one recent auction a 1909SVDB, listed as "AU whizzed" went for $165—about half of what it would have brought had it not been whizzed. However, it was bought by the original consignor as "BU" at a price well above the $165 level several years earlier.

There a number of substances on the market today which are useful in protecting the surface of the Lincoln Cent. One of them is Coin Care. It coats the surface with a stable oil which not only blocks oxidation and protects the coin against moisture but it also enhances the appearance. Check the supply ads in the coin publications for other products that protect coins.

For the new collector, a few points are worth noting. One, NEVER touch your fingers to the surface of an uncirculated coin. Fingerprints are long-lasting and harmful to coins. Never rub the surface of an uncirculated coin even with tissue. Wear gloves or use tongs in handling uncirculated cents.

In removing BU coins from the roll, use a soft surface such as a towel to lay them out—avoiding clattering them. Place them individually into safe holders—2x2 mylar flips, treated 2x2 envelopes, or coin holder using tongs or gloves.

Proof coins require the most care in handling since every mark shows. For proofs minted since 1968, their original mint holders are usually safe for long term storage. Earlier dated sets should be examined periodically to see if they are doing well. The plastic holders used from 1955-1964 tend to crack open and permit spotting and in many cases (if heated above 90°), tend to form oily residues which harm the coins.

To examine the surfaces of coins, a binocular microscope is recommended using both 30x and 60x oculars. A quality 17x or 20x hand held lens will also do. Learn to see the coruscation features of newly minted coins. This is the feature of new coins that is referred to as "mint frost" or "mint bloom." It is caused by the momentary expansion of the surfaces of the coin as it is struck by the dies under tremendous pressure. The planchet from which the coin is struck is slightly smaller in diameter than the coin-to-be. This is to allow expansion from the impact and in the process of expansion, the coin's surfaces break into this feature called coruscation. Although this is not a scientific explanation for the phenomenon, it explains in essence the causes of the mint bloom of newly minted coins versus the shiny surfaces of other metals which were made by casting, plating, or polishing.

By examining many, many coins, you can train your eye to see the subtle differences between mint bloom and the results of various processes aimed at imitating the mint bloom effect.

1979S Typ II Proof

Chapter 8 - CURRENT STATUS OF THE LINCOLN CENT

Since the Lincoln Cent has been issued for so long, much has changed in the way collectors see this series. In the past decade alone, such unheard of issues as "Population Data" and "slabbing" have come into common use. This has impacted how collectors, dealers, and investors look at coins in general. The closer scrutiny of coins in general has created a whole new collecting arena of errors and error collecting.

The issues touched upon in this final chapter include: Die States, a study by Della Romines, The Error Index by James Wiles, The Ultimate Lincoln Cent Set by Stewart Blay, a look back to 1964 with Robert Svensson, Robert Zuecher, and Walt Laub, Exhibiting Lincoln Cents, Lincoln Cent Value Guide, Outlook for the Lincoln Cent, additional Lincoln Cent trivia, and the pricing history of the Lincoln Cent by Stephen J. Cohen.

There is little doubt that there is enough additional material to include triple the number of pages in this edition. Perhaps an expanded edition is down the road. The editing process has often to set aside good material which otherwise would be used. Space and use factors determined the optimum limits on book size and content. Less emphasis has been placed on auction results due to the rapidly fluctuating prices one finds in the 1990s at auctions--high in one sale and down in another. This is not a catalogue and thus prices would be obsolete before the copies came off the press. The companion volumes listed in the text are vital adjuncts to the serious collector of Lincoln Cents. No doubt new books will be published in time as more material is accumulated through discoveries, sales, research, and correspondence.

August, 1992

DIE STATES

The grading of United States coins is so closely tied to dollar value, that more than a single number can describe a coin. Author Delma K. Romines published a four-part series in THE NUMISMATIST in 1991 on "A Guide to Die States". This aspect of a coin's quality is often not mentioned in a certificate or a slab, but certainly weighs heavily upon one's price of the coin. The illustrations show one small area of the Lincoln Cent to illustrate the metal flow and letter sharpness (or lack thereof) per die state.

According to Romines, the VERY EARLY DIE STATE (VEDS) is limited to perhaps no more than the first 2,800 strikings. After that, the die begins to show some metal flow, wear on the high points, and small superficial die cracks.

The EARLY DIE STATE (EDS) for bronze coins is about 30,000. Thus only the first 32,800 coins of any die life are VEDS or EDS. For Lincolns, this is a very small percentage of all strikings.

The MID DIE STATE (MDS) also referred to as, Medium Die State, Average Die State (ADS), runs for about 115,000 strikings. These numbers were taken by actual striking tests on bronze planchets. This state is recognized by metal flow lines near the rim and the sharp corners of letters nearest the rim begin to round off.

The LATE DIE STATE (LDS) show actual flow of letters closest to the rim (see photo #4). This runs for some 450,000 strikings. Many dies are retired when the coins begin to show these features.

However, for many years, especially at the branch mints, these dies were kept well past this state and into the next. The most common examples are the Denver and San Francisco Mint coins dated 1918 through 1930.

The VERY LATE DIE STATE (VLDS), is found only in a few dates since most dies are retired after they begin to reach this stage. Modern issues since 1959 rarely achieve this late die state. Most cents between 1930 and 1958 were produced up to and including late die state. Very few dies were left on the line past the 500,000 strikings to result in VLDS coins. But for each year, chances are one or more dies did see service well past their working life and did produce some VLDS. These are often incorrectly referred to as "very weakly struck". In fact, they are normal strikes from very worn dies.

1

2

3

4

1) **Very Early Die State (VEDS).** All details are extremely sharp, with virtually no metal flow lines.

2) **Early Die State (EDS).** Details display only very minor metal flow lines.

3) **Mid Die State (MDS).** Heavy metal flow lines are evident on most or all of the lettering near the rim. The lettering has rounded, rather than sharp, edges.

4) **Late Die State (LDS).** The lettering, date and parts of the design have little, if any, sharpness. Lettering near the rim appears "fuzzy."

5) **Very Late Die State (VLDS).** Most major detail is lost, and metal flow lines are extremely heavy.

5

The Truly Scarce

(Reprinted from the November, 1991 LINCOLN SENSE)

Based upon current PCGS Population report date, the scarcest Lincoln Cents are as follows:

(Only those dates with ten or less certified by PCGS as MS65 Red (or better) are listed.)

1909 VDB Matte proof	(2)	1912 Matte proof	(4)
1915 Matte proof	(8)	1916 Matte proof	(4)
1913S	(10)	1914S	(5)
1916D	(9)	1916S	(2)
1917S	(5)	1918S	(2)
1919s	(5)	1920S	(3)
1921S	(5)	1922 Plain	(0)
1923S	(9)	1924D	(4)
1924S	(2)	1925D	(8)
1925S	(1)	1926D	(8)
1926S	(0)	1927S	(7)
1928S	(9)	1944D/S (Both)	(7)
1969S Doubled Die	(2)		

These numbers will grow as more coins are being submitted, but the relatively low numbers are strong indicators of their scarcity. Most collectors have these coins on their "wanted" lists.

It is interesting to note that most of the "keys" are not on the list: 1909S VDB, 1909S, 1914D, and 1931S.

NO MORE RPMs?
Starting with 1992, the branch mints will have the mint mark included in the master hub from which the dies are made. This will preclude the practice of applying the mintmark by hand which is accountable for the phenomenon of the repunched mintmark.

THE ERROR INDEX

James Wiles of Fort Worth, Texas has published the ERROR INDEX (1990). This series of volumes covers all the errors by denomination as found in various error publications. For a list of each volume, contact James Wiles, 9017 Topperwind Ct., Ft. Worth, TX 76134.

Compiled in Volume I are all the published repunched mintmarks in the Lincoln Cent through 1989. Most are listed in Wexler's THE RPM BOOK. Many are not--having been discovered since 1982. Only a few of these RPMs and OMMs are included in Chapter 5.

The publications cited in this Index include: ERRORGRAM, EVN/NUMISTAKE, EVN, ERRORGRAM, ONEC ERRORSCOPE, and the price lists of several error specialists, including Joja Jems.

A single page is reproduced herein to illustrate the type of data compiled under each year and mintmark.

Sample page from THE ERROR INDEX

1989-D

RPM # 1 D/D SOUTHEAST
NO STAGES KNOWN, NO IDENTIFYING MARKERS
SHOWS STRONG OUTSIDE BOTTOM LOOP
MINT MARK IS WELL CENTERED AND TILTED SLIGHTLY TO THE RIGHT
REPORTED BY MIKE ELLIS

RPM # 2 D/D EAST
NO STAGES KNOWN, NO IDENTIFYING MARKERS
SHOWS STRONG VERTICAL UPRIGHT INSIDE MAIN MINT MARK
REPORTED BY MIKE ELLIS
PICTURED IN ERRORSCOPE, MAY 1990, PAGE 18

RPM # 3 D/D WEST
NEED SPECIMEN FOR STUDY
REPORTED BY PHIL MAGANBUA

RPM # 4 D/D
NEED SPECIMEN FOR STUDY

RPM # 5 D/D WEST
NO STAGES KNOWN, NO IDENTIFYING MARKERS
REPORTED BY JAMES WILES

RPM # 6 D/D
NEED SPECIMEN FOR STUDY

RPM # 7 D/D NORTH
NO STAGES KNOWN, NO IDENTIFYING MARKERS
REPORTED BY JOHN CONWAY

RPM # 8 D/D WEST
NO STAGES KNOWN, NO IDENTIFYING MARKERS
REPORTED BY JOHN CONWAY

RPM # D/D SOUTH
NEED SPECIMEN FOR STUDY
REPORTED BY KEITH ZERRLAUT

THE ULTIMATE LINCOLN CENT SET

One of the goals of collecting any series is to assemble "The World's Finest Set of . . . " Apparently, one (perhaps more) collector of Lincoln Cents, Stewart Blay of New York has staked his claim that his set of encapsulated Lincoln Cents is the "World's Finest" set of Lincoln Cents. Completed in 1991, the set has been exhibited at the 100th anniversary convention of the American Numismatic Association in Chicago in 1991. The following pages include the coins in this collection. for each date and mint, the coin in the set is graded the highest grade assigned by the various grading services. In addition, each coin was compared (where possible) to others with similarly high grades for the best features in terms of eye appeal, die state, brightness, color, and planchet quality. This goal can only be achieved by very few individuals since for many dates, only a single coin has achieved let us say a grade of MS67 Red or even MS66 Red or MS65 Red.

WORLD'S FINEST
CERTIFIED LINCOLN CENTS
COLLECTION

1909 VDB	M.S. 67 RD	P.C.G.S.
1909-S VDB	M.S. 66 RD	P.C.G.S.
1909	M.S. 66 RD	P.C.G.S.
1909-S	M.S. 67 RD	N.G.C.
1909 S/S	M.S. 65 RD	A.N.A.C.S.
1910	M.S. 67 RD	P.C.G.S.
1910-S	M.S. 65 RD	N.G.C.
1911	M.S. 66 RD	P.C.G.S.
1911-D	M.S. 66 RD	P.C.G.S.
1911-S	M.S. 66 RD	P.C.G.S.
1912	M.S. 66 RD	P.C.G.S.
1912-D	M.S. 65 RD	P.C.G.S.
1912-S	M.S. 65 RD	P.C.G.S.
1913	M.S. 66 RD	P.C.G.S.
1913-D	M.S. 66 RD	P.C.G.S.
1913-S	M.S. 65 RD	P.C.G.S.
1914	M.S. 66 RD	P.C.G.S.
1914-D	M.S. 66 RD	P.C.G.S.
1914-S	M.S. 65 RD	P.C.G.S.
1915	M.S. 66 RD	N.G.C.
1915-D	M.S. 66 RD	P.C.G.S.
1915-S	M.S. 66 RD	P.C.G.S.
1916	M.S. 66 RD	P.C.G.S.
1916-D	M.S. 65 RD	P.C.G.S.
1916-S	M.S. 65 RD	P.C.G.S.
1917	M.S. 66 RD	P.C.G.S.
1917-D	M.S. 66 RD	P.C.G.S.
1917-S	M.S. 65 RD	P.C.G.S.
1918	M.S. 66 RD	P.C.G.S.
1918-D	M.S. 66 RD	P.C.G.S.
1918-S	M.S. 65 RD	P.C.G.S.

WORLD'S FINEST
CERTIFIED LINCOLN CENTS
COLLECTION

1919	M.S. 67 RD	P.C.G.S.
1919-D	M.S. 65 RD	P.C.G.S.
1919-S	M.S. 65 RD	P.C.G.S.
1920	M.S. 66 RD	P.C.G.S.
1920-D	M.S. 65 RD	P.C.G.S.
1920-S	M.S. 65 RD	P.C.G.S.
1921	M.S. 66 RD	N.G.C..
1921-S	M.S. 65 RD	P.C.G.S.
1922 NO D	M.S. 65 RD	N.G.C.
1922-D	M.S. 65 RD	P.C.G.S.
1923	M.S. 66 RD	P.C.G.S.
1923-S	M.S. 65 RD	P.C.G.S.
1924	M.S. 66 RD	P.C.G.S.
1924-D	M.S. 65 RD	P.C.G.S.
1924-S	M.S. 65 RD	P.C.G.S.
1925	M.S. 66 RD	P.C.G.S.
1925-D	M.S. 65 RD	P.C.G.S.
1925-S	M.S. 64 RD	P.C.G.S.
1926	M.S. 66 RD	P.C.G.S.
1926-D	M.S. 65 RD	P.C.G.S.
1926-S	M.S. 65 RB	N.G.C.
1927	M.S. 66 RD	P.C.G.S.
1927-D	M.S. 65 RD	P.C.G.S.
1927-S	M.S. 65 RD	P.C.G.S.
1928	M.S. 66 RD	P.C.G.S.
1928-D	M.S. 66 RD	P.C.G.S.
1928-S	M.S. 65 RD	P.C.G.S.
1929	M.S. 66 RD	P.C.G.S.
1929-D	M.S. 66 RD	P.C.G.S.
1929-S	M.S. 66 RD	P.C.G.S.
1930	M.S. 66 RD	P.C.G.S.
1930-D	M.S. 66 RD	P.C.G.S.

WORLD'S FINEST
CERTIFIED LINCOLN CENTS
COLLECTION

1930-S	M.S. 66 RD	P.C.G.S.
1931	M.S. 66 RD	P.C.G.S.
1931-D	M.S. 66 RB	P.C.G.S.
1931-S	M.S. 65 RD	P.C.G.S
1932	M.S. 66 RD	P.C.G.S
1932-D	M.S. 66 RD	P.C.G.S.
1933	M.S. 66 RD	P.C.G.S.
1933-D	M.S. 66 RD	P.C.G.S.
1934	M.S. 66 RD	P.C.G.S.
1934-D	M.S. 66 RD	P.C.G.S.
1955/55	M.S. 65 RD	P.C.G.S.
1972/72	M.S. 67 RD	P.C.G.S.
1909 VDB	P.F. 65 RD	N.G.C.
1909	P.R. 66 RD	P.C.G.S.
1910	P.F. 66 RD	N.G.C.
1911	P.R. 66 RD	P.C.G.S
1912	P.R .65 RD	P.C.G.S
1913	P.R. 65 RD	P.C.G.S.
1914	P.F. 67 RD	N.G.C.
1915	P.R.67 RD	P.C.G.S.
1916	P.F. 65 RD	P.C.G.S.
1936 Type I	P.R. 66 RD	P.C.G.S.
1936 Type II	P.R. 65 RD	P.C.G.S.
1937	P.R. 65 RD	P.C.G.S.
1938	P.R. 65 RD	P.C.G.S.
1939	P.F. 66 RD	N.G.C.
1940	P.F. 65 RD	N.G.C.
1941	P.F. 65 RD	N.G.C.
1942	P.R. 65 RD	P.C.G.S
1950	P.R. 66 RD	P.C.G.S
1964	P.R. 68 RD	P.C.G.S

A 1964 Booklet with some interesting views of the Lincoln Cent. See next two pages from this booklet. Collection of the author.

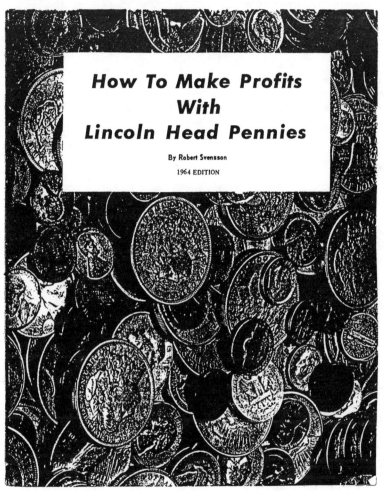

How To Make Profits
With
Lincoln Head Pennies

By Robert Svensson

1964 EDITION

INVESTING IN PENNIES

The Lincoln Head Penny is an interesting coin for investment. For the more sophisticated collector, the field of investment offers interesting possibilities. Indeed, this is being done today on a scale never before known in numismatics.

It must be remembered that investing in coins, pennies or any other, requires capital which is immediately tied up. A safe place for keeping the coins is required and pennies can begin to use up space at a terrific rate.

One thing is certain, you cannot lose on this type of investment. You can, of course, run the risk of losing interest on your money. But investing in coins has proved profitable for the roll investor over the years.

We mention rolls because these are the most profitable form of investing. You will note from the table of valuations that rolls have increased considerably over face value through the years. There is a speculative side to this, too. Roll buyers have often been delighted to find that they have bought rolls with mint errors, or other pecularities which sends roll prices sky high in a comparatively short time.

Rolls should be UNCIRCULATED COINS. These are available at face value only during the year of issue. And again we point out, usually they must be held for several years before they begin to acquire "premium" value ... unless, of course, some error or other factor, as mentioned, crops up. There are many such factors. The 1955-S penny is a good example. This was the last year of the San Francisco Mint -- as a result this coin has skyrocketed in value and profits of 1000% on Uncirculated rolls are not uncommon. It is still going up.

It is dangerous --- indeed unwise --- to pay premium prices for current Uncirculated rolls. Try to get them from your bank if possible. Banks get them from the local Federal Reserve banks and they ARE obtainable in this way. Of course if you want previous years you will have to buy them from a dealer who is already making a profit when he sells them to you ... but they may go still higher.

These are average _retail_ prices charged by dealers. _Dealers_ buy at _wholesale_ prices, which are less than those shown. Buying and selling prices vary in different parts of the country and with different dealers, depending on their stocks on hand, supply and demand, etc. This table will give you an approximate idea of current 1963 prices.

Year	Quantity Minted	Good	Very Good	Fine	Very Fine	Ex. Fine	Unc.
1909 VDB	27,995,000	$ .40	$ .55	$ .75	$ 1.00	$ 1.50	$ 4.00
1909-S VDB	484,000	100.00	130.00	140.00	170.00	180.00	300.00
1909	72,702,618	.35	.40	.60	.85	1.25	5.50
1909-S	1,825,000	25.00	30.00	35.00	40.00	50.00	60.00
1910	146,801,218	.20	.30	.50	.75	1.00	6.00
1910-S	6,045,000	3.00	4.00	5.00	7.50	10.00	40.00
1911	101,177,787	.25	.35	.60	.90	1.25	8.00
1911-D	12,672,000	1.20	2.00	3.00	6.00	9.00	30.00
1911-S	4,026,000	8.00	10.00	13.00	17.00	20.00	45.00
1912	68,153,060	.20	.30	.55	1.15	1.75	7.75
1912-D	10,411,000	1.35	2.40	4.50	8.75	13.00	38.00
1912-S	4,431,000	4.00	5.00	6.00	9.00	13.50	40.00
1913	76,532,352	.20	.30	.60	1.00	1.50	6.75
1913-D	15,804,000	.60	1.50	3.25	6.25	9.00	40.00
1913-S	6,101,000	3.00	4.00	6.00	8.00	12.00	42.50
1914	75,238,432	.50	1.20	2.40	3.75	5.00	17.50
*1914-D	1,193,000	34.50	45.00	57.50	105.00	150.00	510.00
1914-S	4,137,000	4.00	5.00	7.00	13.75	22.00	85.00
1915	29,092,120	.50	1.60	3.50	6.00	10.00	75.00
1915-D	22,050,000	.60	1.35	2.50	4.00	6.00	22.50
1915-S	4,833,000	3.00	4.00	6.00	8.00	11.00	40.00
1916	131,833,677	.20	.40	.60	.85	1.25	6.75
1916-D	35,956,000	.40	.70	2.25	3.35	4.70	17.50
1916-S	22,510,000	.70	1.40	2.50	4.15	6.75	30.00
1917	196,429,785	.20	.35	.55	.85	1.25	6.00
1917-D	55,120,000	.40	.80	1.50	4.75	7.00	23.50
1917-S	32,620,000	.40	.85	1.50	4.75	7.00	23.50
1918	288,104,634	.20	.35	.55	1.00	1.75	6.00
1918-D	47,830,000	.35	.85	1.85	4.25	6.50	27.50
1918-S	34,680,000	.35	.85	1.85	4.25	6.50	30.00
1919	392,021,000	.20	.30	.50	1.00	1.50	6.50
1919-D	57,154,000	.40	.75	1.40	3.25	5.00	17.50
1919-S	139,760,000	.25	.55	1.00	2.75	4.00	17.50

* Beware of Altered Date. No VDB on Lincoln's Shoulder on Genuine 1914-D Coin

Although the Lincoln Cent has undergone changes in its long life, it has always held an attraction for collectors. Starting somewhere along the 1930s it also held an attraction for investors. The hoards of cents put away in 1931 (the 1931S) and hoards of rolls put away every year since 1934 were more a phenomenon of investing than collecting. The cover of a 1964 booklet by Robert Svensson points to the interest in Lincoln Cents as a profit-maker. The 16 page booklet highlights the humble origins of the Lincoln Cent and some points on grading. One key sentence of p. 7 says,

> "We mention rolls because these are the most profitable form of investing. You will note from the table of valuations that rolls have increased considerably over face value through the years. There is a speculative side to this, too. Roll buyers have often been delighted to find they have bought rolls with mint errors, or other peculiarities which sends roll prices sky high in a comparatively short time."

From the numismatic publications of 1964 and well into the 1970s, this logic prevailed and rolls of every denomination from the cent through the half dollar were advertised often in full page ads. And for many of these years, it was true that prices tended to move strongly upward with the exception of some of the most recent issues which went up and down.

Under a headline "The Big Ones", author Svensson listed the key Lincoln Cents in date order: 1909S VDB, 1909S, 1914D, 1914S, 1922D, 1924D, 1926S, 1931D, 1931S, 1933D, 1955 double strike, 1960 small date, 1960D small date.

In addition, author Svensson recommended 15 circulated rolls to acquire (either by buying from dealers or perhaps locating in change)

1935D	1936S	1938D	1942S	1954
1935S	1937D	1938S	1948S	1954S
1936D	1937S	1939D	1949S	1955S

The price chart of Lincoln from 1909-1919 give an idea of the retail market in 1964. Also, note that "Unc" did not break down into "BU" or other grades as has become the mode since 1980.

PRICES OF THE PAST

The heyday of sales by the roll was the mid-1960s. The following two pages of ads are from issues of THE NUMISMATIST of 1966 and 1967. They are fairly typical of many other dealers who offered coins for sale by the roll. Today, it would be less likely to find even a very few dealers who offered circulated rolls by the grade for the range of dates in the Zurcher ad.

The brilliant uncirculated rolls ad by Walt Taub again is typical of other dealers who stocked quantities (often bag lots) of BU rolls of coins from 1934 to date. Some dealers in this era advertised every date and denomination from 1934-1966 in their ads. Due to massive hoarding in the 1950s and 1960s, most dates were readily available (see Ch. 5) for several decades later.

The 1945 issue from Ben's Stamp and Coin Company typifies how mail order firms sold coins. Numberical grading was unknown and there were only two categories of mint state, namely "uncirculated" and "brilliant unc.".

From collection of the author.

ROLL LIST March 1, 1966
LINCOLN CENT ROLLS

	Good	VG	F-VF
09-VDB	42.50	45.00	47.50
1909-P	....	....	11.50
1909-S	....	....	1395.00
1910-P	....	4.50	9.75
1910-S	....	149.50	177.50
1911-P	2.75	4.75	24.50
1911-S	....	345.00	525.00
1912-P	....	8.75	....
1912-S	....	195.00	285.00
1912-D	61.50	....	....
1913-P	5.50	8.50	....
1913-S	115.00	120.00	185.00
1913-D	38.50	....	....
1914-P	2.75	5.75	42.50
1914-S	195.00	199.50	275.00
1915-P	26.50	....	....
1915-S	170.00	180.00	225.00
1915-D	25.50	29.50	59.50
1916-P	....	2.25	9.75
1916-S	25.00	27.50	42.50
1916-D	10.75	11.75	44.50
1917-P	....	2.25	9.75
1917-S	....	....	16.75
1917-D	5.75	7.25	34.50
1918-P	1.75	2.00	8.50
1918-S	4.75	6.50	14.50
1918-D	4.40	9.50	34.50
1919-P	1.25	1.50	3.50
1919-S	....	2.50	7.50
1919-D	5.50	7.50	....
1920-P	1.25	1.50	3.75
1920-S	3.75	6.75	34.50
1920-D	3.75	6.75	34.50
1921-P	....	....	35.00
1921-S	22.50	26.50	79.50
1922-D	117.50	147.50	....
1923-S	42.50	49.50	99.75
1924-P	1.75	2.00	5.50
1924-S	22.50	25.50	59.50
1924-D	395.00	445.00	715.00
1925-P	1.25	1.50	4.50
1925-S	4.75	5.25	12.50
1925-D	8.75	9.75	32.50
1926-S	127.50	137.50	....
1926-P	1.25	1.50	3.50
1926-D	6.75	7.75	24.50
1927-P	1.25	1.50	3.50
1927-S	12.50	13.50	24.50

	Good	VG	F-VF
1927-D	5.25	8.75	13.50
1928-S	8.75	9.75	16.75
1928-D	3.75	5.75	8.75
1929-S	1.95	2.10	2.75
1930-S	3.75	4.25	....
1930-D	2.25	2.50	6.00
1931-P	8.95	9.95	13.75
1931-S	....	1375.00	1425.00
1931-D	....	175.00	205.00
1932-P	33.50	42.50	57.50
1932-D	26.50	28.50	....
1933-P	26.50	28.50	49.50
1933-D	92.50	99.50	120.00
1934-D	5.75	6.75	9.75
1935-S	2.25	2.50	3.25
1935-D	1.75	2.00	3.50
1936-S	3.75	4.00	4.75
1936-D	3.50	3.75	4.25
1937-S	2.75	3.00	3.25
1937-D	1.75	2.00	2.75
1938-S	13.75	14.00	14.25
1938-D	10.75	10.85	11.50
1939-S	1.65	1.75	1.95
1939-D	....	24.50	26.50

	VG	F-VF	AU
1940-S	1.00	1.25	11.75
1940-D	1.25	1.50	....
1941-S	1.25	1.75	....
1941-D	1.25	1.50	....
1942-S	1.50	2.00	....
1942-D	1.00	1.25	....
1943-P	1.25	1.50	....
1943-S	4.25	4.95	12.75
1943-D	3.75	4.25	....
1944-S	1.00	1.25	4.00
1945-S	1.00	1.25	....
1946-S	1.00	1.25	3.95
1947-S	1.00	1.25	11.75
1948-S	1.25	1.40	12.75
1949-S	2.50	2.75	17.75
1950-S	1.00	1.25	8.50
1951-S	1.00	1.25	8.75
1952-S	1.00	1.25	3.75
1953-S	1.00	1.25	2.25
1954-P	4.50	4.75	....
1954-S	1.10	1.25	3.75
1955-S	....	14.50	16.00
60-D SD	....	1.75	2.25

JEFFERSON NICKEL ROLLS

	VG	F-VF		VG	F-VF		VG	F-VF
1939-S	29.50	32.50	1944-D	3.75	5.75	1949-S	8.50	9.50
42-P II	3.50	5.50	1945-P	2.85	3.85	1951-S	17.50	19.50
1942-S	3.75	5.75	1945-S	2.85	3.85	1952-S	2.50	3.00
1943-P	2.85	3.85	1945-D	3.75	5.75	1953-S	2.65	3.25
1943-S	2.85	3.85	1946-S	3.85	5.85	1953-S	2.50	3.00
1944-P	2.85	3.85	1947-S	2.50	3.00	1955-P	19.50	22.75
1944-S	5.75	7.75	1948-S	4.95	5.95			

ROOSEVELT DIME ROLLS

	VG	F-VF	EF-AU		VG	F-VF	EF-AU
1946-S	5.95	6.95	19.95	1951-S	5.95	6.95	39.50
1947-S	5.95	7.25	23.50	1952-S	5.95	6.95	17.50
1948-S	5.95	7.25	23.50	1953-S	5.95	6.95	17.00
1949-P	6.25	8.25	....	1954-S	5.95	....	17.75
1949-S	21.50	27.50	77.50	1955-P	....	39.50	....
1949-D	5.95	6.95	....	1955-S	12.75	14.75	....
1950-S	6.25	7.95	59.50	1955-D	15.75	16.75	....

Satisfaction Guaranteed

ROBERT ZURCHER INC.

Box 126-A   Cornelius, Oregon 97113

BRILLIANT UNCIRCULATED ROLLS

CENTS	
1934P	..... 70.00
1934D	..... 275.00
1935D	..... 48.50
1935S	..... 120.00
1937P	..... 17.00
1938P	..... 32.50
1938D	..... 75.00
1939D	..... 125.00
1939S	..... 29.00
1940P	..... 13.00
1940S	..... 14.00
1941P	..... 16.00
1941D	..... 26.00
1943P	..... 9.50
1943D	..... 16.50
1943S	..... 32.00
1944P	..... 5.00
1944S	..... 8.00
1945D	..... 7.50
1945S	..... 9.00
1946P	..... 5.00
1946D	..... 6.50
1946S	..... 7.00
1947P	..... 15.00
1947D	..... 6.00
1947S	..... 12.00
1948P	..... 8.00
1948S	..... 29.00
1949D	..... 12.00
1949S	..... 34.00
1950P	..... 8.25
1950S	..... 17.50
1951P	..... 14.50
1951D	..... 3.50
1951S	..... 17.00
1952S	..... 14.00
1953P	..... 5.50
1953D	..... 3.00
1953S	..... 8.00
1954P	..... 17.00
1954D	..... 3.00
1954S	..... 7.25
1955P	..... 4.25
1955D	..... 3.50
1955S	..... 17.50
1956P	..... 3.25
1957P	..... 3.00
1958P	..... 2.75

CENTS	
1959P,D	... 1.05
1960P,D	... 1.00
1961P,D	... 1.00
1962P,D	... 1.00
1963P,D	... 1.00
1964P,D	... .95
1965	...... .90
1966	...... .85
1967	...... .80

NICKELS	
1937P Buf. .	95.00
1938D Buf. .	100.00
1938P	..... 49.00
1938D	..... 145.00
1938S	..... 195.00
1939P	..... 29.00
1940S	..... 40.00
1942P	..... 31.00
1942 T-2	... 180.00
1942S	..... 72.50
1943P	..... 45.00
1943D	..... 80.00
1943S	..... 33.00
1944P	..... 67.50
1944D	..... 62.50
1944S	..... 67.50
1945P	..... 70.00
1945P	..... 39.00
1945S	..... 33.00
1946P	..... 6.95
1946D	..... 18.00
1946S	..... 32.00
1947P	..... 6.50
1947S	..... 25.00
1948D	..... 32.00
1949P	..... 19.00
1949S	..... 65.00
1950P	..... 62.50
1950D	..... 450.00
1953P	..... 7.00
1953D	..... 5.50
1953S	..... 22.00
1954D	..... 4.50
1955P	..... 55.00
1958P	..... 15.00
1958D	..... 3.00

NICKELS	
1959P	..... 5.75
1960P,D	... 3.00
1961P,D	... 2.85
1962P,D	... 2.75
1963P,D	... 2.70
1964P,D	... 2.65
1965	...... 2.90
1966	...... 2.85

DIMES	
1946S	..... 40.00
1947P	..... 21.00
1947D	..... 22.00
1947S	..... 40.00
1948D	..... 24.00
1948S	..... 45.00
1949S	..... 325.00
1951P	..... 27.00
1951D	..... 19.50
1952P	..... 14.00
1952D	..... 22.00
1952S	..... 65.00
1953S	..... 19.00
1954P	..... 8.00
1955D	..... 31.00
1955S	..... 22.00
1956D	..... 7.00
1957P	..... 7.50
1958P	..... 18.50
1958D	..... 7.00
1959P,D	... 6.50
1960P,D	... 6.40
1961P	..... 7.50
1961D	..... 6.00
1962P,D	... 6.75
1963P,D	... 6.00
1964P,D	... 5.90
1965	...... 5.80
1966	...... 5.75
1967	...... 5.50

QUARTERS	
1941P	..... 50.00
1941S	..... 165.00
1943P	..... 35.00
1943D	..... 70.00
1944P	..... 24.00

QUARTERS	
1946S	..... 109.00
1947S	..... 90.00
1948D	..... 35.00
1950P	..... 30.00
1951S	..... 160.00
1952D	..... 18.00
1953P	..... 35.00
1954D	..... 15.00
1955P	..... 26.00
1955D	..... 110.00
1957P,D	... 13.50
1958P	..... 42.50
1958D	..... 13.50
1959D	..... 13.00
1960P,D	... 13.75
1961P,D	... 15.00
1962P,D	... 14.00
1963P,D	... 13.00
1964P,D	... 12.50
1965	...... 11.50
1966	...... 11.25
1967	...... 11.00

HALVES	
1936P	..... 92.50
1941P	..... 90.00
1943P	..... 72.50
1952S	..... 105.00
1953P	..... 180.00
1953D	..... 22.50
1955P	..... 137.50
1956P	..... 42.50
1957P	..... 30.00
1958P	..... 42.50
1958D	..... 17.50
1959P	..... 27.00
1960P	..... 25.00
1961D	..... 18.00
1957D	..... 16.50
1962P	..... 20.00
1962D	..... 14.00
1963P	..... 13.25
1963D	..... 12.50
1964P	..... 12.00
1964D	..... 14.50
1965	...... 11.50
1966	...... 11.25
1967	...... 11.00

★

Postage and insurance included in above prices. Satisfaction guaranteed as always. Please add 75c on orders under $50. WANTED CHOICE BU ROLLS, please state quantity and price in first letter or will quote you.

★

WALT LAUB

1532 Broadway   ANA 34957   Denver, Colo. 80202

FLYING EAGLE CENTS AND INDIAN CENTS

1905	Very Good-Fine	.05
	Very Fine-Ex. Fine	.15
	About Uncirculated	.40
	Brilliant Unc.	1.00
1906	Very Good-Fine	.05
	Very Fine-Ex. Fine	.15
	Brilliant Unc.	1.00
	Brilliant Proof	4.50
1907	Very Good-Fine	.05
	Very Fine-Ex. Fine	.15
	Uncirculated	1.50
	Brilliant Unc.	2.00
1908	Fine	.05
	Very Fine-Ex. Fine	.15
	Proof	3.50
	Brilliant Proof, GEM	4.50
1908 S	Fine	3.00
	Very Fine	3.50
	Brilliant Unc.	7.50
1909	Very Good-Fine	.10
	Very Fine-Ex. Fine	.25
	Uncirculated	1.00
	Brilliant Unc.	1.25
	Proof	6.00
	Brilliant Proof	7.50
1909 S	Fine	12.50
	Very Fine	15.00
	Unc., slight abrasion in field	21.50
	Brilliant Unc.	28.50

500 INDIAN HEAD CENTS

Mixed dates from 1880-1909, Good-Very Fine .... $10.00 postpaid

LINCOLN CENTS

1909 VDB	Fine	.10
	Brilliant Unc.	.25
1909 S VDB,	Fine	9.00
	Very Fine	10.00
	About Uncirculated	11.00
	Uncirculated	13.50
	Brilliant Unc.	15.00
1909	Very Good-Fine	.05
	Brilliant Unc.	.25
1909 S	Good-Very Good	.75
	Very Fine	1.25
	Brilliant Unc.	3.50
1910	Very Good-Fine	.05
	Brilliant Unc.	.50
	Proof	2.50
1910 S	Good-Very Good	.20
	Uncirculated	1.25
	Brilliant Unc.	1.50

LINCOLN CENTS

1911	Very Good-Fine	.05
	Uncirculated	.40
	Brilliant Unc.	.50
1911 S	Good-Very Good	.20
	Very Fine	1.50
	Uncirculated	3.00
1911 D	Good-Very Good	.15
	Brilliant Unc.	2.00
1912	Very Good-Fine	.05
	Proof	2.50
1912 S	Good-Very Good	.20
	Brilliant Unc.	4.00
1912 D	Good-Very Good	.20
	Fine	.75
	Red Uncirculated	5.00
1913	Very Good-Fine	.05
	Brilliant Unc.	.50
	Brilliant Proof	3.50
1913 S	Good-Very Good	.20
1913 D	Good-Very Good	.10
	Extremely Fine	2.00
	Uncirculated	6.00
1914	Very Good-Fine	.05
	Very Fine-Ex. Fine	.50
	Uncirculated	2.50
	Brilliant Proof	6.00
	Brilliant Proof, GEM	6.75
1914 S	Good-Very Good	.20
	Very Fine	2.50
1914 D	Good	2.00
	Very Good	2.25
	Fine	3.00
1915	Very Good-Fine	.10
	Brilliant Proof	7.50
1915 S	Good-Very Good	.20
1915 D	Good-Very Good	.10
	Very Fine-Ex. Fine	.50
	Brilliant Unc.	2.00
1916	Very Good-Fine	.05
	Very Fine-Ex. Fine	.15
	Brilliant Unc.	.50
1916 S	Good-Very Good	.10
	Very Fine-Ex. Fine	.85
1916 D	Good-Very Good	.05
	Very Fine-Ex. Fine	.50
1917	Very Good-Fine	.05
	Very Fine-Ex. Fine	.15
	Red Uncirculated	.50
	Brilliant Unc.	.65
1917 S	Good-Very Good	.10
1917 D	Good-Very Good	.05
	Very Fine-Ex. Fine	.65

EXHIBITING LINCOLN CENTS

Most major conventions encourage numismatic exhibits. And many of the finest collections known has won awards as competitive exhibits. In the past two or three decades, few exhibitors have focused on Lincoln Cent collections. In fact, in reviewing the ANA exhibit awards over that period, no Lincoln Cent exhibit was even mentioned, no less a winner.

A Lincoln Cent exhibit is not only worthwhile but a potential winner. Here are a few suggestions:

1. The LINCOLN MEMORIAL SERIES - This series has the potential for completeness, high quality, information, and beauty. Since many exhibitors are graded for these features, any serious collector can assemble a choice to gem set of 1959-date Lincolns. Next one can compile a nice exhibit format so each coin is properly highlighted, described, and positioned. Finally, the narrative can be tastefully and artfully done to frame the exhibit.

2. A COMPLETE WHEAT BACK SET IN BU - Though much more of a challenge, this too can compete for awards at major shows. Complete BU sets can be assembled and suitably exhibited. The coins need not all be MS65 Red, but most can be. And of the very scarce coins MS63 Red and MS64 Red look (almost) as good in an exhibit case to the judges and the public.

3. THE LINCOLN CENT ERROR - Here's a chance for real imagination. A good exhibit can be made from a few choice coins:
   1. One or two RPMs
   2. One or two OMMs
   3. An off metal strike--such as on a dime planchet or if available, an extremely popular 1943 copper cent
   4. An off center cent--or several of various degrees of off-centering
   5. A blank planchet--perhaps one in bronze and one in zinc
   6. One or two strong laminations
   7. One or two double struck cents
   8. One or two errors including a famous doubled die such as 1955/55 or 1972/72

Many other possibilities exist and it is only up to the collector to be inventive on what to include and how to display it. Since everyone knows of the Lincoln Cent, exhibits should be encouraged. Exhibit rules are available from ANA and other regional organizations.

1984 **I-O-IV**
Doubled Ear

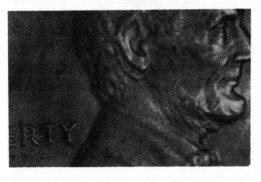

AU	$ 75.00
MS63	$120.00
ANACS 65/65	$195.00
PCGS 65RD	$235.00
PCGS 66RD	$335.00

LINCOLN CENT VALUE GUIDE

GRADE	COLOR	DIE STATE	MINTAGE	POPULATION
MS67-70	Red (Bright)	VEDS	Very Low Under 100	0-1
MS65-66	Red (Dull)	EDS	Low 101-1000	2-10
MS63-64	Red Brown (Lustrous)	MDS	Low 1001-10,000	11-50
MS60-62	Red Brown (Dull)	LDS	Low 10,000-50,000	51-100
AU55-58	Brown (Lustrous)	VLDS	Low 10,000-50,000	51-100
AU55-58	Brown (Lustrous)	VLDS	Low 10,000-50,000	51-100
1-3	Brown (Dark, dull)	VLDS	Billions	Over 500

The value of a Lincoln Cent lies in these five phases. The grade is perhaps the most important value guide. Thus a coin graded MS67 would have a higher value than a coin of the same date grade MS65 regardless of the other features. However, a coin graded MS64RB would have very high value as compared to other coins of similar mintage and color if the population of such a coin were as small as one or two. This would indicate its very scarce or rare nature. Likewise the very same coin would decline in value if it turned brown.

For certain dates, especially mintmarked coins from 1918-1929, the early die state is very uncommon. Thus a 1926D EDS in Red would be worth much more than a 1926D in VLDS graded the same grade and color.

A coin with one high feature such as red, would have more value than a comparable coin with red-brown color. Likewise a coin of very early die state would have more value than a comparable coin with all the same features but medium die state. This accounts often for the wide discrepancies noted in two seemingly identical coins such as the 1909S VDB MS65 Red where one was sold at an auction for $950 and the other for $2500.

Outlook for the Lincoln Cent

The Lincoln Cent has been and still is the most widely collected coin in the world. Among the more serious collectors, the hunt for mint state red or mint gold coins has become a passionate challenge. Many members of SLCC have been pursuing this goal for decades. And for each collector of Lincoln Cents today there may well be dozens tomorrow. The logic is twofold: 1. It's quite easy and inexpensive to build a respectable or even complete collection and 2. It's far less expensive to build an exhibit quality collection of Lincoln Cents than almost any other series except for the modern of series (coins starting after 1932).

The true red or mint gold coins of each date are still the major challenge facing collectors and these coins will continue to rise in value as collectors are vying for nicer and nicer specimens. With age, a goodly number of earlier Lincolns (before 1934) will age poorly—toning, spotting, and fading.

In 1940 no Lincoln Cent retailed for more than $100. In the 1960s a very few passed the $350 level. By the mid-1970s a handful passed the $1,000 mark—BU specimens of the 1909S VDB, 1914D, and 1922 had passed that mark. In the 1980s many Lincolns had passed the $2,000 mark, but some early winners had fallen back—BU 1909 S VDB cents were available for under $1,000. On the other hand Pf64 or Pf65 matte proofs all were touching and passing the $1,000 level.

The BU rolls which were traded like so much commodities in the 1960s and 1970s have basically been broken down to single coins ranging in quality from subpar MS60 to a few gem MS65s. These rolls covering the period from 1934 through the remainder of the wheat back series (1958) have all but disappeared from the coin show displays and dealer stock boxes by 1988. The more modern rolls (1959 to date) still can be found in solid rolls.

The popular coin folders still have more Lincoln Cent buyers than any other series. And as the novice collectors fill 90-99% of the holes, the hunt begins to fill the missing holes and to upgrade the quality of those coins already in the album. This cycle repeated by almost every adult collector alive today will more than likely continue for decades to come. The data from surveys of collectors in SLCC and many coin clubs indicate that regardless of the adult interest—ancients, currency, tokens, or medals, the early interest was the Lincoln Cent (or for older collectors, the Indian Head Cent).

The values of MS65 coins will undoubtedly continue to rise with time. The few hoarded MS65 coins (1909 VDB, 1909 S VDB) notwithstanding, collectors will have to pay more and more for these very select bright BU coins. Time alone will shrink the supply. Poor care will further reduce the quality of older collections. Each decade will see new price records for elusive BU coins.

Some of the record prices known for Lincoln Cents include the 1922P MS65RB (PCGS) sold in November, 1988 for $20,900. The Walter D. Greer 1943 copper specimen was reportedly sold privately for $40,000 in 1958. Another 1922P in January, 1988 sold at auction for $15,000, in PCGS MS64. (See 1943 for other top prices.)

For late date Lincolns, some high prices include a dealer-to-dealer sale of a ANACS 1960 sm/lg Pf67 Red went for $750 in mid-1991. Two others also brought $750 from the same dealer in Oregon. A Pf66 Cameo (ANACS) sm/lg sold for $500--six others were also sold for $500. In the same transaction, a Pf66 Red (ANACS) sm/lg sold for $400. All the coins were part of a hoard of 1960 small date proof sets owned by an Oregon coin dealer who discovered 17 small over large date varieties.

A 1915 LIncoln Cent is described as being struck on a gold planchet intended for a $2 1/2 gold Pan-pacific commemorative. The owner in 1947 was J.V. McDermott who displayed the coin at the Chicago Coin Club. The estimated value (in 1990) was $20,000. Another Lincoln Cent, 1909S VDB is also known to exist on a $2 1/2 gold planchet, it is last purported to be in a Los Angeles coin collection.

Various unplated (pure zinc) cents are known for almost all dates form 1982 to the present. A recent investigation (in 1992) is focused on the manufacturer as being lax in control of the planchets which may elude security before reaching the designated U.S. mint. Prices for unplated 1986 to 1991 cents have dropped in value as quantities have been offered to dealers across the country. Lightly and partially plated zinc cents are seen for sale.

There are far more Lincoln Cents catalogued by RPM, doubled die, die crack (Cohen), off-metal planchet (mostly struck on dime planchets), lamination, broadstruck, misaligned die, and different date and mintmark.

As more than three million coins have been encapsulated by 1992, and the numbers slowly rising, the reliance upon the form of preservation and grading will play an important role in the future. Since these coins are sonically sealed, they will age better than coins in albums or other holders. Perhaps in time, slabbed coins will hold a premium only for the protection afforded the coin. For Lincolns, this is crucial as most collectors know, Lincolns tend to lose their luster and color in time. Since the encapsulated plastic holder has only been with us a few years, only time will tell if bright BU red cents will still be bright BU red in twenty-five or fifty years from now.

If the cent becomes obsolete and many of the circulated hoards are redeemed, the collecting of the cent may become more of a challenge insofar as searching through change for the more common circulated specimens. As of 1992, one cannot hope to assemble even a full Memorial back set. But most of the dates from 1959 can be found by searching through bags of cents. In fact, many RPMs and the minor doubled dies can still be located in circulated bags--providing they have not been searched by other cherrypickers.

Most hobbies have a starter course--such as stamp collectors buying mixed packets and skiers starting on the beginner slopes. Into the next century collectors of coins will more than likely be cutting their teeth on the Lincoln Cent. And as supplies of both the high quality pieces shrink and the number of better quality circulated pieces get squirreled away in private collections, the next generation of collector will undoubtedly have to pay more for what he or she wants.

Late date Lincolns (after 1935) are generally not shown in any quantities in Population Reports because they have a market value far less than the usual $20 (or more) charged for encapsulation. Thus very low numbers in late date coins are not factors in pricing. In Chapter 5, only a few dates indicate Population Report data where it may impact a coin's value. This is especially noted for the 1935S, 1943S, 1955 doubled die, 1972 doubled die, 1983 doubled die, and 1984 doubled die. Scattered low numbers appear for almost all other dates from 1935 to date.

The Lincoln Cent is the only series:
   a. to run more than 79 years
   b. to have the same person appear on both sides of the coin (Lincoln is seated within the Memorial on the reverse.)
   c. to not use the "P" mintmark in the modern (1964-date) coinage series.
   d. to have the designer's initials appear in two different locations (1909 VDB reverse and 1918-date obverse).
   e. to be struck in three coinage metals: bronze, zinc-coated steel, and copper coated zinc.

The Society of Lincoln Cent Collectors was begun at a coin show in Long Beach with a quartet of collectors in April, 1982. By year's end, 1991 membership card number 950 had been issued.

The D mintmark applied in 1987 is the largest mintmark used on any Lincoln Cent.

LINCOLN CENT TRENDING DURING THE 1980'S AND 1990'S
INCLUDES REGULAR ISSUES FROM 1909 THRU 1934 ONLY (NO 1922 PLAIN)

	MS60				MS63				MS64	MS65		
	CDN BUY	C.W. SELL	N.N. SELL	REDBOOK SELL	CDN BUY	C.W. SELL	N.N. SELL	REDBOOK SELL	CDN BUY	CDN BUY	C.W. SELL	N.N. SELL
1980	$2,951.50			$4,134.00	*N/A*	*N/A*	*N/A*	*N/A*	*N/A*	$13,617.00		
1981	$3,203.50			$4,872.50	*N/A*	*N/A*	*N/A*	*N/A*	*N/A*	$13,998.00		
1982	$3,784.50			$5,472.50	$6,487.65	*N/A*	*N/A*	$9,559.50	*N/A*	$17,597.00		
1983	$3,779.00			$5,511.00	$6,909.00	*N/A*	*N/A*	$9,731.00	*N/A*	$24,016.00		
1984	$3,780.00			$5,166.50	$6,889.00	*N/A*	*N/A*	$9,312.50	*N/A*	$24,016.00		
1985	$3,758.00	$4,468.00	$4,849.25	$5,166.50	$6,764.00	*N/A*	*N/A*	$9,312.50	*N/A*	$23,052.50	$26,860.75	
1986	$3,476.50	$4,159.10	$4,849.25	$5,100.50	$6,330.50	*N/A*	*N/A*	$9,255.00	*N/A*	$17,796.00	$21,064.00	
1987	$3,481.50	$4,208.45	$4,849.25	$5,085.50	$6,376.50	$7,907.25	*N/A*	$9,255.00	*N/A*	$22,816.00	$24,544.00	
1988	$3,517.00	$4,062.25	$4,831.25	$5,060.50	$6,352.50	$7,600.35	*N/A*	$9,205.00	*N/A*	$26,006.00	$28,519.50	$28,702.00
1989	$3,513.00	$4,361.15	$4,831.25	$4,860.50	$6,332.50	$8,304.75	*N/A*	$9,005.00	*N/A*	$25,291.00	$31,100.00	$28,702.00
1990	$3,496.50	$4,052.90	$4,831.25	$4,860.50	$6,193.50	$7,189.25	*N/A*	$8,905.00	*N/A*	$29,261.00	$40,196.50	$28,702.00
1991	$3,492.00	$3,998.95	$4,864.50	$4,721.50	$5,684.50	$7,207.50	$8,170.00	$8,492.50	$14,562.50	$35,750.00	$62,701.00	$51,061.00
1992												

Track history of MS60 Lincoln compiled by Stephen J. Cohen

YEAR MINT	1935	1940	1945	1950	1955	1960	1965	1970	1975	1980	1985	1990	1992
1909 VDB	$0.15	$0.15	$0.15	$0.25	$0.60	$2.10	$7.75	$5.25	$11.00	$12.50	$13.00	$13.00	$13.00
1909 SVDB	$1.50	$2.50	$9.00	$12.50	$30.00	$97.50	$350.00	$200.00	$275.00	$400.00	$550.00	$475.00	$475.00
1909 S	$0.15	$0.20	$0.25	$0.30	$1.00	$3.50	$9.00	$5.75	$8.50	$10.00	$13.00	$12.00	$14.00
1910	$0.40	$1.50	$2.50	$4.00	$8.50	$32.50	$120.00	$65.00	$75.00	$95.00	$190.00	$175.00	$165.00
1910 S	$0.20	$0.25	$0.60	$2.00	$4.50	$17.50	$11.50	$7.25	$9.50	$11.00	$13.00	$13.00	$13.00
1911	$0.50	$0.60	$0.75	$0.60	$1.25	$3.50	$60.00	$40.00	$45.00	$53.00	$95.00	$95.00	$95.00
1911 D	$0.20	$0.25	$0.40	$2.50	$5.50	$14.00	$12.00	$8.50	$11.00	$15.00	$18.00	$18.00	$18.00
1911 S	$0.35	$1.25	$1.25	$3.50	$8.50	$23.00	$42.50	$32.00	$47.50	$60.00	$100.00	$100.00	$100.00
1912	$0.35	$2.50	$2.55	$0.60	$1.25	$4.50	$85.00	$50.00	$60.00	$75.00	$115.00	$115.00	$120.00
1912 D	$0.25	$0.30	$0.40	$6.00	$13.50	$32.50	$15.50	$11.50	$17.50	$22.50	$25.00	$25.00	$25.00
1912 S	$0.55	$1.90	$3.50	$5.00	$10.00	$25.00	$60.00	$45.00	$57.50	$70.00	$110.00	$110.00	$110.00
1913	$0.50	$3.00	$2.50	$0.60	$1.25	$3.50	$60.00	$45.00	$60.00	$75.00	$110.00	$110.00	$110.00
1913 D	$1.15	$3.75	$3.50	$6.50	$10.00	$25.00	$15.00	$11.00	$17.50	$21.00	$20.00	$20.00	$20.00
1913 S	$1.25	$3.75	$4.50	$5.50	$9.00	$22.00	$57.50	$40.00	$52.50	$67.50	$70.00	$70.00	$70.00
1914	$1.15	$1.50	$2.00	$3.00	$5.00	$10.50	$62.50	$40.00	$52.50	$67.50	$100.00	$100.00	$100.00
1914 D	$2.15	$7.00	$7.00	$20.00	$80.00	$275.00	$37.50	$24.00	$29.50	$750.00	$1,000.00	$800.00	$750.00
1914 S	$1.65	$4.25	$4.75	$8.50	$6.00	$60.00	$775.00	$560.00	$675.00	$92.50	$165.00	$165.00	$165.00
1915	$0.85	$2.00	$3.00	$3.50	$6.00	$10.00	$115.00	$75.00	$80.00	$80.00	$110.00	$110.00	$85.00
1915 D	$0.50	$1.00	$1.25	$1.75	$3.50	$10.00	$125.00	$65.00	$65.00	$37.50	$45.00	$45.00	$40.00
1915 S	$0.55	$2.00	$4.00	$4.00	$7.50	$10.00	$60.00	$42.00	$52.50	$65.00	$100.00	$100.00	$100.00
1916	$0.40	$0.40	$0.35	$0.50	$0.90	$4.00	$30.00	$7.25	$9.50	$12.00	$12.00	$12.00	$12.00
1916 D	$0.55	$1.20	$1.50	$2.00	$5.00	$10.00	$25.00	$19.00	$25.00	$32.50	$50.00	$50.00	$50.00
1916 S	$0.60	$1.35	$2.30	$2.30	$8.00	$18.00	$40.00	$26.00	$30.00	$35.00	$60.00	$60.00	$60.00
1917	$0.25	$0.35	$0.40	$0.50	$1.25	$3.50	$10.00	$6.75	$10.00	$11.00	$12.00	$12.00	$12.00
1917 D	$0.50	$0.95	$2.00	$2.75	$6.00	$14.00	$35.00	$24.00	$30.00	$37.50	$50.00	$50.00	$55.00
1917 S	$0.60	$1.35	$0.50	$3.50	$6.50	$15.00	$35.00	$25.00	$30.00	$37.50	$55.00	$55.00	$55.00
1918	$0.25	$0.35	$3.00	$0.50	$1.25	$4.75	$11.50	$8.25	$10.50	$13.00	$13.00	$13.00	$13.00
1918 D	$0.50	$1.80	$3.50	$4.50	$8.00	$20.00	$42.00	$26.00	$31.00	$37.50	$50.00	$50.00	$50.00
1918 S	$0.60	$1.80	$0.40	$6.00	$10.00	$20.00	$44.00	$28.00	$31.00	$37.50	$55.00	$55.00	$55.00
1919	$0.25	$0.30	$1.35	$0.50	$1.25	$3.50	$10.00	$7.00	$9.00	$10.00	$11.00	$11.00	$11.00
1919 D	$0.50	$1.20	$1.25	$1.50	$3.50	$10.50	$25.00	$18.00	$21.00	$26.00	$40.00	$40.00	$40.00
1919 S	$0.55	$1.50	$0.30	$1.50	$3.25	$10.50	$25.00	$17.50	$18.50	$22.00	$30.00	$30.00	$30.00
1920	$0.25	$0.30	$2.00	$0.50	$1.25	$3.50	$10.00	$6.50	$8.00	$10.00	$10.00	$10.00	$10.00
1920 D	$0.55	$1.15	$1.35	$3.00	$7.50	$25.00	$46.50	$30.00	$30.00	$37.50	$50.00	$50.00	$50.00
1920 S	$0.50	$1.35	$0.75	$4.50	$8.50	$25.00	$50.00	$30.00	$30.00	$36.00	$65.00	$65.00	$65.00
1921	$0.25	$0.45	$0.45	$2.00	$4.50	$10.00	$30.00	$21.00	$25.00	$31.00	$40.00	$40.00	$40.00
1921 S	$0.65	$3.75	$7.00	$16.00	$40.00	$115.00	$200.00	$155.00	$160.00	$195.00	$125.00	$125.00	$125.00
1922 D	$0.60	$1.15	$2.25	$3.00	$6.00	$20.00	$57.50	$47.50	$52.00	$65.00	$80.00	$80.00	$80.00

1922 ERROR	$4.00	$10.00	$23.00	$26.00	$50.00	$165.00	$800.00	$700.00	$1,100.00	$2,300.00	$3,100.00	$3,000.00	$3,000.00
1923	$0.30	$0.35	$0.40	$0.50	$1.10	$3.50	$11.00	$7.00	$8.50	$9.50	$10.00	$10.00	$10.00
1923 S	$1.35	$5.50	$7.50	$15.00	$40.00	$140.00	$285.00	$225.00	$225.00	$260.00	$175.00	$175.00	$175.00
1924	$0.20	$0.45	$0.60	$1.75	$4.50	$11.00	$20.00	$13.00	$19.00	$22.00	$22.00	$22.00	$22.00
1924 D	$0.90	$6.00	$5.50	$9.50	$20.00	$60.00	$250.00	$180.00	$275.00	$200.00	$235.00	$235.00	$200.00
1924 S	$0.85	$3.75	$4.50	$9.50	$17.50	$45.00	$105.00	$90.00	$105.00	$125.00	$110.00	$110.00	$100.00
1925	$0.20	$0.30	$0.40	$0.50	$1.10	$3.50	$8.75	$5.75	$7.50	$9.00	$10.00	$10.00	$10.00
1925 D	$0.35	$1.50	$1.60	$2.50	$5.00	$10.50	$32.00	$25.00	$33.00	$40.00	$50.00	$50.00	$50.00
1925 S	$0.60	$3.00	$4.50	$6.50	$10.00	$20.00	$40.00	$27.50	$33.00	$40.00	$60.00	$60.00	$60.00
1926	$0.25	$0.50	$0.50	$0.60	$1.25	$2.50	$7.75	$5.50	$7.25	$9.00	$8.00	$8.00	$8.00
1926 D	$0.35	$1.40	$1.50	$2.50	$5.00	$10.50	$30.00	$24.00	$31.50	$37.50	$50.00	$50.00	$50.00
1926 S	$1.15	$5.00	$5.35	$7.50	$13.50	$55.00	$169.00	$100.00	$120.00	$165.50	$100.00	$100.00	$100.00
1927	$0.20	$0.25	$0.35	$0.50	$1.10	$2.75	$7.50	$5.25	$7.00	$8.50	$8.00	$8.00	$8.00
1927 D	$0.45	$1.85	$2.50	$5.35	$13.10	$28.00	$21.00	$19.00	$21.00	$25.00	$26.00	$26.00	$25.00
1927 S	$0.45	$1.50	$3.00	$6.00	$12.00	$25.00	$52.00	$38.50	$37.00	$50.00	$65.00	$65.00	$65.00
1928	$0.15	$0.25	$0.35	$0.50	$1.00	$2.00	$6.00	$4.75	$6.75	$8.00	$8.00	$8.00	$8.00
1928 D	$0.45	$1.45	$1.50	$2.50	$9.50	$17.50	$15.00	$15.00	$18.00	$22.00	$22.00	$22.00	$22.00
1928 S	$0.40	$1.50	$2.50	$3.50	$6.50	$15.00	$30.00	$28.00	$27.50	$37.50	$45.00	$45.00	$45.00
1929	$0.15	$0.15	$0.40	$0.85	$2.00	$6.00	$6.00	$4.25	$5.50	$7.00	$7.50	$7.50	$7.50
1929 D	$0.25	$0.70	$0.75	$1.50	$4.50	$10.00	$10.00	$5.25	$9.75	$11.00	$18.00	$18.00	$18.00
1929 S	$0.25	$0.25	$0.25	$0.90	$2.25	$7.00	$7.00	$5.25	$6.25	$8.50	$9.00	$9.00	$9.00
1930	$0.10	$0.15	$0.10	$0.45	$1.00	$4.00	$4.00	$3.25	$4.00	$5.00	$5.50	$5.50	$5.50
1930 D	$0.25	$0.40	$0.60	$0.75	$1.50	$3.75	$10.00	$7.25	$8.00	$9.00	$12.00	$12.00	$12.00
1930 S	$0.20	$0.20	$0.20	$0.35	$0.75	$2.00	$10.00	$5.75	$6.00	$7.00	$9.00	$9.00	$9.00
1931	$0.15	$0.40	$0.50	$1.50	$2.50	$6.50	$22.50	$16.00	$13.00	$16.00	$17.00	$17.00	$17.00
1931 D	$0.20	$1.00	$2.00	$3.50	$6.50	$28.50	$87.50	$45.00	$47.50	$55.00	$55.00	$55.00	$50.00
1931 S	$0.40	$0.50	$1.00	$1.60	$4.50	$21.00	$95.00	$50.00	$50.00	$52.50	$75.00	$75.00	$65.00
1932	$0.15	$0.30	$0.50	$2.00	$5.50	$20.00	$20.00	$15.00	$13.50	$16.00	$18.00	$18.00	$18.00
1932 D	$0.20	$0.35	$0.45	$2.50	$6.00	$20.00	$26.00	$14.00	$13.00	$16.00	$16.00	$16.00	$16.00
1933	$0.15	$0.40	$0.55	$2.25	$8.00	$26.00	$37.50	$17.00	$14.00	$17.50	$18.50	$18.50	$18.50
1933 D	$0.20	$0.20	$0.25	$1.75	$6.50	$20.00	$20.00	$20.00	$17.00	$20.00	$25.00	$25.00	$25.00
1933 S	$0.10	$0.10	$0.10	$1.25	$4.50	$2.75	$4.50	$2.75	$2.25	$3.00	$4.00	$4.00	$4.00
1934	$0.10	$0.10	$0.10	$0.30	$0.30	$1.25	$15.00	$8.75	$15.00	$18.50	$23.00	$23.00	$23.00
1934 D	$0.20	$0.15	$0.25	$0.75	$3.25	$15.00	$23.00	$8.75	$15.00	$18.50	$23.00	$23.00	$23.00
EXCL 1922	$34.50	$99.95	$137.30	$235.10	$536.55	$1,567.10	$4,282.75	$2,931.25	$3,499.25	$4,134.00	$5,166.50	$4,860.50	$4,721.50
INCL 1922	$38.50	$109.95	$160.30	$261.10	$586.55	$1,732.10	$5,082.75	$3,631.25	$4,599.25	$6,434.00	$8,266.50	$7,860.50	$7,721.50

Lot #57 from the May, 1992 Mike Aron Rare Coin Auction held in Van Nuys. The coin was housed in a custom plastic holder with the information regarding the possible origins of the 1917 matte proof. The coin was brown with some golden planchet streaks and a mildly matte finish. Since the rims were not visible, that aspect could not be examined. There were bids from the floor and the top mail bid was $2,200. With a 10% buyer's fee, the hammered price was $2,420. The opinion of the few floor bidders who examined the coin was that the coin was probably not a matte proof.

---

57   **1917   Matte Proof62, Red & Brown!**

Officially, Matte Proof coinage was suspended in 1916. Although no mintage figures are available, an estimated half a dozen Proof cents and Buffalo nickels were clandestinely made. The texture and finish of this example is quite similar to the Proof Lincolns of 1916.

Discovered in 1989, this piece did not appear on the market prior to the Long Beach convention held during October, 1991. It was sold for a medium four-figure price at that time.

Although ANACS has certified at least one example, some of the other major grading services do not recognize the existence of a 1917 Matte Proof. We can offer only a limited warranty that the present coin was produced by the U.S. Mint, but any other warranty is expressly disclaimed, Including any determination as to it's status as a business strike or a Proof.

A once-in-a-lifetime opportunity for the advanced specialist that should not be taken lightly!   .... $6000+

Encouraging the Next Generation of Collectors

One truism in collecting is, "Without collectors of the next generation, the value of today's collectibles is nil." So we must do our part to encourage the next generation of collectors. Ideal birthday gifts for beginners aged 7-10 include: coin folders, numismatic books and subscriptions, small accumulations of coins to be sorted, and kindly helping hands from collector adults. Many youth projects are available from various sources. SLCC Vice President John Iddings writes "Lincoln Youth Project" for Lincoln Sense. Write to John at P.O. Box 963, Victorville, CA 92392 for reprints and ideas.

Memberships in coin clubs, the ANA, or regional organizations also will encourage a budding collector. Many a collector got his or her start when taken to a coin exhibit, a coin show, or in this author's case, a tour of the Philadelphia Mint (in 1940).

Each April includes National Coin Week. The ANA sponsors this national week to encourage collectors and the public at large to better understand numismatics. Many local clubs will hold exhibits in public libraries and banks. Some clubs will hold seminars and open houses. Other will sponsor coin clinics. This author was instrumental in starting the annual Whittier Coin Club Clinic held each year at a local bank. Club members offer the public free evaluations of their numismatic (and other) holdings—coins, medals, tokens, currency, and related memertoes.

Most public and private schools have hobby days, "show and tell" programs, and other programs which encourage local citizens to share with the youngsters special skills, knowledge, hobbies, and activities. This author has presented "Beginning Coin Collecting" to school children for over twenty years. The typical program runs 15-20 mintues. Each child is given a Lincoln Cent coin folder, a roll of mixed Lincoln Cents "salted" with at least one 1960D small date, 1974S, one wheat cent, one steel cent, and a random mix of dates from change. The lesson consists of showing the album and explaining its function. The mintage figures are explained. The mint marks are explained. A large card (about

16x20 inches) shows enlargements of the "D" and "S" mintmarks plus the "V.D.B." on the truncation of the bust. Then each youngster is given a roll of cents and the balance of the session is spent filling as many holes as possible and answering questions. The remaining or unused coins are put in the class fund—they always seem to have some project which needs funding. And in recent years, the youngster who filled the most holes won a prize—either a magnifier loupe or a copy of The Standard Guide to Lincoln Cents. Each local school library also has received one or more copies of this book.

To answer one of the most often asked questions, "What is the best coin investment you can recommend?" This author's answer has typically been, "Invest in the next generation of collectors."

MULTIPLE-DENOMINATION coins are nothing new. This undated Lincoln cent was struck a second time by Standing Liberty quarter dollar dies sometime between 1918 and 1930.

Chapter 9 — BIBLIOGRAPHY

All the references listed in this book are available through the American Numismatic Association Library, P.O. Box 2366, Colorado Springs, CO 80901. We are indebted to the ANA for making these references available to allow us to complete this book.

BOOKS
1. ANA - Official Grading Guide to United States Coins
2. Barker, F.B. - Cracked Dies and Flaws in the Lincoln Cent
3. Cohen, Jean - The Spiked Head - A Study of Die Cracks...
4. Hardy, Howard O. - BIE Handbook
5. Harsche, Bert - Detecting Altered Coins
6. Haylings, George W. - The Profit March...
7. Jewett, E.G. - Mistrikes and Oddities in the Lincoln Cent...
8. Kolman, Michael - The Numismatic Lincoln Cent Error
9. Kolman, Michael - The Numismatic Flying Eagle
10. Manley, Stephen G. - The Lincoln Cent
11. Marvin, Paul and Arnold Margolid - The Design Cud
12. Morgan, Carl E. - Lincoln Cent Oddities...
13. Schmeider, Thomas K. - Collecting and Investing in U.S. Cents
14. Taxay, Don - The U.S. Mints and Coinage
15. Wallace, E.V. - The Numismatography of the Lincoln Head Cent
16. Wexler, John, The Lincoln Cent Doubled Die, 1984
17. Wexler, John, & Tom Miller, The RPM Book, 1983
18. Yeoman, Richard S. - A Guidebook of United States Coins

PERIODICALS & JOURNALS

1. Coin World - Dec. , 1976 p. 48
2. Coin World - Sep. 26, 1979
3. CoinAge - April, 1976, p. 70
4. CoinAge - January, 1973, p. 78
5. CoinAge - July 1980, p. 16, June 1967, Aug. 1968, April 1970
6. The Numismatist - Vol. 22 p. 225 The Lincoln Cent
7. The Numismatist - Vol. 44 p. 144, Lincoln Head Cent.
8. The Numismatist - Vol. 52, p. 805 The Lincoln Cent
9. The Numismatist - Vol. 91, p. 2245, The Lincoln Cent
10. NASC Quarterly, Fall, 1974 Albert K. Hall, Victory D. Brenner and the Lincoln Cent
11. NASC Quarterly, Spring, 1973, Sol Taylor, The Fine Art of Grading
12. NASC Quarterly, Winter, 1973, Sol Taylor, Lincoln Sense
13. Numismatic Scrapbook, August, 1973, p. 692
14. Private Coin Collector, March 1983, New Boom in Lincoln Cents?, Ed Reiter
15. Society of Lincoln Cent collectors, Lincoln Sense, Vol. 1-VI, 1982-1992
16. What Are Doubled Dies? A Handbook, 24 pp. J.T. Stanton, 1985
17. Joja Jemz (Georgia Gems), Retail Coin Price List by Bill Fivaz and J.T. Stanton, 1988-1991
18. Error Nibble, Quarterly, lists errors and varieties, retail prices, articles. Lou Coles, P.O. Box 21110, Carson City, NV 89721.
19. EVN News, Lonesome John, 3481 Old Conejo Rd. Newbury Park, Ca. 91320

Plus articles published in the U.S. Coin Exchange by the author.

Data from several issues of the COIN DEALER NEWSLETTER are used with permission of the publishers.